Terrorism
Biographies

Terrorism
Biographies

**James L. Outman
and Elisabeth M.
Outman**

Matthew May and
Diane Sawinski, Editors

Detroit • New York • San Diego • San Francisco • Cleveland • New Haven, Conn. • Waterville, Maine • London • Munich

THOMSON

GALE

TM

Terrorism: Biographies
James L. Outman and Elisabeth M. Outman

Project Editors
Diane Sawinski and Matthew May

Permissions
Margaret Chamberlain

Imaging and Multimedia
Robert Duncan, Christine O'Bryan, Robyn Young

Product Design
Pamela A. E. Galbreath, Tracey Rowens, Kate Scheible

Manufacturing
Evi Seoud

Composition
Rita Wimberley

For permission to use material from this product, submit your request via Web at http://www.gale-edit.com/ permissions, or you may download our Permissions Request form and submit your request by fax or mail to:

Permissions Department
The Gale Group, Inc.
27500 Drake Rd.
Farmington Hills, MI 48331-3535
Permissions Hotline:
248-699-8006 or 800-877-4253, ext. 8006
Fax: 248-699-8074 or 800-762-4058

Cover photograph reproduced by permission of AP/Wide World Photos.

Library of Congress Card Number: 2002113130
ISBN: 0-7876-6567-3

Printed in the United States of America
10 9 8 7 6 5 4 3 2 1

Contents

Reader's Guide

W ho are the individuals who wreak havoc and violence upon society? What are their motivations? What are their backgrounds? *Terrorism: Biographies* profiles twenty-six people who figure prominently in the story and history of terrorism. Included are terrorists from the Middle East such as Osama bin Laden, Ramzi Yousef, and Abu Nidal; individual actors such as Theodore "Ted" Kaczynski and Timothy McVeigh; those involved in terrorizing minority classes such as Robert M. "Bobby" Shelton; and people some view as freedom fighters, such as John Brown and Michael Collins. In addition, statesmen such as George J. Mitchell and Tom Ridge are profiled, reflecting the efforts of negotiators and protectors of peace in response to terrorism. Informative sidebar boxes as well as more than seventy photographs and maps augment the text. Each entry concludes with a list of further readings. Also included in the volume are a timeline, a "Words to Know" section, and an index providing easy access to subjects discussed throughout *Terrorism: Biographies.*

Related Reference Sources

- *Terrorism: Almanac* presents a history of terrorism from the French Revolution until today. The volume examines the motivation behind various forms of terrorism, as well as the strategies governments use to combat terrorism.

- *Terrorism: Primary Sources* presents fifteen full or excerpted speeches and written works that illuminate the philosophy behind individuals and groups that practice terrorism, thos who have been victims of terrorist acts, and those who fight it. Each entry includes an introduction, things to remember while reading the excerpt, the excerpt itself, information on what happened after the work was published or the event took place, and a list of further reading.

Acknowledgments

The authors extend their thanks to U•X•L senior editor Diane Sawinski and U•X•L publisher Tom Romig at the Gale Group for their assistance throughout the production of this series.

Comments and Suggestions

We welcome your comments on *Terrorism: Biographies* and suggestions for other topics in this area to consider. Please write: Editors, *Terrorism: Biographies*, U•X•L, 27500 Drake Road, Farmington Hills, Michigan 483313535; call toll-free 800-877-4253; fax to 248-414-5043; or send email via http://www.gale.com.

Timeline

January 28, 1793 Maximilien Robespierre is elected to the Committee of Public Safety in France, emerging as its leader.

March 1794 Maximilien Robespierre solidifies his power on the Committee of Public Safety by arresting and executing his two chief rivals.

July 28, 1794 Maximilien Robespierre is put to death by guillotine.

1851 Mikhail Bakunin is sentenced to prison in Russia for revolutionary activities.

May 24, 1855 John Brown and his gang of abolitionists attack a pro-slavery settlement on Pottawatomie Creek in Kansas, killing five.

October 16, 1859 John Brown leads a raid on the armory at Harpers Ferry, Virginia.

December 2, 1859 John Brown is hanged in Charlestown, Virginia.

1866 Mikhail Bakunin publishes *Revolutionary Catechism*.

1909 Michael Collins joins a Irish independence group, the Irish Republican Brotherhood (IRB).

April 24, 1916 Irish nationalists, including Michael Collins, stage an uprising in Dublin, Ireland. A few days later, British forces retaliate; 450 people die and more than 2,600 are injured.

August 22, 1922 During an attack by the Irish Republican Army (IRA), Michael Collins is killed by a gunshot.

July 22, 1946 The King David Hotel in Jerusalem is bombed on the orders of Menachem Begin, leader of the Israeli resistance group Irgun Zvai Leumi.

1948 Yasir Arafat leaves the university and joins in combat against the new state of Israel.

1954 Edward Abbey publishes his first novel.

1961 Robert M. "Bobby" Shelton, influential member of the Ku Klux Klan in Alabama, is placed under a court order not to interfere with whites trying to integrate interstate bus transportation.

1962 Edward Abbey's novel *The Brave Cowboy* is made into a motion picture starring Kirk Douglas and Walter Mattheau.

1963 Robert M. "Bobby" Shelton seeks to quell violent tactics of the Ku Klux Klan, but a bomb planted by the Klan explodes at the Sixteenth Street Baptist Church in Birmingham, Alabama.

1964 Gerry Adams begins working actively with Sinn Féin.

1966 The U.S. House of Representatives Committee on Un-American Activities finds Robert M. "Bobby" Shelton in contempt of Congress when he refuses to answer questions during the committee's investigation of the Klan. Shelton serves a year in prison.

1967 The Popular Front for the Liberation of Palestine (PFLP) is formed by George Habash.

1968 The PFLP stages its first terrorist attack, hijacking an El Al (Israel's national airline) flight from Rome, Italy, forcing it to land in Algiers.

1969   Yasir Arafat becomes chairman of the Palestine Liberation Organization (PLO) and appoints Abu Nidal to represent the PLO in Baghdad, Iraq.

1969   Andreas Baader and Gudrun Ensslin are convicted of arson, but flee Germany to escape from serving a prison sentence.

1970   Carlos the Jackal arrives at a Palestinian guerrilla training camp in Jordan.

May 1972   The Japanese Red Army, under the direction of Fusako Shigenobu in the Middle East, attacks the Lod Airport in Israel with hand grenades and machine guns, killing twenty–six people.

May 11, 1972   Andreas Baader, Gudrun Ensslin, and two others set off pipe bombs at the Frankfurt, West Germany, headquarters of the U.S. Army to protest U.S. involvement in Vietnam.

May 12, 1972   Bombs planted in a police station in Augsburg, West Germany, injure five policemen; Andreas Baader and Gudrun Ensslin take credit for the violence.

1975   Edward Abbey publishes his novel *The Monkey Wrench Gang*.

1976   Mu'ammar Qaddafi publishes *The Green Book*, an exhaustive explanation of his political philosophies and hopes for the Arab world.

1977   Menachem Begin is elected prime minister of Israel.

June 1977   The Japanese Red Army claims responsibility for attacks on the U.S. and British embassies in Rome.

1978   Menachem Begin, prime minister of Israel, and Anwar el-Sadat, president of Egypt, share the Nobel Peace Prize after the two leaders negotiate a peace treaty between the two nations.

May 25, 1978   The first package containing a bomb sent from Theodore "Ted" Kaczynski, the Unabomber, is opened, injuring a Northwestern University patrolman.

1980   The terrorist group Shining Path, led by Abimael Guzman, begins armed conflict against army installations in Peru.

1983 Gerry Adams becomes president of Sinn Féin.

April 1983 Shining Path members round up villagers in Lucanamarca, Peru, and execute almost seventy people.

December 31, 1983 Carlos the Jackal claims responsibility for bombing two trains in France in response to a French air strike in Lebanon.

1984 James Kopp helps found a "pregnancy crisis center" in San Francisco, California, that advocates alternatives to abortion.

September 1985 Abu Nidal masterminds the hijacking of an Egyptian plane; sixty people die in a botched rescue attempt by Egyptian forces.

December 1985 Hugh Scrutton, a computer company owner, is the first person killed by a bomb planted by Theodore "Ted" Kaczynski.

April 5, 1986 A Libyan terrorist plants a bomb in a West Berlin, Germany, discotheque, killing two American servicemen, a Turkish woman, and injuring over two hundred others. Mu'ammar Qaddafi is blamed for the attack.

1987 The religious cult Aum Shinrikyo, headed by Shoko Asahara, is founded.

1987 Ahmed Yassin founds the Palestinian terrorist group Hamas.

1988 James Kopp joins the antiabortion group Operation Rescue.

December 21, 1988 Pan American Flight 103 from London, England, to New York City explodes in midair over Lockerbie, Scotland, killing 259 people. Mu'ammar Qaddafi refuses to hand over Libyan agents found responsible.

1989 Ahmed Yassin is convicted by an Israeli court of taking part in a plot to kill Palestinians who collaborated with the Israeli army.

1989 *Secrets of Developing Your Supernatural Powers,* a book by Shoko Asahara, is published.

January 1989 George J. Mitchell is elected majority leader of the United States Senate.

September 1992 Abimael Guzman is arrested in Peru, convicted of murder, and sentenced to life in prison.

September 1, 1992 Ramzi Yousef arrives in the United States on a Pakistani airliner, avoids detention by American immigration officials, and takes residence in Jersey City, New Jersey.

February 26, 1993 A bomb explodes in the underground parking garage beneath the World Trade Center towers in New York City. Ramzi Yousef is the prime suspect and, after eluding authorities, is arrested in 1995 and sentenced to life in prison in November 1996.

April 19, 1993 Federal agents stage a raid on the compound of a religious sect called the Branch Davidians, in Waco, Texas, killing eighty people and motivating Timothy McVeigh to seek revenge on the federal government.

1994 Along with Yitzhak Rabin and Shimon Peres, Yasir Arafat is awarded the Nobel Peace Prize.

1994 U.S. president Bill Clinton asks former senator George J. Mitchell to help negotiate a settlement between parties in Northern Ireland on the issue of independent rule.

August 1994 Carlos the Jackal is captured by French agents and convicted for the murder of two policemen in 1975; he is sentenced to life in prison.

November 1994 Tom Ridge is elected governor of Pennsylvania.

March 20, 1995 More than five thousand people are sick or injured and twelve die as a result of a poison gas attack in the Tokyo, Japan, subway system organized by the religious cult Aum Shinrikyo headed by Shoko Asahara.

April 19, 1995 The Murrah Federal Building in Oklahoma City, Oklahoma, is destroyed in an explosion that kills 168 people. Timothy McVeigh is arrested and later convicted of the act.

September 19, 1995 The *Washington Post* and *New York Times* share the cost of publishing the "Unabomber Manifesto" written by Theodore "Ted" Kaczynski in the hopes he will cease sending package bombs.

1997 Ahmed Yassin is released from an Israeli prison as part of an agreement with Jordan to release jailed Palestinian resistance leaders.

1998 Catholic and Protestant leaders agree to share power in Northern Ireland and observe a cease-fire after negotiations involving Gerry Adams, George J. Mitchell, and David Trimble.

October 23, 1998 Barnett Slepian, a doctor who performed abortions, is shot through his kitchen window. James Kopp is the prime suspect and charged with second degree murder in 2002 after an intense manhunt by the Federal Bureau of Investigation (FBI).

2000 George Habash formally announces his resignation as head of the People for the Liberation of Palestine (PFLP) terrorist organization.

June 11, 2001 Timothy McVeigh, the man convicted of planning and carrying out the bombing of a federal building in Oklahoma City, Oklahoma, is executed in a federal prison.

September 11, 2001 Agents of the Al Qaeda terrorist group masterminded by Osama bin Laden fly hijacked airliners into the twin towers of the World Trade Center in New York City, and one into the Pentagon outside Washington, D.C. Another hijacked flight crashes in a field in rural Pennsylvania after it was believed that passengers overtook their captors, avoiding a crash into another American landmark. More than three thousand people are killed in the attacks.

September 20, 2001 U.S. president George W. Bush names Pennsylvania governor Tom Ridge as director of Homeland Security in the wake of the September 11, 2001, terrorist attacks on the United States.

November 2001 Fusako Shigenobu, head of the Japanese Red Army, is arrested by Japanese authorities.

August 18, 2002 Abu Nidal is found shot to death in Baghdad, Iraq. Reports vary on whether it was a murder or suicide.

Words to Know

A

Abolitionist: A person who wants to outlaw slavery.

Abortion: The act of ending a pregnancy by removing the fertilized egg from a woman's uterus.

Absentia: In their absence.

Anarchism: A theory that says society should be organized around voluntary associations, rather than large government organizations.

Anarchist: A person who believes that society should be organized around voluntary associations, rather than large government organizations.

Anthrax: An infectious disease that can be fatal unless a person gets treatment soon after he or she has been exposed.

Antisocial personality disorder: A condition in which a person does not have a conscience about his or her actions. People with this disorder are aggressive and more concerned with their needs than with the needs of others.

Aristocracy: A class of people with special privileges inherited from birth.

Aristocrats: The upper classes of society that controlled some governments.

Armory: A place where weapons are stored.

Atheist: A person who believes there is no God.

Autism: A mental disorder beginning in infancy. Its symptoms include an inability to interact socially, repetitive behavior, withdrawal from reality, and being absorbed in mental activities such as daydreams, fantasies, and delusions.

B

British Commonwealth: Association of countries that were formally British colonies or possessions that continue to maintain close governmental, military, and legal ties to Great Britian.

Buddhism: A religion of eastern Asia based on the teachings of Gautama Buddha; it teaches that suffering, though a part of life, can be overcome by mental and spiritual purification.

C

Capital crimes: Crimes for which execution is a possible penalty.

Capitalism: An economic system in which factories and other businesses are owned and controlled by private individuals.

Chronic schizophrenia: A form of schizophrenia in which the altered thought processes are constant.

Civil rights: The nonpolitical rights of citizens protected under the law.

Class: A group of people in society who share the same political and economic status.

Communist: A person who believes in an economic theory that does not include the concept of private property; instead, the people—represented by a central government—owns the goods and means of production.

Conservative: A person who seeks to maintain traditions, preserve established institutions, and promote a strong, authoritative government.

Coup d'etat: The takeover of a government by force, usually by the military.

Cult: A group of people who believe in unorthodox ideas or concepts.

D

Democracy: A form of government in which the citizens vote for their representatives.

Depression: A feeling that everything is hopeless. Depressed people may decide that they are unlovable or that they have ruined a relationship and withdraw from contact with others.

E

Ecoterrorists: Environmental activists who use terrorist tactics to help their cause.

F

Fetus: A developing unborn baby in the mother's uterus.

Figurehead: A symbolic leader who has no real power.

Fundamentalist: A person who believes in following a strict set of moral principles.

G

Genetics: The study of how people and animals inherit their traits, such as eye and hair color.

Guerrilla: A combat soldier who fights in nontraditional ways, using ambushes and surprise attacks, usually to oppose larger armies.

Guillotine: A machine that used a falling metal blade to cut off a person's head.

H

Hermit: A person who lives alone, away from civilization.

Hinduism: The dominant religion in India; one of its basic beliefs is the immortality of the soul and its reincarnation after the death of the human body.

Home rule: A system that put the Irish in charge of affairs in Ireland but left the British in charge of international affairs.

I

Indolent: Lazy.

Infanticide: Baby killing.

Infitada: Mass uprising by Palestinians.

Insanity defense: Telling a court of law that the person accused of a crime is not responsible for his or her own actions because he or she is insane.

Islamist: Someone who believes that Islam should play a central role in the organization of a government.

J

Job discrimination: When employers refuse to hire certain types of people, such as Catholics or women.

K

Koran: Islam's holy book.

L

Left-wing: People associated with radical solutions to social problems, especially in the interest of gaining greater freedoms and equality for average citizens and the poor.

Leukemia: An often fatal disease affecting the blood, which causes an abnormal increase in the number of white blood cells.

Lynching: The execution of someone by a mob.

M

Manifesto: A statement of principles and ideas.

Martyr: Someone who is killed for a cause.

Metaphor: A figure of speech that suggests a likeness or similarity to something else.

Middle class: People who have some money and political rights.

Militiaman: Historically, part-time soldiers who could take up arms in an emergency, somewhat like the National Guard.

Mosques: Religious meeting places in Islam, similar to churches.

N

Nationalist: A person who believes his or her nation is superior in all ways.

New Left: A group of radicals demanding swift changes and more government involvement in social issues.

Nihilism: A nineteenth-century political philosophy in Russia that supported the use of terrorism to bring about revolution.

Nomadic: Referring to people who move from place to place.

P

Palestinian nationalism: The desire to found a new Palestinian nation on the land controlled by Israel.

Pan-Arabism: The idea that all Arabs should unite in a single nation.

Paranoid personality disorder: A personality disorder in which the patient is very distrustful of others and suspicious of their motives. People with this disorder tend to avoid close relationships, constantly search for hidden meanings in what others say or do, and carry grudges for a long time.

Paranoid schizophrenia: A mental disorder in which the patient imagines people's words and actions are intended to be harmful. Patients may believe that people, including complete strangers, are plotting against them or controlling their thoughts in some way.

Personality disorder: A set of traits that make it more difficult for a person to succeed or be happy in everyday life. A personality disorder refers to fairly constant behavior that goes outside the range of what most people experience, and that causes problems in a person's daily life and relationships with other people.

Phoenix: In mythology, a bird that burned to ashes only to be reborn.

Prejudice: Irrational dislike.

Proletariat: The working class; people without property or political rights.

Q

Quadriplegic: A person who is unable to move his arms or legs.

R

Racial segregation: A system in which black people and white people did not share public services such as schools or transportation.

Radicals: People who want rapid changes in society.

Revelation: A sudden realization of a new perception of reality.

S

Sabotage: Destroying someone's property to interfere with their operations.

Saboteurs: People who commit sabotage.

Schizophrenia: A severe disturbance of the brain's functioning that can sometimes be treated with drugs.

Secular: Nonreligious.

Socialist: A person who believes in popular democratic control of the economy as well as the government.

Subversive: Attempting to overthrow or destroy the political or social order.

Synonymous: Having the same meaning.

W

White supremacists: People who believe that the white race is superior to the other races, particularly blacks.

Working class: People without property or political rights.

Z

Zionism: The movement with the goal of creating a Jewish homeland in Palestine.

Terrorism
Biographies

Edward Abbey

January 29, 1927
Indiana, Pennsylvania
March 14 , 1989
Near Tucson, Arizona

Writer, environmental activist

"The forests and mountains and desert canyons are holier than our churches. Therefore let us behave accordingly."

Photograph reproduced by permission of Warner Books, Inc.

On May 7, 2000, two hundred protesters in Franc-Waret, Belgium, gathered for a picnic and then walked through a field where the Monsanto Corporation was growing an experimental variety of corn. They destroyed several parcels of the corn while a rock band played from a nearby truck. Earlier in the year, a woman in Lancaster, England, had gone on trial for damaging equipment and painting slogans on a U.S. submarine while it was docked in Barrow, England, in 1991.

These were just two out of dozens of events supported by Earth First!, a radical environmental organization devoted to taking direct action against corporations and governments that they believe are harming the environment.

Some members of Earth First! were inspired by the work of Edward Abbey, an American writer whose most famous work is *The Monkey Wrench Gang* (1975), a novel about a group of people in the American Southwest who try to block a road-building project through the desert.

Abbey did not directly support **saboteurs** (people who commit **sabotage**, or who destroy someone's property to interfere with their operations), but his writing—especially *The Monkey Wrench Gang*—presented them in a very good light. Regardless of his intentions, many people adopted such tactics as their own, unofficial environmental protection acts.

Is it acceptable to use the term "terrorists" to describe people who sabotage equipment as a way to protect the wilderness or other parts of the environment? Some would argue that "terrorism" involves violence, and that sabotage is not the same thing. Others have described Abbey as an "environmental **anarchist**," someone who believes that society should be organized around voluntary associations, rather than large government organizations. These people argue that direct action, rather than working through democratic channels such as voting to change government policy, qualifies as a form of terrorism.

Childhood and youth

Abbey was born in 1927 in the western Pennsylvania town of Indiana, northeast of Pittsburgh. Later, his family moved to the small town of Home, Pennsylvania, about 10 miles (16 kilometers) away. Abbey was one of five children of Paul and Mildred Abbey. When he was just two years old, the country fell into a deep economic depression. His father worked as a lumberjack, a farmer, and a school bus driver. His mother was a schoolteacher and church organist. His relatives remembered Abbey's early efforts at becoming a professional writer: he used to charge his brothers and sister a penny to read stories he wrote called "The Adventures of Lucky Stevens."

Abbey attended public schools near Home and later in Indiana, Pennsylvania. He was remembered as a loner in high school; he didn't make many friends.

As a young boy, Abbey loved to watch the cowboy movies that were popular in the era. The movies were his first introduction to the American West, and apparently he fell in love with the region and its rugged heroes. It was a place he adopted as an adult and a philosophy he embraced in his fiction.

In the summer of 1944, between his junior and senior years in high school, Abbey hitchhiked from Pennsylvania to Seattle, Washington, and then south to New Mexico. He later told *EcoNews* that the trip was a turning point in his life: "I became a Westerner at the age of 17, in the summer of 1944, while hitchhiking around the USA. For me it was love at first sight—a total passion which has never left me." In his book *The Journey Home* he wrote: "On the Western horizon, under a hot, clear sky sixty miles away crowned with snow (in July), was a magical vision, a legend come true: the front range of the Rocky Mountains. An impossible beauty . . . the image of those mountains struck a fundamental [basic] chord in my imagination that has sounded ever since."

On that trip, he first spotted the red, rocky desert and canyons of the Southwest in New Mexico. It was the region he returned to a few years later, and where he spent the rest of his life. In the meantime, he took a train home to Pennsylvania and finished high school, a minor hero for having taken his adventure. His father wholly approved of the trip; he had gone on a similar adventure in his own youth.

Life as an author

Abbey graduated from high school as World War II (1939–45) was ending. He was drafted into the army and sent to Italy, where he spent most of his time as a military policeman.

Back in the United States, he enrolled in Indiana University of Pennsylvania for a year and then transferred to the University of New Mexico. He graduated from New Mexico in 1951 and later received a master's degree in philosophy from the same university. Abbey also received grants to study at the University of Edinburgh, in Scotland, and at Stanford University in California. He also entered Yale to study writing but dropped out after just two weeks.

Abbey published his first novel, *Jonathan Troy,* in 1954. It was an autobiographical novel set in West Virginia, in a thinly disguised version of Abbey's own boyhood town of Home, Pennsylvania. Like Abbey, the book's hero, Jonathan

The Works of Edward Abbey

Fiction:

Jonathan Troy (1954)

The Brave Cowboy (1956)

Fire on the Mountain (1962)

Black Sun (1971)

The Monkey Wrench Gang (1975)

Good News (1980)

The Fool's Progress (1988)

Hayduke Lives! (1990)

Nonfiction:

Desert Solitaire (1968)

Appalachian Wilderness (1970)

Slickrock (1971)

Cactus Country (1973)

The Journey Home (1977)

The Hidden Canyon (1977)

Abbey's Road (1979)

Desert Images (1979)

Down the River (1982)

In Praise of Mountain Lions (1984)

Beyond the Wall (1984)

One Life at a Time, Please (1988)

A Voice Crying in the Wilderness: Notes from a Secret Journal (1989)

Confessions of a Barbarian: Selections from the Journals of Edward Abbey 1951–1989 (1994)

Troy, dreams of the American West as a place where he can escape the limitations of modern life. Abbey later came to dislike the book and refused to let it be reprinted, with the result that it has become very rare, and very valuable.

Two years later, Abbey published *The Brave Cowboy*. Its hero, John Burns, refuses to compromise with modern civilization. Burns escapes from jail and, on horseback, tries to escape a posse chasing him in cars, helicopters, and airplanes. The story was a **metaphor** for the way Abbey believed that civilization harasses the individualist. (A metaphor is a figure of speech that suggests a likeness or similarity to something else.) In the book, Burns escapes the posse, but dies crossing a new superhighway when he is hit by a truck filled with bathroom fixtures. The book was made into a film, *Lonely Are the Brave* (1962), starring Kirk Douglas and Walter Matthau.

Over a period of fifteen years, Abbey also worked as a park ranger and fire lookout during the summer in several national parks, including the Arches National Monument (later a national park) in Utah. His experiences in the desert led to one of his best-known books, *Desert Solitaire* (1968), a collection of widely admired nonfiction essays about the country he loved. In the book Abbey expressed his anger with the National Forest Service, whose policy of building roads into national forests he criticized as trying to serve the "**indolent** [lazy] millions born on wheels and suckled on gasoline who expect and demand highways to lead them in comfort, ease and safety" into the wilderness.

Abbey's essays were written in an era when most Americans liked the idea of industrial society and ever-expanding roads and resorts. He foreshadowed a time in the late twentieth century when environmentalists argued for preserving a wilderness free of gasoline engines. Abbey's writing, particularly *Desert Solitaire* and the novel that followed it, *The Monkey Wrench Gang,* is credited with giving direction to the environmental protection movement that arose in the last third of the twentieth century.

The Monkey Wrench Gang

Abbey's best-known book was the novel *The Monkey Wrench Gang* (1975). It tells the story of four people in the desert determined to stop a new highway from being built through the wilderness. To stop the road builders, the four pull out surveyors' stakes and sabotage their road graders and other heavy equipment.

The story of their campaign is mostly a comedy, not intended to be taken seriously. But the book later served as a rough how-to manual for ecological terrorists who were quite serious about the same issues that drove the characters in Abbey's book. The so-called **ecoterrorists** were on a collision course with road builders, resort developers, and timber and mining companies, who see in the wilderness a source of income. (Ecoterrorists are environmental activists who use terrorist tactics to help their cause.) Most often, federal agencies like the Forest Service, assigned to manage the millions of acres of government-owned wilderness in the West, sided with the developers. The acts of sabotage—for example, dam-

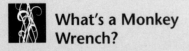

What's a Monkey Wrench?

A monkey wrench is both an actual tool and a figure of speech.

The tool is a kind of wrench that can be adjusted to fit different sizes of nuts and bolts. It consists of a handle with grooves along one edge and a head that can move up and down the handle, using the grooves as gears.

The metaphor is the expression "throw a monkey wrench into the works," meaning the act of interfering with a process. It is similar to the throwing of wooden shoes (sabots, pronounced sa-BOHS, in French) into machinery, an act from which we get the word "sabotage."

aging or destroying bulldozers, or driving spikes into trees to make it difficult or impossible to cut them down for lumber—cast these "monkey-wrench" environmentalists in the role of "terrorists" fighting the legal use of the land.

After *The Monkey Wrench Gang,* Abbey wrote three more novels, including a sequel to *The Monkey Wrench Gang* called *Hayduke Lives!* (1990), as well as books of nonfiction.

The influence of Edward Abbey

Almost from the beginning, ecoterrorists operated differently from more traditional political environmentalists. They struck by night, often working in distant wilderness areas, but sometimes attacking laboratories or facilities owned by corporations that they felt were threatening the environment.

To avoid arrest, some of these saboteurs announced their acts through individuals who had no knowledge of the specific people engaged in sabotage. A system of secret code words was developed so the public spokesmen could recognize "genuine" claims of actions without knowing the identity of the people who were claiming responsibility for the attacks.

Abbey was never accused of personally engaging in illegal activities. But the colorful characters he created in *The Monkey Wrench Gang* served as role models and guides to underground combat against developers.

In March 1989 Abbey died from complications after an operation. He died at home, near Tucson, Arizona. Following his instructions, friends took his body into the desert and buried it in an unmarked grave, ignoring laws about the disposal of human remains. He is said to have written, "I want my body to help fertilize the growth of a cactus or cliff rose or sagebrush or tree."

For More Information

Books

Abbey, Edward. *Desert Solitaire: A Season in the Wilderness*. New York: Ballantine Books, 1968.

Abbey, Edward. *The Journey Home: Some Words in Defense of the American West*. New York: Plume, 1981.

Bishop, James, Jr. *Epitaph for a Desert Anarchist: The Life and Legacy of Edward Abbey*. New York: Atheneum, 1994.

Cahalan, James M. *Edward Abbey: A Life*. Tucson: University of Arizona Press, 2001.

Loeffler, Jack. *Adventures with Ed: A Portrait of Abbey*. Albuquerque: University of New Mexico Press, 2002.

Periodicals

"Ed Abbey: Tearing . . . Down with Words." *EcoNews,* January 1981, p.6.

"Edward Abbey" (interview). *Whole Earth Review,* Winter 1988, p. 17.

Petersen, David. "Where Phantoms Brood and Mourn." *Backpacker,* September 1993, p. 40.

Warshall, Peter. "Spadefoot Packrat Havahart; Eulogy for Ed Abbey." *Whole Earth Review,* Summer 1989, p. 114.

Gerry Adams

October 6, 1948
Belfast, Northern Ireland

Leader of Sinn Féin

"When with the advantage of distance the history is written of Ireland in the years in which I have lived, I know that an Everest amongst the mountains of traumatic events the Irish people have experienced will be the republican hunger strikes of 1980–1981."

Gerry Adams, long accused of being a terrorist and a member of the Irish Republican Army (IRA), is most often credited with guiding one side of Northern Ireland's warring communities of Catholics and Protestants to give up arms in favor of a peaceful political solution to their long-standing differences.

Tall and thin, Adams is usually seen wearing glasses, Irish tweeds, and a bulletproof vest, a constant reminder that violence is never long absent from the bitter political quarrels of Northern Ireland.

Adams's official role is as the leader of Sinn Féin (pronounced shin fain, Gaelic for "We Ourselves"), a political party with close ties to the terrorist IRA. Both organizations have fought a long campaign to unite the six counties of Northern Ireland (also called Ulster) with the twenty-six counties of the Irish Republic to the south. The struggle for Irish independence from England, and then the joining of Northern Ireland with the rest of the island, has been going on since 1916, and really for centuries before that (see box on pp. 12–13). Even after a peace agreement was reached in 1998, in which Adams played a central role, the IRA's refusal to give up its weapons has frustrated a permanent peace in Ulster. Similarly, Adams's own history combines diplomacy with widely held suspicions about his role in the IRA.

Birth and childhood

Gerard Adams was born in 1948, the first of ten children born to his father, also named Gerard, who was a building laborer, and his mother, Annie Hannaway, who worked in a linen factory. Both parents were from Belfast, the largest city in Northern Ireland. His life was difficult due to a lack of money and the fact that his family was Roman Catholic in an area where most of the residents were Protestants. (Northern Ireland had been set up as a separate political entity for Irish Protestants who did not want to join the largely Roman Catholic Irish Republic, which became somewhat independent from Britain in 1923.)

Adams's father had been active in the Irish republican cause, which wanted to join the six counties of Northern Ireland with the Irish Republic. He had been jailed for five years for his political activities and was released just a year before his first child was born. Annie also believed in the republican cause; she was the daughter of a trade-union organizer who fought for the rights of workers in Northern Ireland.

Housing was scarce in Belfast when Adams was born, and at first the Adams family shared a four-room house with his maternal grandmother and two of his uncles in the Falls section of West Belfast. It was an area inhabited mainly by Catholics. Later, Adams, his father and mother, and a younger brother and sister moved into a single large room in an old house, the five of them sharing water and a toilet with the other residents.

Eventually the family moved into a newly built house with three bedrooms, which was part of a public housing pro-

 Words to Know

British Commonwealth: association of countries that were formally British colonies or possessions that continue to maintain close governmental, military, and legal ties to Great Britain.

Civil rights: the nonpolitical rights of a citizen.

Job discrimination: when employers refuse to hire certain types of people, such as Catholics or women.

Prejudice: irrational dislike.

Radicals: people who want rapid changes in a society.

ject. Adams remembered having one sheet and one blanket on each mattress. If the weather got cold the children pulled coats over themselves to stay warm at night.

Getting involved in politics

As a child Adams was quite familiar with the mixture of religion and politics that formed Northern Ireland society. In high school he learned not to reveal his religion while shopping in mainly Protestant areas of Belfast; doing so could lead to a beating. Adams once tried to get a job washing dishes in a pub in a Protestant neighborhood. ("Pub" is short for "public house," the British term for a bar: a place that serves alcoholic drinks and some food.) As soon as he announced that he attended St. Mary's High School, a Catholic school, he was told there was no job. That proved true in every pub where he applied; Catholics were not welcome as workers.

Despite this **prejudice** (irrational dislike), day-to-day relations between Protestants and Catholics were generally peaceful until the mid-1960s. But there were underlying concerns. Many Protestants in Northern Ireland feared Catholic efforts to unite with the Catholic Irish Republic. Catholics, on the other hand, thought that problems such as the ones Adams faced would end if Northern Ireland were part of a majority Catholic country.

Politicians on both sides who were looking for popular support fed these tensions. But in the mid-1960s the problems suddenly got worse. In September 1964 the green, white, and orange flag of the Irish Republic was posted in the Belfast shop where the republican political party Sinn Féin had offices. A Protestant preacher, Ian Paisley, who for years had expressed his dislike of Catholics, threatened to lead a mob to the shop and remove the flag if the police would not. The next day police broke into the shop and took down the flag.

The Catholic community objected to the police's actions. Several thousand people held a protest, which turned violent. Several city buses were set on fire, and more rioting broke out the following day. It was made worse when the Sinn Féin put up another Irish flag. Police stepped in and used armored cars to put down the rioting.

Adams was sixteen years old at the time, and the clash made a major impression on him. He volunteered after school to help in the election campaign of Sinn Féin candidate Liam McMillen.

After graduating from high school Adams became increasingly active in Sinn Féin. Sinn Féin was widely considered the legal, political arm of the IRA. The IRA had been banned in Northern Ireland because it had been connected with terrorist attacks against British rule over any part of Ireland.

Fighting British rule

In April 1966 supporters of Sinn Féin celebrated the fiftieth anniversary of the Easter Monday uprising of 1916, when the IRA started a protest in Dublin that the British military put down (see box on pp. 12–13), with a parade in Belfast. Although the demonstration was peaceful, the Protestant government saw it as a new campaign to force Northern Ireland to join the Irish Republic.

Thus pro-British newspapers and some Protestant activists stirred up feelings against Catholics, and Sinn Féin in particular. Protestant organizations held many demonstrations in Belfast, which made Catholic residents feel unwanted. Worse, some Protestants attacked Catholic property with gasoline bombs. Any reaction from Catholics to these attacks was put down by the Royal Ulster Constabulary, a part-time police force known for its use of violence.

In response to the rising tensions, Adams wrote in his autobiography, *Before the Dawn,* he began actively working for Sinn Féin 1964. Over time Adams became a well-known actor in the ongoing struggle between those who wanted Northern Ireland to join the Irish Republic and those who wanted to remain part of Britain.

Adams's autobiography compares his struggle on behalf of Catholics in Northern Ireland to Martin Luther King Jr.'s (1929–1968) struggle for **civil rights** for African Americans in the United States or Nelson Mandela's (1918–) fight for the rights of black citizens in South Africa. Sinn Féin borrowed techniques from both of these movements.

A Thousand Years of "Troubles"

Since the first invasion of Ireland by the English in 1170, Irish resistance to English rule—often called "the Troubles"—has continued for nearly a thousand years.

Throughout the 1800s Irish leaders called for independence from Britain. On Easter Monday (April 24) in 1916, an armed group calling itself the Irish Republican Army (IRA) started an uprising in Dublin, the capital city of Ireland, hoping to start a rebellion and achieve independence. English troops put down the revolt, after which the IRA launched a campaign of terrorism and guerrilla warfare. The campaign resulted in the Irish Free State. The Free State (1922–37) had a status similar to Canada: a self-governing part of the British Empire, but not fully independent. Nor did it include six counties in Northern Ireland, where the Protestant majority wanted to remain part of Britain.

The IRA and Sinn Féin continued to press for full independence and for uniting all Ireland. A popular vote in 1937 resulted in the state of Eire, which moved Ireland another step closer to complete independence. Twelve years later, on Easter Monday (April 18), 1949, the Irish Dáil (parliament) declared Ireland a fully independent republic, no longer a member of the **British Commonwealth**. (The British Commonwealth was an association of countries that were former British colonies or possessions. They continued to have close connections with the government of Britain, including special trade relationships, military ties, and a common legal system.) Britain went along with the Dáil but passed a bill in Parliament approving the continuing status of Northern Ireland as a part of Britain.

This formal separation of Northern Ireland from the rest of the country set the stage for a long campaign by the IRA to reunite the two halves of Ireland—and on the part of Irish Protestants in the North to maintain their union with Britain.

In August 1969 British troops were called in to put down pro-republican riots in the cities of Londonderry and Belfast. Over the next thirty years Northern Ireland was rocked almost constantly by riots, terrorist attacks, and violent police crackdowns. Hundreds of civilians died in bombings, both in Northern Ireland and in England itself.

Adams and Sinn Féin campaigned for better housing and an end to **job discrimination** (employers refusing to hire certain types of people, such as Catholics or women), as well as the right for Sinn Féin to take part in politics and to publish a newspaper that supported the unification of Ireland.

In 1972 British soldiers fired into a crowd of Catholics marching for civil rights in Londonderry, killing fourteen people. The day became known as "Bloody Sunday" and marked an increase in hostilities between Catholics on one side and the British Army and Irish Protestants on the other. In March 1972 Britain took on direct rule of Northern Ireland, upsetting both Catholics and Protestants. In 1984 the IRA claimed responsibility for setting off a bomb that nearly killed British Prime Minister Margaret Thatcher (1925–). The next year Britain and the Irish Republic signed an agreement that gave the Republic a say in the affairs of Northern Ireland, which Protestants bitterly opposed. More than a decade of peace negotiations and terrorist attacks by both Catholics and Protestants followed.

Although Britain and the Irish Republic reached a tentative (not fully developed) agreement in 1993, the next nine years were marked by a succession of peace talks, temporary agreements, and more terrorist attacks. Sinn Féin, led by Gerry Adams and closely tied to the IRA, negotiated on behalf of those who supported uniting the Irish Republic and Northern Ireland. The United States tried to help the process in 1995 by sending former senator George J. Mitchell (1933–) of Maine to help the two sides negotiate.

Finally, in April 1998, the two sides signed an agreement that called for reforms in the Northern Ireland government giving Catholics more say. But four months later a terrorist attack blamed on a group that had split off from the IRA— called the Real IRA—killed twenty-nine people in Omagh, Northern Ireland, and wounded more than two hundred others. It was the worst single terrorist attack in Northern Ireland in three decades.

In November 1999 the long Mitchell talks finally produced an agreement between the Ulster Unionists (the leading Protestant political party) and Sinn Féin that could mean a new government for Northern Ireland and a possible end to the terrorist attacks. Even then, **radicals** (people who want rapid changes in a society) on both sides vowed to continue their struggle, and a generation of mistrust kept delaying a final agreement.

By 1969 Northern Ireland was in a virtual civil war between Catholics and Protestants. The British army was brought in to try to stop violence on both sides. The army quickly earned the hatred of Catholics, who did not see it as a neutral force. Civil rights, such as the right of assembly and the right to print newspapers, were taken away in the interest of ending violence. In the Catholic community, Adams wrote in his autobiography, "many people involved with the defense committees flocked to the IRA, which speedily mushroomed out of all proportion to its previous numbers."

Gerry Adams and the IRA

The IRA already had a long history of using violence to achieve its political aims. In the 1970s and 1980s, the IRA built on its reputation with a long string of bombings, assassinations, and shoot-outs with the British army and Ulster police. In turn, anti-republican organizations in Northern Ireland (called Unionists, for their desire to maintain a union with Britain) boasted their own string of terrorist attacks.

Although Adams emerged as a leader of the pro-republican forces in Northern Ireland, he has never admitted to being a member of the IRA, which was illegal. But many observers of Northern Ireland's history during the 1970s and 1980s insist that Adams was a senior leader of the IRA. According to several writers, Adams joined the IRA at about age seventeen and became commander of the IRA unit based in Ballymurphy, the area of Belfast where Adams lived. By 1971, they claim, Adams was in charge of the Belfast Brigade and was the commanding officer of IRA operations by 1979, when he was thirty-one years old.

Leading negotiations

As the situation in Ulster got worse a group called the Provisional IRA appeared that seemed willing to raise the level of violence against the British army. In response, the Northern Ireland authorities began arresting people suspected of being involved with the Provisional IRA and holding them in jail, often without a trial. This was called "internment."

In 1971, after a six-week romance in the middle of the rising violence, Adams married Colette McArdle. They eventually had three children.

The following year, on January 30, 1972, about twenty thousand people marched in favor of civil rights in the Northern Ireland town of Derry. Although the cause is uncertain,

during the march troops began shooting at the crowd. At the end of the day thirteen civilians were dead and twenty-nine were injured. (Another died several months later.) The day became known as "Bloody Sunday" and heightened emotions on both sides throughout all of Ireland.

In March 1972 Adams was arrested and "interned" aboard a British prison ship and later at a prison near Belfast called Long Kesh. The authorities had long suspected that Adams belonged to the IRA, but it was never proved. Adams himself has maintained that his activities in favor of unification were limited to politics.

Adams was released from prison in mid-1972 so he could take part in negotiations with the British secretary of state for Northern Ireland, William Whitelaw (1918–1999). The aim was to negotiate a cease-fire between the British army and the IRA and eventually a peaceful solution to the situation in Northern Ireland. The fact that Adams was chosen to take part in these talks is often pointed to as evidence of his connection to the IRA.

Shortly after the talks took place in London, the truce collapsed. What amounted to an all-out guerrilla war between Irish republicans and the British army resumed. In 1973 Adams was arrested again; this time he was held for four years. Also in the internment camp at Long Kesh were many members of the IRA and Sinn Féin. Many of them had never been charged with a crime or found guilty in a trial.

Adams, using the name "Brownie," began writing opinion articles for a Sinn Féin newspaper published in Belfast. The articles added to his reputation as a political leader of the republican forces. He was finally released from prison in 1977, having never been convicted of membership in the IRA.

Politics

The following year Adams was elected vice president of Sinn Féin. (Some sources say Adams also became commander of IRA operations, but Adams has denied this.) In 1983 he became president of Sinn Féin, a position he would hold for at least twenty years.

It was as president of Sinn Féin that Adams became well known in Ulster. Although his party generally received less than one-fifth of the popular vote in elections, it was the "aboveground" arm of the "underground" IRA, and as such was central to the issue of terrorist violence in Northern Ireland. Adams himself supported negotiating a solution to the long Troubles of Ulster.

Thanks in part to sympathy for political prisoners, who staged repeated hunger strikes (sometimes resulting in their death), Sinn Féin's popularity grew significantly in the late 1970s. In 1983 Adams also was elected to represent his district of Belfast in the British Parliament. But like other Sinn Féin members who had been elected to the British legislature, Adams refused to swear loyalty to the British queen. He was thus not allowed to take his seat, even though he was reelected in 1987.

Although Adams became increasingly diplomatic in his public statements, terrorist violence continued in Ulster. In 1984 three Protestant gunmen tried to assassinate Adams on a Belfast street. He was seriously wounded in the attack.

In 1987 Adams took part in secret talks with representatives of Britain aimed at a truce in Ulster. The talks were held in secret because tensions were so high on both sides that some saw any effort at compromise as disloyal.

In 1993 British Prime Minister John Major (1943–) publicly declared that he was willing to negotiate the future of Ulster if the IRA would first give up the use of violence.

Little progress was made, and in 1994 Sinn Féin rejected Major's demand. Nevertheless, later that year, the IRA announced a cease-fire. Adams, along with the prime minister of the Republic of Ireland, Albert Reynolds, and John Hume, the leader of Ulster's largest Catholic party (the Social Democratic Labor Party), issued a statement that declared: "We are at the beginning of a new era in which we are all totally and absolutely committed to democratic and peaceful methods of resolving our political problems."

Peace?

On Good Friday in 1998, Catholic and Protestant leaders reached an agreement to share power in Northern Ireland

Sinn Féin leader Gerry Adams helps carry the coffin of IRA member Terrence Clark, 2000. The funeral attracted thousands and made its way through republican areas in north and west Belfast. *Photograph reproduced by permission of AP/Wide World Photos.*

and to observe a cease-fire. The agreement was negotiated with the help of former U.S. senator George J. Mitchell (1933–) of Maine, who was sent to Ulster by President Bill Clinton (1946–) to help bring an end to nearly thirty years of warfare.

The agreement called for new elections to a Northern Ireland parliament, as well as a cabinet called the Executive. The agreement also required armed groups on both sides to surrender their weapons by May 2000. The IRA was reluctant to give up its weapons, and the peace agreement nearly collapsed after the Protestants refused to name ministers to the Executive until Sinn Féin and the IRA gave specific details on their plans to disarm.

However, the two sides managed to keep the Good Friday peace accords alive. For some in the IRA, the peace agreement betrayed the long-held hope for uniting Ulster with the Irish Republic. But for some on the Protestant side, the agreement was a step toward unification, and they thought they could trust the IRA to put down its guns and live in peace.

In 2002 Adams continued to lead Sinn Féin, sometimes speaking on behalf of the IRA and other times declaring that he could not do so, especially when the IRA refused to agree to a firm schedule for giving up its arms.

For More Information

Books

Adams, Gerry. *Before the Dawn: An Autobiography*. New York: William Morrow & Co., 1996.

Adams, Gerry. *Cage Eleven*. Boulder, CO: Roberts Rinehart Publishers, 1994.

Coogan, Tim Pat. *The IRA*. New York: Palgrave for St. Martin's Press, 2002.

Taylor, Peter. *Behind the Mask: The IRA and Sinn Fein*. New York: TV Books, 1997.

Periodicals

Hillenbrand, Barry. "Gerry Adams under the Gun." *Time,* February 26, 1996, p. 50.

"Struggling to Make History." *Time,* August 1, 1994, p. 40.

Yasir Arafat

August 24, 1929
Cairo, Egypt or Palestine

Leader of the Palestine Liberation Organization

Yasir Arafat has represented the Palestinian people on the world stage since the 1960s, first as a terrorist leader and later as a peace negotiator in an area that has seen almost constant warfare since the end of World War I (1914–18). He has caused controversy every step of the way.

Childhood

Arafat was born on August 24, 1929, and given the name Mohammed Abdel-Raouf Arafat As Qudwa al-Hussaeini. As a boy, he was called Yasir (meaning "easygoing"). The controversy surrounding him begins with his birthplace. The Nobel Prize committee and the Palestinian Academic Society for the Study of International Affairs say he was born in Cairo, Egypt. The Palestine Liberation Organization (PLO) says it was Jerusalem, which was then located in what was called the Palestine Mandate, controlled by Britain. Arafat himself declared in a speech to the United Nations General Assembly in November 1974 that "Palestine was the cradle of the most ancient cultures and civilizations. . . . As a son of Jerusalem, I treasure for myself and my people beautiful memories and

"I have come bearing an olive branch and a freedom fighter's gun. Do not let the olive branch fall from my hand."

Photograph courtesy of the Library of Congress.

Words to Know

Communist: a person who believes in an economic theory that does not include the concept of private property; instead, a central government owns the goods and means of production.

Fundamentalist: a person who believes in following a strict set of moral principles.

Guerrilla: a combat soldier who fights in nontraditional ways, using ambushes and surprise attacks, usually to oppose larger armies.

Intifada: mass uprising by Palestinians.

Islamist: someone who believes that Islam should play a central role in the organization of a government.

Nationalist: a person who believes his or her nation is superior in all ways.

vivid images of the religious brotherhood that was the hallmark of our Holy City before it succumbed to catastrophe," meaning the creation of Israel in 1948 (see below).

Regardless of his birthplace, both of Arafat's parents were Palestinians. His father was a wealthy businessman who lived in Egypt. His mother came from a leading Palestinian family. She died when he was still a young child, and at age five he was sent to live with relatives in Jerusalem. Four years later Arafat moved back to Cairo to live with an older sister and other siblings. Arafat's father was frequently absent, and when he died in 1952 Arafat did not attend his funeral.

To war against Israel

As a teenager in Cairo Arafat became active in efforts to influence events in Palestine, where Jewish immigrants were organizing what was to become the state of Israel. Arafat helped smuggle arms to Palestinian Arabs who were struggling against similar Jewish organizations, including Jewish terrorist groups.

The British, who governed Palestine as a result of the treaty that ended World War I, tried to prevent the Jews from immigrating in large numbers. However, public opinion in the West (especially in the United States) began to support the Jews as details of the Holocaust (the murder of six million Jews by Nazi Germany during World War II [1939–45]) became more widely known.

In 1948, three months before Arafat's nineteenth birthday, Israel declared its independence. Almost immediately Arab armies on its borders attacked, while Palestinians inside Israel also fought the newly formed Jewish state. Arafat left the University of Faud I (later Cairo University) to join in

Yasir Arafat: Timeline of Major Events

1929: Born, either in Egypt or Palestine (sources differ).

1948: Joins Arab attacks on the new independent state of Israel.

1952: Becomes leader of the General Union of Palestinian Students in Egypt.

1956: Fights with Egyptian army in war against Israel, France, and Britain.

1958: Forms al-Fatah, whose goal is to replace Israel with an Arab-ruled Palestine. Fatah operates as both a political and military organization.

1969: Becomes chairman of the PLO, the main organization leading Palestinian opposition to Israel.

1970–71: Leads fighting between PLO and government of Jordan. Forced to move his headquarters to Lebanon, from where PLO launches guerrilla attacks on Israel.

1978: Egypt and Israel agree on a peace treaty, taking away one of Arafat's major allies in the Arab world.

1982: Israel invades Lebanon, forcing Arafat to move his headquarters to Tunis, Tunisia, in North Africa.

1988: PLO declares an independent state of Palestine and gives up violence as a tactic, effectively recognizing the right of Israel to exist.

1990: Supports Iraqi leader Saddam Hussein's (1937–) invasion of Kuwait.

1991: With loss of financial aid from wealthy Arab oil-producing states, Arafat opens peace talks overseen by the United States in Madrid, Spain.

1993: Palestinians and Israelis begin secret peace talks in Oslo, Norway. In September 1993 Arafat and Israeli Prime Minister Yitzhak Rabin (1922–1995) sign the Oslo Accords in Washington, D.C., giving Arafat control over the Gaza Strip and part of the West Bank. Arafat shakes hands with Rabin for the first time.

1994: Shares Nobel Peace Prize with Rabin and Israel's foreign minister, Shimon Peres (1923–).

1998–2000: Series of peace negotiations with Israel fail to advance Oslo Accords.

2000: Second **Intifada** (mass uprising by Palestinians) launched in Israel. The level of violence rises, lowering hopes of a permanent peace accord.

the fighting and saw combat in the area of the Gaza Strip (an area in southwestern Palestine).

After Israel's armed forces drove back the invading Arabs, Arafat returned to the university as an engineering student.

Freedom Fighters or Terrorists?

Yasir Arafat is praised as a "freedom fighter" or "guerrilla" in some places and condemned as a "terrorist" in others. Which word is correct?

"Terrorist" is usually a negative phrase, designed to link the subject with people who routinely use violence to get their way politically. On the other hand, "freedom fighters" implies patriots fighting against an alien power or a harsh government that oppresses people. "Guerrilla" refers to fighters who do not always wear uniforms or follow regular military procedures. French guerrillas became famous for resisting German Nazi rule during World War II (1939–45), for example, and the term is often a form of praise.

Governments attacked by people calling themselves "guerrillas" or "freedom fighters" often describe their attackers as "terrorists." The three terms often are used to describe the same armed men or women; the choice reflects whether the speaker supports or opposes them.

There he founded and led the General Union of Palestinian Students.

Struggle for Palestinian independence

After graduating with a degree in engineering, Arafat took a job in Kuwait for a few years, but he was never far from the Palestinian independence movement. In 1958 he and another Palestinian nationalist, Abu Jihad, founded the first cell of al-Fatah, which was to become a leading Palestinian guerrilla organization. The next year, he began publishing a magazine that supported armed struggle against Israel. In 1964 Arafat left Kuwait and began working full time to replace Israel with an Arab Palestinian state.

Arafat based his operations in the country of Jordan, east of Israel. Jordan held a large population of Palestinians who had left Israel in 1948. From there Arafat and fellow Fatah members launched raids into Israel. From the Israeli standpoint, Fatah was the largest terrorist organization conducting attacks against Israel. From Arafat's viewpoint, he was trying to free Palestine from the Jews who had taken the country from its rightful owners.

In his speech to the United Nations General Assembly in 1974, Arafat compared the Palestinian Arabs to black citizens of Africa who were fighting for independence from British and Portuguese colonial rule. He complained that the Jews were really invading Europeans acting on behalf of a British government that wanted to continue controlling the region. He asked for the support of other nations to restore Arab control, including the right of Palestinians to return to the homes from which they fled in 1948.

From the 1960s until the 1980s Arafat made it clear that his goal was to get rid of the government of Israel and replace it with a government of Palestinian Arabs, headed by himself. He described Fatah as a nationalist organization willing to accept people of many religions, including Judaism.

Fatah gains influence

In 1964 the major Arab states founded the Palestine Liberation Organization (PLO) to coordinate the efforts of various Palestinian groups. Fatah was not a member of the PLO at first. It was, however, the largest Palestinian group making armed raids against Israel.

This changed after the Six Day War (June 1967) between Israel and surrounding Arab states. In less than a week Israel defeated the combined armies of Egypt, Syria, and Jordan and seized control of key territories, including the Golan Heights in Syria and the Sinai Peninsula and Gaza Strip in Egypt. The Six Day War was a turning point in the conflict between Israel and the Palestinians. First, it made military attacks on Israel much less attractive to surrounding Arab countries. Second, the Fatah joined the PLO and became its largest member organization. Third, terrorist attacks became the preferred Palestinian tactic. And fourth, Arafat emerged as the leading figure in the Palestinian fight against Israel.

The terrorist years: 1967–1984

Arafat became chairman of the PLO in 1969. From his new headquarters in Amman, Jordan, Arafat launched dozens of attacks by Fatah against targets in Israel. But Fatah was only one of several terrorist organizations working against Israel. Although Arafat did not personally control every terrorist group, as the public spokesman for the Palestinian cause he was closely tied to the continuing terror campaign.

Arafat built a significant military organization, which began to seem threatening to the government of King Hussein (1935–1999) in Jordan. Frequent clashes between the Jordanian armed forces and the Palestinians became outright war in the autumn of 1970. The immediate cause was a series of plane hijackings, in which Palestinian terrorists took over three

The 1967 Six Day War between Israel and surrounding Arab states resulted in a rapid Israeli victory and the Israeli occupation of territory in the Golan Heights, the Sinai Peninsula, and the Gaza Strip. This territory became the focus of the Arab/Palestinian campaign against Israel, which has increasingly taken the form of terrorist attacks in the occupied regions.

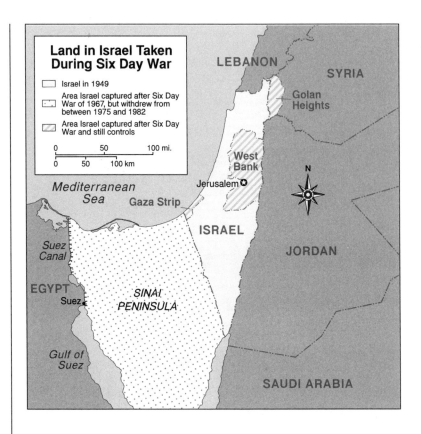

European passenger planes and forced them to land in Jordan. This brought Jordan into conflict with the European countries whose planes had been seized. Two days after the hijacked planes were blown up in Jordan by the hijackers (after the hostages had been set free), the Jordanian army attacked the Palestinian terrorists.

At first the outcome seemed in doubt. But slowly the Jordanians gained the upper hand, and other Arab states arranged a peace negotiation in Cairo. A tense standoff in Jordan lasted until July 1971, when Jordanian forces again attacked Arafat's Palestinians and forced Arafat to leave Jordan for nearby Lebanon.

Throughout the fighting and negotiations, Arafat was highly visible. He also demonstrated a high degree of flexibility in negotiations, a tendency that in later years would annoy diplomats.

Exile in Lebanon: 1973–82

The next significant event in Arafat's struggle to create a Palestinian nation barely involved the Palestinians at all. On October 6, 1973 (the Jewish religious holiday of Yom Kippur), the armies of Egypt and Syria launched surprise attacks on Israel. Their goal was to retake all the territory they had lost in 1967. Although the attacks were successful at first, Israel eventually drove back the Egyptian and Syrian forces and started to advance into the invading countries. Egypt's failure in the so-called Yom Kippur War, in addition to that country's severe economic problems, led President Anwar el-Sadat (1918–1981) to negotiate a peace treaty with Israel in 1978. The treaty recognized Israel's right to exist and set up diplomatic relations between the two countries. With the treaty, Arafat and the Palestinians lost an important Arab ally.

Allies in the communist camp

In the meantime Arafat was actively organizing raids against Israeli targets and campaigning for international support. Arafat allied himself with the Soviet Union (today, Russia and its neighboring countries) and its communist allies. While this alliance helped Arafat in his campaign against Israel (which the United States, then the firm enemy of the Soviet Union, strongly supported), it eventually proved to be a dead end. The breakup of the Soviet Union in 1991 again took a key source of support from Arafat.

More defeats and a change in strategy

In 1982 Israel invaded southern Lebanon, which was an important launchpad for Palestinian guerrilla attacks. Arafat and the PLO were forced to move their operations to the North African country of Tunisia.

In 1987 Palestinians launched a popular revolt, called the "Intifada," against Israeli rule in the Gaza Strip and the West Bank of the Jordan River. The Intifada included throwing stones at Israeli soldiers, labor strikes, and boycotts of Israeli businesses. It took both Arafat and Israel by surprise; Arafat had to move quickly to gain control over the popular uprising.

The following year, on November 15, 1988, Arafat persuaded the PLO to declare an independent state of Palestine.

The declaration said that Palestine "announces itself to be a peace-loving State, in adherence to the principles of peaceful co-existence" and "rejects the threat or use of force, violence and terrorism against its territorial integrity or political independence, as it also rejects their use against territorial integrity of other states"—meaning Israel. The next year Arafat was declared head of the government-in-exile of Palestine.

The Iraqi invasion of Kuwait in 1990 that sparked the Persian Gulf War turned out to be a major event in Arafat's political life, and the cause of a political misjudgment. Kuwait was strongly supported by its wealthy fellow oil-producing states, such as Saudi Arabia, Bahrain, and Qatar. But Arafat decided to support Iraqi leader Saddam Hussein (1937–), and his support for Iraq cost him the backing of the oil producers. After the United States and Britain drove Iraq out of Kuwait, an important source of Arafat's funding dried up. The PLO was forced, partly for financial reasons, to begin peace negotiations with Israel.

Peace talks with Israel and a new role

The first round of peace talks with Israel began with meetings in Madrid, Spain, in 1991, with the assistance of the United States. No progress was made at the talks, but in February 1993 Arafat's representatives began meeting secretly with Israelis in Oslo, Norway. Their goal was to negotiate a peace treaty that would found a new state of Palestine and recognize Israel's right to exist. The following September Arafat came to Washington, D.C., to sign the Oslo Accords with Israeli Prime Minister Yitzhak Rabin. For the first time Arafat shook hands with an Israeli leader, giving rise to hopes that the long battle between Palestinians and Israelis might be coming to an end. Two months later Arafat, Rabin, and Israel's foreign minister, Shimon Peres, shared the 1994 Nobel Peace Prize.

Arafat's role changed significantly. As the newly recognized Palestinian Authority gained control over a limited territory, Arafat moved from being a guerrilla (or "terrorist") leader to the head of an official government.

At the same time Arafat faced another challenge: the rising influence of Islamic fundamentalists. Islamic fundamentalists are strict Muslims who believe that the moral principles of the religion of Islam should play a central role in the

In 1994 Yasir Arafat won the Nobel Peace Prize along with Israeli Prime Minister Yitzak Rabin and Israeli Foreign Minister Shimon Peres for their work in negotiating a partial peace agreement (the Oslo Accords). The agreement did not lead to lasting peace, however, and Arafat continued to be torn between directing a terrorist war against Israel and reaching a permanent settlement. *Photograph reproduced by permission of AP/Wide World Photos.*

government. For the Islamists, the fight between Palestinians and Israelis was a religious issue. They did not support any peace negotiations that would leave Israel intact. Islamists had significant financial support, in particular from the Iranian government, which they used to fund terrorism against Israel and to set up charitable groups in nearby countries. The Islamists were a significant challenge to Arafat's control of the Palestinian cause.

As a result, in 1995 Arafat formed a new semi-military organization, the Fatah Tanzim, within the areas controlled by the Palestine Authority (which had its own armed forces). One effect of Tanzim was to provide Arafat with a military force that could act independently of the Palestine Authority without bringing on international criticism of the organization that was intended to become the government of a new Palestinian state. Critics of Arafat saw Tanzim as an example of double-dealing: Arafat was negotiating for peace on one side and building up a new potential terrorist organization on the other.

Moving to the next step

The Oslo Accords gave Arafat a partial victory. On the one hand, he was the elected leader of an organization that governed territory. But on the other hand, the Palestinian Authority was not quite a full-fledged country, and it did not control all the territory Arafat thought it should.

In 1998 a new round of negotiations between Palestinians and Israelis started with the goal of a permanent peace agreement, under which Palestinians and Israelis would each recognize the right of the other to live in a secure nation. The exact boundaries of the proposed state of Palestine, and the rights of Arab Palestinians to return to the homes they had abandoned when Israel was founded in 1948, proved to be extremely difficult to agree upon. In December 2001 Arafat, Israeli Prime Minister Ehud Barak (1942–), and U.S. President Bill Clinton met to try to push through a final agreement. In the end, however, Arafat refused the terms Israel offered, and the meetings ended without a final agreement.

In the Middle East, Palestinians living under Israeli rule in territory that Israel had occupied in 1967 launched a second Intifada in September 2000. Attacks against Israeli soldiers resumed with a new tactic: suicide bombing. Increasingly, young Palestinians volunteered to go on suicide missions, carrying explosives strapped to their bodies and setting them off inside Israeli stores, nightclubs, and buses. The new tactic increased the level of suspicion between the two sides, as ordinary Palestinians began to be viewed as potential bomb carriers. This new tactic showed the rising influence of Islamist groups like Hamas and Hezbollah, which promised an eternity in paradise to the suicide bombers. These groups, which were strongly opposed to any peace agreement with Israel, also challenged Arafat's leadership and raised doubts about the chances of reaching a permanent peace settlement with Israel.

The new wave of terrorism, combined with a new and more conservative Israeli government headed by Prime Minister Ariel Sharon (1928–), began a new chapter in the long history between Palestinians and Israelis.

For More Information

Books

Gowers, Andrew. *Behind the Myth: Yasser Arafat and the Palestinian Revolution*. New York: Olive Branch Press, 1991.

Hart, Alan. *Arafat, A Political Biography*. Bloomington: Indiana University Press, 1989.

Kiernan, Thomas. *Arafat, the Man and the Myth*. New York: Norton, 1976.

Mishal, Shaul. *The PLO under Arafat: Between Gun and Olive Branch*. New Haven, CT: Yale University Press, 1986.

Reische, Diana L. *Arafat and the Palestine Liberation Organization*. New York: Franklin Watts, 1991.

Wallach, Janet, and John Wallach. *Arafat: In the Eyes of the Beholder*. New York: Carol Publishing Group, 1990.

オウム真理教
麻原彰晃代表

Shoko Asahara (Chizuo Matsumoto)

March 2, 1955
Yatsushiro, Japan

Leader of Aum Shinrikyo

"From now [1993] until the year 2000, a series of violent phenomena filled with fears that are too difficult to describe will occur. Japan will turn into waste land as a result of a nuclear weapons attack."

Photograph reproduced by permission of AP/Wide World Photos.

On the morning of March 20, 1995, thousands of people riding the subway to work in Tokyo, Japan, suddenly felt terribly ill. Some could not stand up and fell down convulsing on the subway platforms. Others could not speak. Some were blinded. Twelve died.

By the end of the morning more than five thousand people had claimed to have been sickened or injured. All were victims of a poison gas attack planned and executed by a religious cult named Aum Shinrikyo, a Japanese name that in English means "Supreme Truth." The organization was headed by a man named Shoko Asahara, who had just had his fortieth birthday three weeks earlier.

Childhood

Making and selling straw mats in southern Japan in the 1950s did not bring in very much money. And the Matsumoto family was large, with five children. When the sixth child was born in 1955, blind in one eye and with limited sight in the other, he was a burden for the struggling family. When he was six years old the boy, named Chizuo, was sent to a boarding school for the blind. He lived there through his teens.

Having some sight was an advantage at the blind school, and it gave Chizuo a certain status. Perhaps his thirst for power dates from these early days. Reportedly, during these school years Chizuo repeatedly said he wanted to become prime minister of Japan.

Chizuo studied acupuncture (an ancient Chinese medical technique that involves inserting small needles into the body at precise points to relieve pain), hoping it might somehow improve his eyesight. At age twenty-one he moved to Tokyo and soon married Tomoko Ishii, with whom he had six children. He applied to study law at Tokyo University but was turned down. Eventually he began selling Chinese herbal cures but got into trouble by illegally marketing them as medicine. In his late twenties, still feeling at loose ends, Chizuo decided that he was experiencing a spiritual pull. It took him to India, where he wandered in a vague quest for spiritual enlightenment. Upon his return to Japan he announced that he had achieved Nirvana, the ultimate state of grace for a Buddhist, and was ready to explain his religion to the world.

 Words to Know

Buddhism: a religion of eastern Asia based on the teachings of Gautama Buddha; teaches that suffering, though part of life, can be overcome by mental and spiritual purification.

Cult: a group of people who believe in unorthodox ideas or concepts.

Hinduism: the dominant religion of India; one of its basic beliefs is the immortality of the soul and its reincarnation after the death of the human body.

Cult leader

Chizuo Matsumoto took on a new name, Shoko Asahara, and started a new cult, which he called Aum Shinrikyo. The cult was founded on a mixture of beliefs taken from the eastern religions Buddhism and Hinduism, with elements of Christianity mixed in. Its chief symbol was Shiva, the Hindu god of destruction and reproduction. The cult's beliefs developed gradually between its founding in 1987 and the poison gas attack on Tokyo in 1995.

At first Aum Shinrikyo was founded on the idea of turning away from worldly materialism (the desire to succeed and acquire things) in favor of a life of meditation using the techniques of yoga (a system of spiritual exercises designed to make the body flexible and teach breath control). In this respect the sect was like many religious groups, and it attracted large numbers of young people who were unhappy with the intense competition that was part of Japanese society. Asahara wore a flowing beard and long Indian robes, and he encouraged his followers to purchase bottles of his bath water (sold under the name "Miracle Pond" for about $300 an ounce) and even his blood to drink as a way to achieve enlightenment. The sect also rented out special headsets, called "Hats of Happiness," at $11,500 per month. These devices promised to reproduce Asahara's brain waves.

In 1989 Asahara published a book, *Secrets of Developing Your Supernatural Powers,* which promised to let readers in on such secrets as seeing the future, reading other people's minds, making wishes come true, developing X-ray vision, and hearing the voice of God. Asahara also wrote, "I hereby declare myself to be the Christ."

Other sect practices included taking hallucinogenic drugs (drugs that cause the mind to perceive things that do not exist), not having sex, and self-starvation. Followers sometimes spent long periods in closed, airless spaces. One police raid on a cult compound turned up a woman in a box, where she had been for at least two months. Followers were encouraged to leave their families and live in religious communities called Lotus Villages, which were scattered around Japan. The cult sometimes ignored local building rules, setting up buildings wherever they wanted.

In 1990 the man who had once vowed to become Japan's prime minister decided to try politics. With two dozen other cult members, Asahara ran for a seat in the Japanese parliament. Their campaign tactics were extremely unusual. The candidates wore Asahara masks or elephant masks and put on song-and-dance shows on the streets of Tokyo. The songs consisted of endless repetitions of Asahara's name. After all of his candidates lost, Asahara accused the government of rigging the voting.

Asahara was quite successful in attracting followers. By 1994, a year before the subway gas attack, there were about ten thousand members of the cult in thirty-six branches in Japan, plus a number of international offices (including some in the United States). Aum Shinrikyo was once thought to have ten thousand to forty thousand members in Russia.

The cult was also successful at making money. It tended to bring in well-educated, wealthy members and typically required them to hand over all their money to the group. Cult members worked in exchange for simple meals and a place to sleep. In addition to the money they got from new recruits, the cult earned money from running chains of discount stores, restaurants, and a factory that put together personal computers.

A darker vision

But there was a darker side to Asahara's beliefs. He taught that the world would end soon. At first he said the end of the world would take place in 1999; later, he decided the world would end in 1997.

And he said he knew how it would take place. In a book called *Disaster Approaches the Land of the Rising Sun* (Land of the Rising Sun is a name for Japan), he claimed that the United States was ruled by Freemasons (a secret society founded in the Middle Ages)—or possibly Jews—and planned to attack Japan. Part of the attack would include a cloud of poison gas sent floating over Japan. A worldwide nuclear war would follow, after which only 10 percent of humanity would survive, including the members of Aum Shinrikyo.

Japanese authorities later uncovered evidence that Asahara had begun planning to make his own prophecy come true by getting what he needed to start a war himself.

The cult began recruiting experts in chemical and biological weapons and sent them around the world in search of materials. In 1992, for example, cult members went to Zaire, where there had been an outbreak of the deadly Ebola virus. (The Ebola virus is the cause of Ebola hemorrhagic fever, an often fatal disease that is highly infectious through blood or other body fluids.) Posing as aid workers, the cult members tried to get a sample of the virus that could be used in biological warfare. Investigators also found evidence that Aum Shinrikyo had bought special gas masks in the United States.

The cult also set up assembly lines inside its main compound to put together automatic rifles. It bought remote-controlled miniature helicopters, at $20,000 each, to distribute poison gas. It tried hard to recruit members from Russia, apparently hoping to get its hands on weapons from the former Soviet Union (today, Russia and its neighboring countries).

A trial run, then the real thing

In June 1994 a panel of three judges was about to rule on a land dispute involving Aum Shinrikyo in the Japanese city of Matsumoto, northwest of Tokyo. About three weeks before the ruling, however, a cloud of sarin gas spread over a neighborhood in the city, killing seven people and injuring two hundred others, including the judges. Although no one was charged in the Matsumoto attack, a few weeks later people living near one of the cult's compounds woke up with sore eyes, feeling ill. There was a bad smell throughout the neighborhood. The cult was given a warning.

Then came March 20, 1995. At about 8 A.M., a man wearing sunglasses, brown pants, and a blue or beige coat got onto an eight-car subway train on the Hibiya line. He was wearing a surgical mask, which was not too unusual during the spring allergy season in Tokyo. He began fiddling with a package wrapped in newspapers.

At the next stop the man set down the package and rushed off the train, which closed its doors and continued toward the center of Tokyo. It was headed for a station that serves government offices.

Soon the package began giving off a bad odor and left a pool of oily water on the floor of the subway car. Eleven minutes after the man with the package first boarded the train, passengers began panicking, realizing that the package was giving off a gas. But by then it was too late for some.

News accounts described a frightening scene of rush-hour commuters being overcome by what later proved to be a poisonous gas called sarin. "I saw several dozen people on the platform who had either collapsed or were on their knees unable to stand up," one witness was reported saying, in *Time* magazine. "One man was thrashing around on the floor like a fish out of water." Some passengers said they had been blinded.

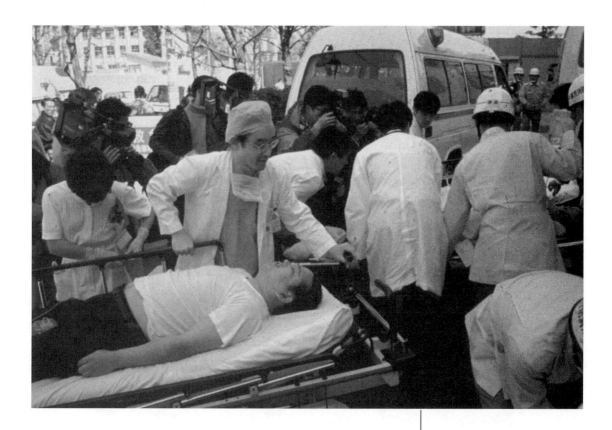

Others were shaking and crying but making no sound—the gas had made them mute.

In all, five subway stations on three different subway lines were affected by gas attacks that morning. A dozen people died from the gas, and about fifty-five hundred reported they were injured. A Japanese government official described it as "a declaration of war against the Japanese government." It appeared that Asahara intended the gas attack to touch off the world war that he had predicted.

What the police found next

Just two days after the subway gas attack, twenty-five hundred police officers raided twenty-five offices of Aum Shinrikyo located throughout Japan. Police dressed in protective suits held cages out in front of them. The cages held canaries. If the birds died as police entered the buildings, the officers planned to run for their lives.

Shoko Asahara was accused of masterminding a poison gas attack on Tokyo subways in 1995. Twelve people died and thousands were sickened by the gas. Here, passengers affected by the gas are unloaded at St. Luke's Hospital in Tokyo. *Photograph reproduced by permission of AP/Wide World Photos.*

Who Joined Aum Shinrikyo?

What sort of person joined the Aum Shinrikyo cult? Although many of the cult leader's claims sound strange—such as the idea that drinking his bathwater would help one reach enlightenment—what shocked many Japanese was the fact that many Aum Shinrikyo members were well-educated and wealthy. Asahara attracted people with Ph.D. degrees who put together a complex system for manufacturing arms, chemical weapons, biological weapons, and drugs. The cult seemed to attract some of Japan's best and brightest. Indeed, it was through recruiting people educated in science and technology that Asahara was able to put into practice many of his programs, such as developing nerve gas and other weapons and setting up a personal computer assembly plant.

In his 1996 book *A Poisonous Cocktail?* author Ian Reader noted that the sect, in addition to disapproving of materialism, argued that it was important to withdraw from society to achieve spiritual progress. This attracted "young, idealistic people who were dissatisfied [with] the materialism, stifling conformity [the requirement that everyone act according to strict standards], rigid structures and competitiveness of Japanese society."

Under Asahara's leadership, cult members' sense of separation from Japanese society gradually became a sense of being persecuted (unjustly mistreated) and then a desire to take action that would bring about the end of the world.

The birds did not die, but inside one Aum Shinrikyo compound the police found large quantities of chemicals that could be used to make sarin. They found fifty cult members suffering from malnutrition (not eating enough food or enough good food) and a young woman lying inside a small, windowless box, where she had been for more than two months.

According to the report in *Time* magazine, Asahara quickly released recorded messages stating his innocence. In a singsong voice, he repeated over and over again: "I didn't do it, I'm innocent. I didn't do it, I'm innocent." In his other message, Asahara appealed to his followers: "Disciples, the time to awaken and help me is upon you. Let's carry out the salvation plan and face death without regrets."

Asahara's lawyer insisted that Aum Shinrikyo practiced religion according to the doctrines of Buddhism and suggested that the U.S. military was somehow involved. Shortly afterward, Asahara released a videotape for his followers in which he insisted that he, along with other Aum Shinrikyo members, were the targets of a poison gas attack by the United States.

Charged with murder

Two months after the subway attack, Asahara was arrested and charged with ordering the attack. Police found him dressed in silk pajamas inside a secret bunker in his compound, with a cassette player, a few books, and $100,000 in cash.

Asahara was charged with being responsible for the deaths caused by the Tokyo gas attack and with several other murders connected to the cult. Japan's criminal justice system is known for being slow, and Asahara's trial was expected to last more than a decade. The prosecution's case alone took six years.

In the meantime the cult continued to earn significant sums of money years after Asahara was sent to jail. Although the membership quickly dropped from around ten thousand to about two thousand, Aum Shinrikyo continued to operate a computer assembly factory, as well as retail stores, that brought in $53 million in 1998. The sect continued to put on rock concerts and seminars. In an effort to distance itself from the gas attack, the organization changed its name to Aleph (after the first letter of the Hebrew alphabet).

For More Information

Books

Kaplan, David E., and Andrew Marshall. *The Cult at the End of the World: The Terrifying Story of the Aum Doomsday Cult, from the Subways of Tokyo to the Nuclear Arsenals of Russia.* New York: Crown Publishers, 1996.

Lifton, Robert Jay. *Destroying the World to Save It: Aum Shinrikyo, Apocalyptic Violence, and the New Global Terrorism.* New York: Metropolitan Books, 1999.

Murakami, Haruki. *Underground: The Tokyo Gas Attack and the Japanese Psyche,* translated by Alfred Birnbaum and Philip Gabriel. New York: Vintage, 2001.

Reader, Ian. *A Poisonous Cocktail? Aum Shinrikyo's Path to Violence.* Copenhagen, Denmark: Nordic Institute for Asian Stidies, 1996.

Periodicals

"The Doom Machine: Inspired by Nostradamus, Aum Shinrikyo's Jailed Leader Guides His Still-thriving Flock toward the End." *Time International,* July 5, 1999, p. 22.

Jerome, Richard. "Japan's Mad Messiah: Jailed in Tokyo's Subway Gassing, a Guru Is Alone with His Grand Delusions." *People Weekly,* June 12, 1995, p. 48.

Walsh, James. "Shoko Asahara: The Making of a Messiah." *Time,* April 3, 1995, p. 30.

Andreas Baader

May 6, 1943
Munich, Germany
October 18, 1977
Stuttgart, Germany

Gudrun Ensslin

August 15, 1940
Bartholomae, Germany
October 18, 1977
Stuttgart, Germany

Leaders of the Red Army Faction,
usually called the Baader-Meinhof Gang

L ike the United States and most Western European countries, Germany experienced a wave of terrorism during the 1970s that challenged the political and economic order. Since the end of World War II (1939–45), in which the United States, Britain, and the Soviet Union (today, Russia and its neighboring countries) defeated Germany, the country had rebuilt its industries to become an economic powerhouse. But members of the generation born at the end of World War II challenged the German **establishment** in a movement called the **New Left.** A small number of these **radicals** (people who want rapid change in society) turned to terrorism to get their point across.

The best known of these radicals-turned-terrorists were members of a group called the Red Army Faction. In the press, they often were called the Baader-Meinhof Gang. But this name misidentified the leaders of the group, who were Andreas Baader and Gudrun Ensslin. The name Meinhof belonged to another member of the group, Ulrike Meinhof (1934–1976), who was never a leader but was well known for her appearances on German television.

"We have found that words are useless without action!"

—*Gudrin Ensslin*

"The gun livens up things."

—*Andreas Baader*

Photograph of Andreas Baader reproduced by permission of AP/Wide World Photos.

Andreas Baader: Growing up after the war

Baader was born in 1943 in Munich, the main city in southern Germany's traditionally conservative state of Bavaria. His father, Berndt Baader, who was a historian, fought in the German army against Russia. When Baader was not quite two years old, in 1945, his father was taken prisoner. Berndt Baader was never heard from again and was presumed killed. In April 1945 Germany surrendered. After five years of war, the country was in ruins, defeated and occupied by the United States, Great Britain, France, and Russia. Germany's famous industrial economy was shattered. Times were hard; food was sometimes in short supply.

Full of energy and believed to be highly intelligent, Baader grew up the center of attention in a household of women. But in school he failed to get good grades. His teachers said it was because he did not try hard. He had the traits of a spoiled child: talented but lazy and often rebellious. His teachers complained that he misled the other children into bad behavior. But his mother and aunts refused to discipline Baader, their only remaining male relative, and he grew up lacking self-discipline as well.

As Baader grew older his rebelliousness grew more serious. It started with cars and motorcycles. Baader did not bother getting a driver's license, even though he loved to drive. If he could not afford a fast car, he stole one. He became a familiar figure in court, answering traffic tickets. He was kicked out of high school, which meant he could not attend a university. He enrolled in art school but quit. He tried writing advertisements but left that too.

Berlin in the swinging sixties

When he was twenty Baader moved to West Berlin. In 1963 the city was divided into a western half, ruled by the non-communist West German government, and an eastern half occupied by Russian forces and ruled by the communist government of East Germany. (Communism is an economic theory that does not include the concept of private property; instead the public—usually represented by the government—owns the goods and the means to produce them in common.) West Berlin was filled with nightclubs and excitement and the anything-goes culture of the "swinging sixties," the perfect place for a young man like Baader.

Young Germans in the 1960s had much in common with young Americans in that decade. The generation born at the end of World War II wanted more social freedoms. It was the decade of "sex, drugs, and rock and roll." Freer social behavior carried over into politics as well, and young people rebelled against the conservative (traditionalist) government of their parents' generation. Opposition to American involvement in the Vietnam War (1955–75) was one thing the young rebels had in common in most Western countries. A general disgust with the "establishment"—the adults in charge of government and business—was another. Street demonstrations often led to battles with the police.

This sense of rebelliousness developed into a political movement called the New Left. It sympathized with communism but disliked the rather dull nature of most communist countries. Young people wanted a new society with greater equality and respect for human rights.

Baader gets political

When Baader arrived in West Berlin, he plunged into the culture of the 1960s. He had many girlfriends and frequently drove too fast in cars that did not belong to him. He met an artist named Ellinor Michel, and the two of them had a daughter in 1965. At the time Michel was married to another man, and for a while Ellinor, Baader, and Ellinor's husband all lived in the same apartment. It was the sort of freewheeling arrangement for which the 1960s became famous. Baader kept several girlfriends and continued to live his life of fast cars and fast driving. But this began to change in 1967, when he met Ensslin. Ensslin was at first just another girlfriend. But she was a very different person from Baader.

Gudrun Ensslin

Ensslin was in some ways an odd match for Baader. The daughter of a clergyman who had strongly opposed Adolf Hitler (the leader of Germany during World War II; 1889–1945) and Hitler's Nazi Party, Ensslin grew up as a serious girl who read the Bible and sang hymns in her father's church, which was part of the Evangelical Church in Germany. The Evangelical Church was founded in 1945 as a counterinfluence to the defeated Nazi Party. The Church, and Ensslin's family, taught her to question the government and to have a strong sense of social justice.

Ensslin was a model child in most respects. She did well in school. She helped around the house. Her family often discussed social injustice, both in Germany and abroad. In high school, she spent a year in the United States as part of an international exchange program. Her experience there was mixed. On the one hand, she found a boyfriend and enjoyed her stay. On the other hand, she objected to what she saw as inequality in American society and the wide gap between rich and poor.

Back in Germany Ensslin studied philosophy at the University of Tübingen, where she met Bernward Vesper. He was involved in a variety of **left-wing** causes, such as opposing nuclear weapons, and studied the writings of well-known communist thinkers such as Karl Marx (1818–1883) and Chinese leader Mao Zedong (also spelled Tse-tung; 1893–1976). Ensslin became a committed communist. She and Vesper moved to West Berlin, where she attended the Free University, even as she became more deeply involved in left-wing politics. (Left-wing politics place importance on finding the solutions to social problems, especially inequality, and believe in democratic control of the economy as well as the government.)

A short family life

In 1965 Ensslin and Vesper married. They seemed an ideal couple: they had the same values and political outlook. In 1967 Ensslin gave birth to their son, Felix Robert. But at this

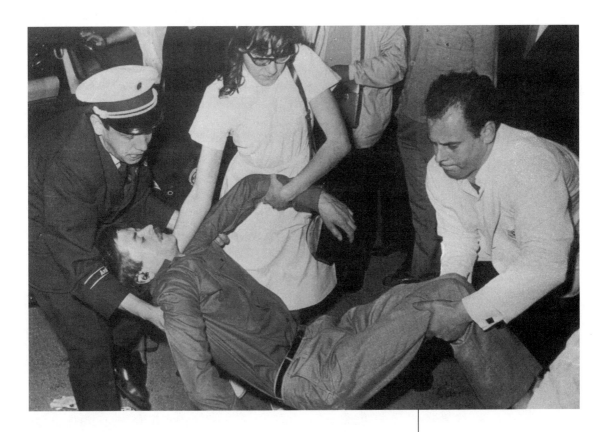

point Ensslin was becoming less interested in family life and more committed to radical politics. She soon left her infant son and husband.

It was in the summer of 1967 that Ensslin met Baader at a gathering. The two fell in love immediately. They were a curious, and eventually dangerous, combination. The "good girl" Ensslin, with her increasingly radical political beliefs, was in many respects the opposite of "bad boy" Baader, who had no strong political beliefs. To Ensslin, Baader brought a sense of daring and a willingness to break the law. To Baader, Ensslin brought a commitment to left-wing politics. As a result, Baader directed his behavior toward politics while Ensslin directed her politics toward rebellious behavior.

The introduction of violence

On June 2, 1967, Benno Ohnesorg, age twenty-six, was shot in the back of the head by a policeman during a protest

A demonstrator at a rally in West Berlin, Germany, Benno Ohnesorg, was shot and killed by a policeman. The event convinced Gudrun Ensslin that political change was possible only through violence—a belief shared by many terrorists throughout history. *Photograph reproduced by permission of AP/Wide World Photos.*

march in West Berlin. Ohnesorg was a college student with a pregnant wife. It was his first political demonstration. His death, and that fact that the policeman who shot him was found not guilty of manslaughter five months later, shocked and enraged young German radicals. According to author Stefan Aust in *The Baader-Meinhof Group,* at the headquarters of one leading organization of young protesters, a thin young woman arrived after the shooting and screamed, "We must organize resistance. Violence is the only way to answer violence. This is the Auschwitz Generation, and there's no arguing with them!" (Auschwitz was the name of a Nazi death camp where thousands of Jews were murdered during World War II. In this case, the woman was referring to the generation of Germans who were young men during the time the Nazis controlled Germany from 1933 to 1945.) The young woman was Ensslin, and ten months later, she took action.

On the night of April 2, 1968, fires broke out at two department stores in Frankfurt, West Germany. A caller who would not give her name told the German Press Agency: "There are flames in the Schneider and Kaufhof [department stores]. It is a political act of revenge." The arson was the first act of a group that called itself the Red Army Faction but later became known as the Baader-Meinhof Gang. Just two days after the fires, Baader, Ensslin, and two other radicals, Thorwald Proll and Horst Söhnlein, were arrested and charged with arson. The charge was made more serious because a night watchman was in one store and might have been injured or killed (in fact, he escaped without injury). At their trial the four were found guilty of setting the fires and sentenced to three years in jail. A few months later they were released pending the outcome of their legal appeal.

But the case had attracted attention, and left-wing journalists were sympathetic to the young arsonists. They argued that the fires had hurt no one and had attracted attention to their cause. One journalist who wrote articles supporting them was a woman named Ulrike Meinhof, who was already well known in Germany for her appearances on television talk shows and for articles she had written to protest the killing of Ohnesorg.

The Baader-Meinhof Gang

In November 1969 their appeals of the guilty verdicts in the arson case were rejected, and the four were ordered to report to jail. Instead, Baader and Ensslin left Germany for Italy, passing through France and Switzerland on the way. A few months later, in the early spring of 1970, they returned to Germany and hid out in Meinhof's apartment. In April 1970 Baader was stopped by a traffic policeman who took him to jail, where he was identified and sent to serve his sentence.

The following month Ensslin persuaded Meinhof to help her carry out a dramatic escape for Baader. The plan used her reputation as a writer to convince authorities that she was helping Baader write a book. On May 14, 1970, Baader was allowed to visit a library outside the prison, supposedly to work on the book with Meinhof. Once the two were inside the library, two young women knocked on the door and asked to use the library. They were told to wait in the lobby until Meinhof and Baader were finished. The doorbell rang again, and the two women in the lobby, who were part of the escape plan, let in a masked man carrying a pistol. While the gunman held off Baader's guards, Meinhof and Baader escaped through a window, followed by their helpers. All four got away, but Meinhof was identified as being in on the escape. Although the group had chosen the name the Red Army Faction (which was the name of a radical left-wing Japanese group), the popular press pounced on Meinhof's involvement and dubbed them the Baader-Meinhof Gang.

Baader, Ensslin, and Meinhof, who were all wanted by the police, fled to East Germany, which was sympathetic to their communist leanings. From there the three went to Jordan, where they joined Palestinians who were being trained in terrorist tactics. At the time, the Popular Front for the Liberation of Palestine, whose main goal was defeating Israel and setting up a Palestinian government in its place, was trying to build alliances with left-wing groups in Europe. (The Jewish state of Israel had been founded in 1948 by the United Nations on Palestinian land.) The Germans thus joined a network of left-wing terrorist groups operating in Europe, the Middle East, and Asia. The Baader-Meinhof Gang was among the most radical of these groups, and in some ways the most successful. But after a few months, the Palestinians were so offended by the Germans' behavior that they asked the group to leave.

The gang became a magnet for young Germans who wanted to rebel against the conservative West German govern-

Ulrike Meinhof (1934–1976)

Ulrike Meinhof, whose name became linked with Andreas Baader in the Baader-Meinhof Gang, was never a leader of the gang, nor was she romantically involved with Baader.

Nine years older than Baader, she was a well-known journalist in Berlin when Baader was convicted of arson. Meinhof was sympathetic to him and Gudrun Ensslin and allowed the two to live in her Berlin apartment after they jumped bail. After Baader was identified by police during a traffic stop, Meinhof agreed to help Baader break out of prison, using her reputation as a journalist as a cover.

Meinhof was born in 1934, shortly after Adolf Hitler came to power in Germany. Her father Werner, an assistant museum director in the town of Jena,

Germany, strongly opposed the Nazis, Hitler's political party. Werner died of cancer when Meinhof was five years old. She grew up a lively child, popular with children and adults alike. She was cared for by her mother, Ingeborg, and a boarder in their house, Renate Riemack.

After the war, the town of Jena became part of Russian-occupied East Germany. Meinhof's mother moved in 1946 to noncommunist West Germany, where, three years later, she died of cancer. Meinhof, then fourteen, was raised by Riemack.

Meinhof was a talented writer and was interested in social issues. At the University of Münster, she became interested in campaigns opposing atomic weapons and German rearmament (the movement to build up Germany's military

ment. Over the next six years, members of the Red Army Faction carried out many attacks on leading West German politicians and businessmen. Some attacks were aimed at individuals. Others were straightforward economic crimes, such as stealing cars or robbing banks, to get money for living and buying guns. The gang was the focus of a massive police manhunt. Many individual members were identified and arrested over time. Some police arrests resulted in gunfire that killed both policemen and gang members. Among the most dramatic incidents laid at the feet of the Baader-Meinhof Gang were these:

- **May 11, 1972:** In Frankfurt, Baader, Ensslin, and two other gang members set off pipe bombs at the headquarters of

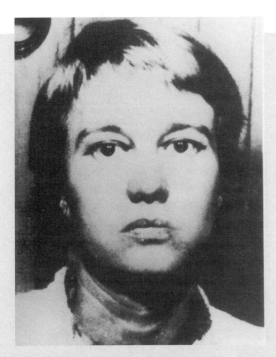

Ulrike Meinhof. *Photograph reproduced by permission of AP/Wide World Photos.*

strength again after World War II). She met Klaus Röhl, the editor of a leftist student newspaper, *konkret* (meaning "concrete" or "real"), and married him in 1961. She became editor in chief of *konkret* and gained a reputation for writing radical articles. She also became the mother of twins.

Meinhof became well known by appearing on television talk shows. She also moved further to the left, getting to know people like Baader, whom she admired as a man of action. In 1970 she helped plan and execute his jailbreak and plunged into a life of terrorism. The Baader-Meinhof Gang, as it became known, was the center of left-wing terrorism in Germany for the next five years. Despite her early involvement, Meinhof was never a leader of the gang that bore her name. Eventually caught, she was standing trial in 1976 when she committed suicide in jail.

the U.S. Army, destroying the officers' dining hall and killing one American. When claiming responsibility, the Baader-Meinhof Gang demanded an end to the American's placing land mines in harbors in North Vietnam.

- **May 12, 1972:** Bombs planted in the Augsburg, West Germany, police department injured five policemen. Later the same day, a car bomb at a police office in Munich, West Germany, destroyed sixty cars.

- **May 24, 1972:** A car bomb left at the headquarters of the U.S. Army Supreme European Command in Heidelberg, West Germany, exploded, killing two Americans. The gang claimed they set off the explosion to protest American bombing in Vietnam.

Captured

The bombing in Heidelberg launched an even more intense police manhunt for the leaders of the Red Army Faction. Their efforts soon paid off. Acting on a tip, on June 1, 1972, police in Frankfurt began keeping watch on a garage. Inside police could see a cache (pronounced cash; a collection) of explosives. Just before 6 A.M., a lilac-colored Porsche stopped outside the garage and three men stepped out. One of them noticed there were dozens of men on nearby roofs and corners, who were obviously police. One man fired a shot before he was tackled and arrested. The other two dashed into the garage. Baader and another gang member, Holger Meins, were cornered.

While a television station filmed the scene, police pumped tear gas into the garage. Three hours later, around 9 A.M., Baader appeared in a doorway, loading a pistol. A police sharpshooter wounded him in the leg. Moments later, Meins surrendered, and police ordered him to strip down to his underwear to make sure he was not carrying a weapon. Soon after Meins surrendered, police stormed the garage and arrested Baader.

One week later, in Hamburg, West Germany, Ensslin stepped into a store to shop for clothes. She put her jacket down to try on a dress, and a sales clerk noticed a bulge in the pocket. It was a pistol. The clerk called the police, who arrested Ensslin without a struggle.

One week after Ensslin's arrest, police received a tip from a woman who had two houseguests: she thought they could be gang members. Police staked out the apartment, and soon one gang member, Gerhard Müller, came out to use a telephone. He was quietly arrested. Eventually he cooperated with authorities and testified against other gang members. With Müller in custody, police knocked on the door of the apartment. Meinhof answered the door and was arrested. She began screaming and fighting, and when her photograph appeared in the newspaper the next day, her face was badly swollen. Police claimed it was because Meinhof had been crying, but many in Germany were sure she had been beaten.

Despite the jailing of the Red Army Faction's main leaders, the gang continued to carry out bombings and robberies. In prison many members of the gang staged hunger strikes. Meins eventually died of starvation, despite being force-fed by prison wardens. His death resulted in widespread protests across Germany; many people believed he had been murdered in jail.

Despite the fact that he was in jail—or perhaps because he was in jail—Baader was able to build sympathy for his cause, and opposition to the government, across Germany. Despite a long string of bombings and kidnappings, Germany's leading terrorist group had won considerable popular support. In 1975 the government passed a special set of laws, called the Baader-Meinhof Laws, that changed Germany's "Basic Law" (its constitution) to limit the rights of accused terrorists like the members of the Red Army Faction.

Deaths of the leaders

The main trial of the captured Baader-Meinhof Gang members began in the spring of 1976, nearly two years after their arrest and after months of pretrial hearings and legal procedures. Meinhof in particular appeared depressed and often decided not to attend the proceedings. On May 9, 1976, her body was found in her cell. Officials said she had hanged herself, but thousands of young Germans staged protests against what they believed to be Meinhof's murder in jail.

Nearly a year after Meinhof's death, on April 28, 1977, Baader, along with Ensslin and another gang member, Jan-Carl Raspe, were convicted of four murders and thirty attempted murders. Each was sentenced to life in prison. Remaining gang members staged several unsuccessful attempts to free the prisoners, such as taking hostages or occupying the West Germany embassy in Sweden, each a dramatic terrorist incident in itself.

On September 5, 1977, gang members in Cologne, West Germany, kidnapped Hanns-Martin Schleyer, one of Germany's leading businessmen. They demanded freedom for Baader, Ensslin, and other imprisoned gang members in exchange for Schleyer's life. The German government began negotiations, asking the imprisoned terrorists where they wanted to fly if they were released and asking foreign governments whether they would accept the released prisoners. Countries listed by the gang members included Vietnam, Algeria, and Libya.

Negotiations dragged on slowly into October. Lawyers for the imprisoned gang members reported they were becoming depressed. To increase pressure on the German government, on October 13, 1977, Palestinian hijackers seized a German plane, forced it to fly to Mogadishu, Somalia, and demanded release of the Baader-Meinhof prisoners in exchange for the plane's ninety-one crew members and passengers. Shortly afterward, a planeload of German army commandos landed in Mogadishu and stormed the plane. In the attack, three of the four hijackers were killed and the fourth was wounded. No hostages were killed and only one, a flight attendant, was hurt.

At the Stammheim Prison, near Stuttgart, West Germany, the Baader-Meinhof Gang members saw the failed hijacking as the loss of their last chance at freedom. Using a secret communications network, they agreed to commit suicide.

According to the official government version of events, on the night of October 17–18, 1977, Baader used a pistol smuggled into his cell by one of his lawyers to shoot himself in the head. Ensslin hanged herself with wire from a speaker. Another Baader-Meinhof prisoner used a smuggled pistol to shoot himself in the head, while a fourth prisoner stabbed herself. (This last prisoner survived the suicide attempt.) This version of events was widely doubted in Germany; many believed the authorities had murdered the prisoners. Soon after the prisoners died, Schleyer's body, shot in the head, was found in France.

However they died, Baader and Ensslin left behind a long string of dead police officers, hostages, and fellow terrorists in a range of kidnappings, bombings, building seizures, and shoot-outs. They also left behind an active terrorist group that continued to carry out attacks for many years after their deaths.

But in the end Baader and Ensslin made little lasting impact on Germany. Their vision of a communist future for West Germany came to an end when the communist government of East Germany collapsed and Germany reunited under a democratic government in 1990. Eight years later the Reuters news agency received an announcement that said the last members of the Baader-Meinhof Gang had decided to disband.

For More Information

Books

Aust, Stefan. *The Baader-Meinhof Group: The Inside Story of a Phenomenon*. Toronto: Random House of Canada Ltd., 1987.

Becker, Jillian. *Hitler's Children: The Story of the BaaderMeinhof Terrorist Gang*. Philadelphia: Lippincott, 1977.

Proll, Astrid, editor. *Baader-Meinhof, Pictures on the Run 67–77*. New York: Scalo, 1998.

Web Sites

Huffman, Richard V. "The Gun Speaks." Available at http://www.baader-meinhof.com/gun/index.htm (accessed October 11, 2002).

Noe, Denise. "The Baader Meinhof Gang." Available at http://www.crimelibrary.com/terrorists/baader/ (accessed October 11, 2002).

Mikhail Bakunin

May 30, 1814
Premukhino, Russia
July 1, 1876
Bern, Switzerland

Philosopher and anarchist

"It is obvious that liberty will never be given to humanity and that the real interests of society, of all groups, local associations, and individuals who make up society will never be satisfied until there are no longer any states."

The world in which Mikhail Bakunin lived was very different from that of the early twenty-first century. When he was active in politics, between about 1840 and 1876, the idea of a sudden uprising by workers seemed real and quite possible, based on actual events that had taken place in 1848 and after. Bakunin thought that his dream—in which poor factory workers and **peasants** would rise up to seize power and found a **communist** society in which all people were equal—was a practical possibility. He spent his adult life trying to make such a revolution take place, and in the process he developed the theory of revolutionary terrorism.

The political idea most closely linked with Bakunin is **anarchism**. This word comes from the same root as "anarchy," or chaos, but it means something very different. Anarchism is a theory, put forward by several nineteenth-century writers, that says society should be organized around voluntary associations, rather than large government organizations. The ideal social structure, in the anarchist's view, is a small village where people voluntarily join in common efforts and decide together on standards of conduct. Anarchists believe that traditional

Words to Know

Anarchism: a theory that says society should be organized around voluntary associations, rather than large government organizations.

Aristocracy: a class of people with special privileges inherited from birth.

Capitalism: an economic system in which factories and other businesses are owned and controlled by private individuals.

Class: a group of people in society who share the same political and economic status.

Middle class: people who have some money and political rights.

Nihilism: a nineteenth-century political philosophy in Russia that supported the use of terrorism to bring about revolution.

Proletariat: the working class; people without property or political rights.

Socialist: a person who believes in popular democratic control of the economy as well as the government.

Working class: people without property or political rights.

governments tend to be forced on people from the outside. These traditional governments, ruling over whole countries, tend to be undemocratic (not allowing its citizens to have a say in government through voting) and coercive (using force to require certain behavior).

A young aristocrat

Mikhail Aleksandrovich Bakunin was born into a well-to-do family of minor aristocrats in Russia, where society had barely changed for hundreds of years. Russia in 1814 was led by the czar (also spelled tsar; king), Alexander I (1777-1825), who was an absolute ruler, meaning he was not subject to any law. Most Russians were poor peasants, living and working on farmland owned by the **aristocracy** (a class of people with special privileges inherited from birth). These peasants had few freedoms, no say in government, and little hope of improving their lives. Most were legally tied to the land on which they lived and worked, unable to travel freely around the country.

Like most young aristocrats, Bakunin became a military officer. At age fourteen he was sent to the Russian capital of St. Petersburg to train as an artillery officer. (Artillery is the part of an army that operates large, heavy guns, like cannon.) He became an officer and went to serve in the towns of Minsk and Grodno (now in Poland but then part of the Russian empire). Bakunin served in the military for three years, until he was twenty-one years old, when he left the army and moved to Moscow to study philosophy.

In 1840 Bakunin went to Berlin (at the time, the center of philosophical studies in Europe) to get an advanced degree. His plan was to return to the University of Moscow and become a professor of philosophy.

Early industrial society

The Industrial Revolution, a time in which goods began to be mass produced with the use of machines, began in England in the second half of the eighteenth century and quickly spread throughout Europe. A new class of wealthy factory owners had arisen, making huge fortunes and gaining strong influence over government. Workers in the new factories were mostly displaced peasants whose status was similar to the landless peasants that Bakunin had seen in Russia. Workers had few rights, received low wages, and had no benefits. Most often they were crammed into cramped houses in the cities that had grown up around the new factories. If a worker fell ill or was injured in the factory and could not work, he was fired and replaced. Workers were often reduced to begging on the streets. Sometimes they starved. Perhaps most important, modern democracy had not yet developed. Most workers did not have the right to vote, so they had little hope of changing the terrible condition of their lives.

Proposed social solutions

These conditions horrified many philosophers, including Bakunin. Another social philosopher of his time who was disturbed by the status of workers was a German named Karl Marx (1818–1883). Both men came to some of the same conclusions:

- Major changes were needed to fix the injustices of the industrial system.

- The governments in industrialized countries had become a tool to protect the interests of factory owners, cracking down on any efforts by workers to make changes.

- The situation was so bad that workers should revolt. This included seizing the factories, the source of wealth, in order to gain democratic control over both the government and the source of economic power.

In Berlin, Bakunin became active in political movements whose members wanted to start a revolution to create a more democratic society. He knew Marx, as well as other leading philosophers of the left wing, which supported popular control over government (led by the people) and the economy to bring about a more equal distribution of power and wealth. He also began writing essays and pamphlets, arguing in support of such changes. His radical politics brought him to the attention of authorities back in Russia. At the time the Russian government held that Russians needed permission to leave the country and claimed the right to order its citizens back home. This is what happened to Bakunin in 1844, the year he left Berlin for Paris, France, which was also a center of left-wing thought. Bakunin refused the Russian government's order to return home. As a result, he was stripped of his aristocratic status, tried in court in absentia (in his absence), and sentenced to hard labor in Siberia, a remote, cold, and unpopulated region in northeastern Russia, should he ever return.

Over the next four years Bakunin became deeply involved in the movement of philosophers and activists supporting a revolution against the existing governments and the economic system called **capitalism.** (Capitalism is an economic system in which factories and other businesses are owned and

Karl Marx also believed in democratic control over factories and farms, but his ideas were the opposite of Bakunin's. Marx advocated a strong government, controlled by workers, to enforce the ideas of communism, while Bakunin advocated voluntary associations. *Photograph courtesy of the Library of Congress.*

controlled by private individuals.) Between 1844 and 1847 Bakunin met various writers, including Pierre Joseph Proudhon (1809–1865), a French anarchist. In 1847 Bakunin made a speech at a banquet in Paris in which he criticized the government of Russia. As a result the French government ordered him to leave the country. He moved to Belgium but returned to Paris just two months later after French workers revolted.

Revolutions of 1848

In both France and Germany the late 1840s was a time of serious social unrest that peaked in 1848. On February 24, 1848, a mob attacked the Tuileries, home of the French king in Paris, forcing the government to flee. A **socialist** leader named Louis Blanc (1811–1882) declared the Second Republic (the First Republic had been founded in 1789, with the French Revolution). Socialism is a political and economic system in which there is no private property, and business and industry is, in theory, owned by the workers. It is the opposite of communism, under which, in theory, the community owns the factories and businesses and the goods they produce. Thus Blanc supported a system of universal voting and a more equal distribution of wealth. (His slogan, "From each according to his abilities, to each according to his needs," was later adopted by Marx.)

One of the most famous results of this time of social unrest was the *Communist Manifesto,* a pamphlet written by Marx and fellow philosopher Friedrich Engels (1820–1895) in 1848, just weeks before the Paris revolt. In it Marx and Engels laid out their ideas for a future society in which equality would be achieved through common ownership of factories and popularly elected legislatures.

The uprising in Paris was followed by revolutions in Germany, Italy, the Austrian empire, and many other European countries. Most of these revolutions were more concerned with national independence than with reforming politics and economics. They were largely led by the **middle class**, or even the aristocracy, who wanted independence from the empires that ruled them. German and Italian revolutionaries wanted to unify their countries, which in 1848 were collections of independent states. Thinkers like Bakunin and Marx tried to shape these revolutions into a social uprising by workers against the owners of land and factories.

From revolution to prison

Bakunin also was busy trying to organize unhappy workers so they could seize power. Bakunin today is remembered for his theories, but between 1848 and 1851 he was actively involved in trying to start revolutions in several countries.

From Paris Bakunin traveled to Cologne, Germany, in March 1848 and met with Marx. Three months later Bakunin took part in a revolution in Prague (then part of the Austrian empire, now in the Czech Republic). Later in the same year Bakunin was thrown out of the German states of Prussia and Saxony and lived for a while in another principality (a small nation ruled by a prince) called Anhalt (later part of Germany). In January 1849 he traveled to Leipzig (then part of the small state of Bohemia, in what is now the western part of Czechoslovakia) to help with an uprising, and then to the German city of Dresden, where he led a popular but short-lived rebellion.

Shortly after the Dresden rebellion Bakunin was arrested in Germany and sentenced to death for his revolutionary activities. In June 1850 his death sentence was commuted (changed) to life in prison, and he was sent to Austria. Jailed in Prague, he was again sentenced to death, and again the sentence was commuted. He was sent back to Russia, where he spent six years in prison before being sent to live in Siberia, to serve the sentence handed down in 1844.

Back into the struggle

In 1861, ten years after he was sent to prison in Russia, Bakunin decided to escape from Siberia. He made his way hundreds of miles to the east coast of Russia and jumped aboard an American ship headed for Japan. From there he sailed to San Francisco, California, traveled to New York, and set sail again for England, where he arrived at the end of December 1861, six months after leaving Siberia.

Bakunin was now a full-time revolutionary. Over the next fourteen-and-a-half years, until his death in July 1876, Bakunin moved among several European cities, constantly writing books and pamphlets, trying to organize revolutionary parties, and quarreling with Marx, who became his bitter rival for leadership of Europe's growing socialist movement.

In His Own Words

"The State, however popular may be the form it assumes, will always be an institution of domination and exploitation, and consequently a permanent source of poverty and enslavement for the populace. There is no other way, then, of emancipating [freeing] the people economically and politically, of giving them liberty and well-being at one and the same time than by abolishing [getting rid of] the State, all States, and, by so doing, killing, once and for all time, what, up to now, has been called 'Politics.'."

From *Politics and the State (1871)*

Basic Bakunin: What he believed

Many intellectuals and writers in the 1800s agreed that social reform was needed. Industrialism had brought poor workers into the cities and made their suffering worse, since there was no way for hungry city workers to grow their own food on tiny plots of land, as they could in the country. Industrialism also concentrated many workers in the same place, where their existence could not be easily ignored.

Many philosophers looking for a solution agreed on the basic concept of "**class.**" A class was a group of people in society who shared the same political and economic status. Some people were born into the aristocracy, a wealthy class of people who owned land. Others were born into the "**working class,**" people without property or political rights. A third class, the "middle class," were people who had some money and political rights. These people tended to be professionals, such as lawyers or doctors, or business owners. In the mid-1800s the biggest class by far was the working class, and people like Bakunin defended their rights.

One of Bakunin's central beliefs was that all governments existed to protect the rights of the upper class (including aristocrats and wealthy factory owners), to the disadvantage of the lower classes. He believed that governments had to be overthrown by violent revolution in order to achieve a fairer and more equal society. In contrast to Marx, who believed that the working class (which he called the "**proletariat**") should seize the government and control it, Bakunin thought government should be destroyed by revolution and not be re-created. It was on this point that Bakunin and Marx most sharply disagreed.

Bakunin also believed that economic power was not the only important factor in people's lives. He thought social controls, including religion, were equally important. Bakunin thought government helped maintain social classes and social controls, as well as economic controls. Most religions, for example, had the financial backing of one government or another in nineteenth-century Europe.

Finally, Bakunin believed that governments tended to look after their own interests above all else. Even though some governments might pass laws to relieve suffering (as had begun to happen after 1850), when the existence of a government was challenged, it would turn immediately to military force to protect itself. Even a socialist government, he thought, would fall into this self-protective behavior. On this, he wrote: "The State [government] never had a morality [system of rules of good and just conduct], and can never have one. Its only morality and justice is its own advantage, its own existence, and its own omnipotence [total power] at any price. Before these interests, all interests of mankind must disappear. The State is the negation of manhood."

Rather than a central government, Bakunin suggested voluntary associations of people who would work for their mutual economic and social benefit. Trade unions were an example of such associations, in Bakunin's view. His idea of society as one without a large central government is known as anarchism. Bakunin spent the last third of his life supporting the cause of anarchism, trying to organize political parties that would destroy existing governments and bring about this new form of society.

Bringing about a revolution

Bakunin had no problem with using violence to put an end to existing governments. He also believed that revolutionaries should attack government institutions as a means of destroying government in general. For this reason, he is often thought of as the author of the idea of "revolutionary terrorism."

In 1866 Bakunin wrote a pamphlet titled *Revolutionary Catechism*. In it he maintained:

> The Revolutionist is a doomed man. He has no private interests, no affairs, sentiments, ties, property nor even a name of his own. His entire being is devoured [consumed] by one purpose, one thought, one passion—the revolution. Heart and soul, not

Bakunin and Russian Nihilism

Mikhail Bakunin is sometimes called the father of Russian **Nihilism** (pronounced NEE-hu-liz-uhm or NYE-hu-liz-uhm). This is a term with different meanings. "Nihilism" sometimes means the belief that life is without meaning, and that there are no real moral "truths." This meaning is often associated with despair and the attitude that "nothing matters, so what's the use?"

The other meaning is a belief that social conditions are so bad that destruction becomes worthwhile for its own sake. When spelled with a capital "N," Nihilist refers to a specific nineteenth-century political party in Russia that supported the use of terrorism to bring about revolution. Bakunin believed that peasants in Russia could start a revolution, and he believed that violence was required to bring down existing governments. These were two points on which he disagreed with the German philosopher Karl Marx.

But other revolutionaries in Russia, particularly Sergei Nechayev, agreed with Bakunin. Nechayev was notable for his support of terrorism—especially assassination—as a means of sparking a revolution. Bakunin was briefly allied with Nechayev from March 1869 until June 1870.

merely by word but by deed, he has severed [broken] every link with the social order and with the entire civilized world; with the laws, good manners, conventions, and morality of that world. He is its merciless enemy and continues to inhabit it with only one purpose—to destroy it.

Bakunin's ideas about anarchism—especially the need to destroy social controls—found an enthusiastic audience, particularly after his death in 1876. Individuals, or small groups of individuals, believed they were acting on his teachings when they used assassinations and bombings to bring about social change. To a significant extent, the actions of anarchists after Bakunin's death influenced the popular understanding of his ideas.

Bakunin and terrorism

Bakunin is often associated with revolutionary terrorism, largely based on his brief association with fellow Russian revolutionary Sergei Nechayev (pronounced nee-CHI-ev; 1847–1882) from 1869 to 1870. But in most of his writings, Bakunin did not specifically suggest terrorism as a way to destroy the state. For the most part, he was vague on exactly how the state would be overthrown. Although Bakunin spent years trying to organize political parties and associations to support anarchism, he pictured an unplanned uprising of workers or peasants that would overthrow the government.

Bakunin often wrote about ideals involving the equality of all people—men and women—and the destruction of classes in a future society that would be governed through democratic "communes," or voluntary communities. He strongly disliked Marx's idea of a "dictatorship of the proletariat," in which society would be led by a group claiming to represent working people. For Bakunin, any control of society by a government, regardless of who was in charge, was unacceptable.

For conservatives (traditionalists), and for many socialists, it was Bakunin's philosophy that was unacceptable. His disapproval of religion in general and his desire to get rid of official state religions was deeply offensive to many. (He did, however, like the American model of religious freedom in which religious organizations depended on their own resources.) Even more shocking were his statements about getting rid of the state. So it was no surprise that his name was linked to terrorism: many people saw it as an example of what would happen if there were no government to prevent crime.

At the same time, terrorists active in Europe toward the end of the nineteenth century, long after his death, often stated their support of Bakunin's ideas. This was sometimes in opposition to the growing communist movement that followed Bakunin's great rival, Marx, who believed a strong revolutionary government was needed to establish a better system of socialism.

For More Information

Books

Aldred, Guy A. *Mikhail Bakunin, Communist*. Glasgow: Bakunin House, 1920.

Bakunin, Mikhail. *Politics and the State*. 1871.

Bakunin, Mikhail. *Revolutionary Catechism*. 1869.

Masters, Anthony. *Bakunin, the Father of Anarchism*. New York: Saturday Review Press, 1974.

Nomad, Max. *Apostles of Revolution*. Boston: Little Brown, 1939.

Pyzuir, Eugene. *The Doctrine of Anarchism of Michael A. Bakunin*. Chicago: Regnery, 1968.

Wilson, Edmund. *To the Finland Section: A Study in the Writing and Acting of History*. New York: Harcourt, Brace, 1940.

Periodicals

Chastain, James G. "Bakunin as a French Secret Agent in 1848." *History Today,* August 1981, p. 5.

Rose, Jonathan. "What 19th-century Terror Tells Us about Today's: What Did Terrorists Hope to Gain from Their Deadly Crimes 100 Years Ago?" *Scholastic Update,* May 16, 1986, p.7.

Menachem Begin

August 16, 1913
Brest-Litovsk, Poland
March 9, 1992
Tel Aviv, Israel

Leader of the Irgun Zvai Leumi,
prime minister of Israel

M enachem Begin emulated his father's passion and commitment to the dream of a Jewish state. His journey led him down paths of violence and diplomacy.

The city of Brest-Litovsk, where the Begin family lived and where Menachem, the youngest of three children, was born, was a border town in Eastern Europe. It was continually shifting from the control of one country to another. Russia, Poland, and Germany all claimed and governed the city at various points, but in 1913, when Begin was born, it was Polish. In a way it did not matter which country the city was in. The Jewish population had been settled there since the 1300s. They created their own world in their section of the city, with a synagogue (a Jewish house of worship), Hebrew-language schools, and community leaders who were their link to whatever country was running the city at the moment.

Ze'ev Dov Begin (pronounced BAY-ghin), Menachem's father, was one of these leaders. The Begin family had once been quite wealthy, controlling great areas of wooded land and making a fortune in lumber profits, but that all disappeared in the constant changes in government. During Begin's child-

"The State for which we have striven from our early youth, the State which will give freedom to the people and assure the future of its sons, that State remains as the goal of our generation."

Photograph reproduced by permission of Archive Photos, Inc.

hood the family was quite poor and sometimes hungry, but the father was respected both inside the Jewish quarter and in the rest of the city, a "doer" who was a talented organizer and who used his abilities to make life in the Jewish quarter better.

Whenever there was an event, a holiday to be celebrated, or a religious festival to be observed, Ze'ev Dov was in the forefront, making things happen. His festivities generally included scheduling a speech for himself, something he loved and at which he was extremely good. The cause of his life was Zionism, the movement that strove to create a Jewish homeland in Palestine, a land in the Middle East that was held holy by Jews, Christians, and Muslims alike.

In his father's footsteps

It was not long before young Begin began following in his father's footsteps. Born in 1913, he was just ten years old when he gave his first speech. The occasion was a festival celebrating the Jewish revolt against ancient Rome in 135 C.E., and Ze'ev provided his son with a speech about Bar Kokhba, the leader of the revolt. This first taste of the power of words made a lasting impression on the boy. In his autobiography Begin recalled making this speech and enjoying his fame. He soon decided that he wanted to become a lawyer.

The Begin children attended the Jewish elementary school in Brest-Litovsk but later went to the local Polish high school. There the education was free, which was important for the family, and career opportunities were better for those educated in the Polish schools. Mixing Polish and Jewish teenagers created problems, though, and the Christian students insulted and humiliated the Jewish students daily. Being small and frail, Begin naturally turned all the more strongly toward his talent for words.

In 1931 Begin graduated from high school and went to Warsaw, Poland, to study law at Warsaw University. But his studies took second place to his Zionist activities, particularly his involvement in the Betar youth movement. Betar had been founded by journalist Vladimir Jabotinsky (1880–1940), whom Begin had heard speak and whom he admired. Its purpose was to prepare young European Jews physically and mentally for moving to Palestine. The leaders of Betar groups were expected to teach self-discipline, good manners, cleanliness, tact, loyalty, courage, self-esteem, and self-denial. The members wore uniforms, marched in parades, and trained with weapons. Before long, young Begin was promoted to head of the movement in Poland. When problems arose within the movement in Czechoslovakia, Begin went to help sort things out there.

By 1939 Jews living in Europe were growing increasingly anxious. The Nazi Party in Germany, headed by Adolf Hitler (1889–1945), was regularly attacking Jews, and this antisemitic poison was spreading throughout Europe. This made the dream of Zionism a matter of immediate importance. Jews in Czechoslovakia were being harassed and mistreated. While visiting there, instead of preaching the official Betar philosophy of the right of Jews to defend themselves, Begin began to urge going on the offensive. Maybe Jews should do some harassing of their own, he declared. For Betar, this was too close to encouraging violence, and Begin was ordered to return to Poland.

In the meantime, though, Arabs in Palestine were increasingly using violence against the Jews who had been settling there. What Begin was saying made sense to many in Betar. The result was Irgun Zvai Leumi (pronounced ear-gun zveye lee-you-mi), a more militant arm of Betar that did not believe that Jews should fight only in self-defense. They immediately began launching and supporting attacks on Arabs. The Irgun faction soon gained control of Betar and made military training its priority.

A dark time

After the German army invaded Poland in 1939, dividing the country with the Soviet Union (present-day Russia and its neighboring countries, with which Germany had a secret agreement), Begin fled to the Soviet Union. There, he was arrested as a troublemaker and spy and sentenced to a Soviet labor camp for eight years. He was freed after only one year as part of a general agreement between the Soviet Union and the Polish government in exile (the Polish government, still recognized as the true Polish government by other countries, fled to London, England, and was operating out of that city). Begin learned that his parents and his brother had disappeared in the

Jews and World War II

World War I (1914–18) changed the face of Europe. In the east Russia was transformed by the Bolshevik Revolution (1917) which replaced the czar (also spelled tsar; king) with a communist government. (Communism is a system in which the state controls the economy, including factories and businesses.) To the west, Germany, which had lost the war, was burdened with huge payments to England and France to make up for the losses those countries had suffered in the war.

In the early 1930s an economic depression gripped Western Europe, which made living conditions much more difficult. Things were particularly bad in Germany because of its huge war debts. A radical political party, the National Socialists (known as the Nazis), gained popularity by blaming Germany's problems on Jews. There was no rational basis for these accusations; the Nazis were using the Jews as scapegoats, or people who are blamed for something that is not actually their fault. In an effort to give a sense of pride to Germans following their defeat in World War I, Nazi leader Adolf Hitler (1889–1945) also invented a theory of German racial superiority, claiming Germans were a "master race," especially compared with Jews. Hitler's followers often seized on

these theories to attack Jews and steal or destroy their property.

In 1933 Hitler became chancellor (prime minister) of Germany. From there he gradually expanded his antisemitic (anti-Jewish) politics. It eventually resulted in the murder of six million Jews during World War II (1939–45), an event known as the Holocaust.

Hitler also wanted to expand Germany's territory to the east, into an area controlled by the Soviet Union (today, Russia and its neighboring countries). Joseph Stalin (1879–1953) had become the dictator of the Soviet Union in 1924. In order to expand the Soviet Union's own territories and keep Hitler from invading it, Stalin entered into a peace pact with Germany under which the two countries divided Poland between them. Although their political philosophies were opposite each other, Hitler and Stalin both ruled as dictators, and they were both willing to take whatever action seemed to be to their immediate benefit. Indeed, opponents of the Soviet Union who ended up in the Soviet part of Poland were quickly rounded up and shipped to prison camps in Siberia, a cold, empty part of northeastern Russia.

Ultimately, the peace agreement did not work out for Stalin: Hitler's armies invaded Russia in 1941.

Holocaust (the systematic killing of the Jews of Europe, as perpetrated by the Nazis), along with tens of thousands of other Polish Jews. Only Begin and his sister, Rachel, survived.

Begin joined the Free Polish Army, which was fighting the German occupation of Poland. The Free Polish Army was allied with the British army. Begin was sent to Palestine (then governed by Britain under the Palestine Mandate, a 1922 agreement negotiated by the League of Nations in the wake of World War I [1914–17] and the defeat of the Ottoman Empire, which had formerly governed much of the Middle East.) There Begin learned English and served as an interpreter for the British army. During these years, his commitment to Zionism, which included calls for violence against Palestinian Arabs and the British, made him leader of the Irgun Zvai Leumi. Irgun members were committed to chasing the British out of Palestine. This angered the official Zionist leadership, the Haganah, which wanted to use diplomacy to achieve the same goal.

Out of this basic split in policy came confusion and bloodshed. Haganah refused to fund violent activities by Irgun, so Irgun turned to robbery and other crimes to raise money for arms. On November 6, 1944, gunmen assassinated Lord Moyne, Britain's minister for Middle East affairs, in Cairo, Egypt. Although a different group was responsible for the murder, the Irgun was blamed. This further destroyed the already shaky trust between Haganah and Irgun and made Begin the focus of an intense manhunt by the British.

After the full horror of what Nazi Germany did to the Jews became known—they murdered more than six million Jews during World War II (1939–45)—Begin issued a statement calling for open revolt against the British rulers in Palestine. He wrote, in part, that Britain had "shamefully betrayed the Jewish people" by not helping make Palestine available for immigration (only a certain number of Jews were allowed to immigrate despite knowledge of the mass killings). In this sense, he argued, the British effectively took part in the murder of Jews by the Nazis. He declared war on Britain "to the end. . . . We shall fight, every Jew in the homeland will fight," he promised.

Nevertheless, as World War II ended and Britain focused more and more on its problems at home, the Haganah and Irgun merged for about a year as the Hebrew Resistance Movement. In a well-planned attack on October 31, 1945, the Resistance sank

Zionism and the Founding of Israel

For centuries the Jewish people had lived in Europe without a country of their own. Most Europeans were Christians. They accepted the Jews in part because the Jewish religion did not prevent them from lending money, as the Christian religion did. The Jews thus filled an important role in the European economy, but they were also resented by many Christians for the money they earned by making loans.

In the late nineteenth century an Austrian Jewish journalist named Theodor Herzl (pronounced HURTS-el; 1860–1904) suggested that Jews should found their own state. It was, in part, a way to end the antisemitic attacks on Jews in Europe that had been going on for hundreds of years. Gradually small numbers of Jews began moving to Palestine to buy and run farms. Palestine, which was roughly in the same area as the ancient Jewish homeland described in the Bible, was ruled by the Turkish Ottoman Empire, which accepted the small migration.

The Ottomans were at war with Britain during World War I, and Britain's prime minister, Arthur Balfour (1848–1930), tried to gain Jewish support by issuing a statement (later called the Balfour Declaration) in 1917, promising to support a Jewish state in the Middle East after the war was over. The Ottoman Empire collapsed during the war, and France and Britain divided up its lands in the Middle East, creating Syria and Lebanon (run by France) and Iraq and Palestine (run by Britain). The stage was set for a struggle between Arabs and Jews living in Palestine to control the territory.

This struggle took on a new dimension at the end of World War II, when the Jews who had survived the Nazi Holocaust realized they could not bear to simply return to their countries (six million Jews were killed by the Germans during the war). Israel, a Jewish homeland since biblical times, was a potential new country that Jews could call their own. Aided by Zionists, thousands of Jewish survivors began pouring out of the Nazi death camps for Israel. The increase in migration threatened to upset the balance of population and power in Palestine.

At the same time some Zionists began organizing armed opposition to Palestinian Arabs, just as the Arabs began their own armed resistance to the Jews.

three police patrol boats, blew up railway lines at 153 points, and destroyed locomotives in a rail yard. They raided British police, army, and air force posts. On February 25, 1946, another raid destroyed twenty British army planes on the ground.

The eventual British response was to round up and imprison Zionist sympathizers, but the Resistance leaders, including Begin, mostly avoided capture. The Irgun continued to stage attacks, sometimes kidnapping British soldiers, which earned Begin a "Wanted for Terrorism" poster. The stage was now set for a truly dramatic gesture, and the Resistance supplied one with "Operation Chick."

Operation Chick

Begin's plan for Operation Chick had been ready for months. Finally, on July 22, 1946, the Resistance decided the time was right. The target was the King David Hotel in Jerusalem. The southern wing of the hotel held the headquarters of the British government in Palestine, the military police, and the special investigations offices. The hotel was also "home away from home" for British in Palestine; the lobby and restaurants were always packed. But on this day, as the usual activity went on upstairs, beneath the restaurant Irgun members were delivering milk cans packed with dynamite.

The Irgun had to overpower the kitchen workers, and a British officer who noticed a disturbance and came to investigate was shot, but the bombs were placed. The kitchen workers were freed and told to run for their lives, which they did, with the Irgun among them, making their getaway. The timers on the milk cans were set to go off in thirty minutes, at 12:37 P.M.

Afterward, the Irgun insisted that they made several phone calls to the hotel and to a local newspaper, warning that there would be an explosion and that the building should be emptied. For whatever reason, nothing was done.

At 12:37 the explosion came. All six floors of the southern wing of the hotel came crashing down, and when the dust finally cleared, ninety-one people were dead in the rubble and forty-five were injured.

Even after this attack, it was almost two years before Israel declared its independence, and the level of violence steadily rose. Both Arabs and Jews were intent on claiming as much territory as possible, in part by driving civilians from the other side off the land. Palestinians were driven from their farms and homes throughout Palestine. In turn, Palestinians attacked Jewish settlements and property in the cities.

British soldiers combing the ruins of the King David Hotel in Jerusalem for survivors following a bomb blast in 1946. The attack, orchestrated by Menachem Begin, was part of what was called "Operation Chick," an open revolt against the British rule in Palestine. *Photograph reproduced by permission of the Gamma Liaison Network.*

In the meantime Jews were flooding into Palestine from the German death camps, increasing the Jewish population of Palestine and laying claim to a kind of moral right to settle somewhere in peace after the horrors of the Holocaust.

In all these activities—attacking Palestinian settlements and helping Jews get around British immigration controls—Begin and the Irgun played a major role.

After independence

After Israel declared its independence in 1948, there was no role for unofficial "terrorist" forces, and Begin dissolved the Irgun. He turned his attention to politics and became the leader of the minority conservative party in Israel's parliament.

In 1965 Begin combined his Herut Party with the Liberal Party, which eventually became known as the Likud Party. Begin continued to play a central role in the government of Israel, insisting that Egyptian President Gamal Abdel Nasser (1918–1970) sign a peace treaty recognizing the state of Israel after the Six Day War of 1967, in which Israel seized significant territory from Egypt and Syria. No treaty was signed, however, and Israel fought another war against Egypt in 1973.

Begin was elected prime minister of Israel in 1977, and he negotiated a treaty with Egypt's President Anwar el-Sadat (1918–1981) in 1978. The two leaders shared the Nobel Peace Prize for 1978 in recognition of the treaty.

Despite the treaty, tensions between Israel and its Arab neighbors continued. In 1981 Begin ordered the Israeli air force to bomb a nuclear power plant in Iraq, which Israel discovered Iraq's leader, Saddam Hussein (1937–), was using to develop nuclear weapons. A decade later, during the Persian Gulf War (1990–91), it was confirmed that the raid did in fact set back Iraq's nuclear weapons program.

Begin's final major act as the leader of Israel was to order an attack on Palestinian positions in Lebanon, in 1982. Palestinians had long used southern Lebanon to launch raids into Israel, and Begin was determined to end the practice. But the attack on Lebanon was highly controversial. On June 6, 1982, army tanks rolled into Lebanon. Six hundred Israeli soldiers

Menachem Begin speaking to a large crowd, Tel Aviv, Israel, 1954. *Photograph reproduced by permission of the Corbis Corporation.*

died and three thousand were wounded. Many more Arabs were killed, and Israel's allies in Lebanon, who were primarily Arab Christians, murdered hundreds of people in a refugee camp.

Begin's wife, Aliza (whom he had married in 1939, and with whom he had three children), died in the winter of 1982. Begin resigned as prime minister shortly afterward. He dropped out of politics, being seen in public only rarely at memorials for his wife or at his grandchildren's weddings.

Begin died on March 9, 1992. He was buried in Jerusalem.

Terrorist or soldier?

The life story of Begin raises the question of whether a man who won the Nobel Peace Prize can be described as a terrorist. This has become a sensitive political issue. Palestinians argue that Begin's organization, Irgun, used terrorist tactics to drive Palestinians off their land and out of their homes

From War to Peace, 1948–1978

Between 1948 and 1973 Israel fought four major wars against its Arab neighbors, in addition to fighting countless terrorist raids across its borders.

1948: War of Israeli Independence. On the morning after Israel declared its independence, armies from surrounding Arab states—Egypt, Jordan, Syria, and Lebanon—all launched attacks. Their aim was to destroy the new Jewish state before it had time to become established. But the Jews of Israel had been organizing for the occasion, and its informal armed forces became a military force that decisively defeated the combined Arab armies.

1956: Israel combined forces with Britain and France to try to seize the Suez Canal, an important waterway in Egypt linking the Mediterranean Sea with the Indian Ocean. By using the canal, ships traveling from Europe to India could avoid the long trip around Africa. Although they succeeded at first, U.S. President Dwight D. Eisenhower (1890–1969) did not support seizing the Suez Canal (which had been built by Britain and was later taken over by Egypt's President Gamal Abdel Nasser [1918–1970]). By threatening to withdraw U.S. support from Israel, Eisenhower forced the invading armies to retreat.

1967: In June Israel launched a lightning strike against the Egyptians in the south and the Syrians in the north. The war was over in just six days, and resulted in Israel holding much of the Sinai Peninsula, the West Bank of the Jordan River, and the Golan Heights of Syria. These territories became a long-standing source of conflict between Israel and its neighbors.

1973: In an effort to regain the territory they had lost in 1967, Egypt and Syria attacked Israel on the Jewish holiday of Yom Kippur. The attack surprised Israel, and at first Egypt and Syria made progress. Within a few days, however, Israel drove the Arabs back and began advancing across the Suez Canal into Egypt and toward Damascus, the capital of Syria. The United States, Israel's strongest ally, helped arrange a truce and persuaded Israel to return some of its newly seized land to Egypt and Syria. A few years later Egypt's President Anwar el-Sadat, who had started the 1973 war, negotiated a peace treaty with Israel, for which he and Menachem Begin shared the Nobel Peace Prize for 1978.

in the months before Israeli independence. His defenders point out that he used terrorist tactics against the British military as a guerrilla fighter for his people, and that even then he took care to warn people away from the targets of bombs.

The question becomes, does winning a battle for independence make the difference between a terrorist and a patriot? The debate continues.

For More Information

Books

Gervasi, Frank. *The Life and Times of Meanchem Begin: Rebel to Statesman.* New York: Putnam, 1979.

Haber, Eithan. *Menachem Begin: The Legend and the Man.* New York: Delacorte Press, 1978.

Hirschler, Gertrude, and Lester S. Eckman. *Menachem Begin, From Freedom Fighter to Statesman.* New York: Shengold Publishers, 1979.

Perlmutter, Amos. *The Life and Times of Menachem Begin.* Garden City, NY: Doubleday, 1987.

Periodicals

Elon, Amos. "Letter from Israel." *The New Yorker,* July 29, 1985, p. 60.

Johnson, Marguerite. "Fighter, First and Last: Menachem Begin: 1913–1992." *Time,* March 23, 1992, p. 42.

"Menachem Begin, RIP." *National Review,* March 30, 1992, p. 14.

Watson, Russell. "The Legacy of a 'Fighting Jew': Menachem Begin Transformed Israeli Politics." *Newsweek,* March 23, 1992, p. 45.

Osama bin Laden

c. 1957
Riyadh, Saudi Arabia

**Leading financial and tactical supporter of
Al Qaeda terrorist network**

S hortly after the terrorist attacks on the World Trade Center in New York City and the Pentagon near Washington, D.C., on September 11, 2001, U.S. President George W. Bush (1946–) declared a "war on terrorism." Osama bin Laden was accused of being the chief organizer of the attacks that killed more than three thousand Americans and injured thousands more. Bin Laden became the symbol of terrorism worldwide.

But for bin Laden, a Saudi Arabian-born millionaire and devout Muslim, the attacks of September 11 were just the latest in a long string of assaults aimed at the United States. Just as America launched its war on terrorism and Bush declared that bin Laden was "wanted, dead or alive," bin Laden years earlier had declared war on the United States. Bin Laden's main complaint has been the presence of U.S. soldiers in Saudi Arabia and the spread of American influence throughout the Muslim world, which stretches from North Africa to Southeast Asia.

Yet despite the enormous impact of 9/11, as the attacks became known, bin Laden remained a figure of mystery and growing myth. Even his date of birth is not known for certain, and after an intense U.S. military campaign in Afghanistan,

"We—with God's help— call on every Muslim who believes in God and wishes to be rewarded to comply with God's order to kill the Americans and plunder their money wherever and whenever they find it."

bin Laden disappeared. Months after the attack, U.S. officials admitted they still did not know whether he was alive or dead.

The son of an important man

Bin Laden is believed to have been born in 1957 in Saudi Arabia. His mother was Syrian. His father, Mohammad Awad bin Laden, was the billionaire owner of a construction business. Like many details of bin Laden's life, the exact details of his father's background are hazy. Mohammad bin Laden apparently came to the Saudi Arabian city of Jeddah, a port on the Red Sea, as a young man from his native Yemen. He arrived just a few years before oil was discovered under Saudi Arabia's vast deserts, when the country was poor and lightly populated. It was, however, the site of Islam's two holiest sites, the cities of Mecca and Medina, which played central roles in the story of Islam's founder, Muhammad (c. 570–632). Mohammad bin Laden became close friends with the ruling Saud family and received construction contracts from the government to rebuild or repair major mosques (Islamic religious meeting places, similar to churches) as well as other government buildings. The contracts made Mohammad bin Laden one of the wealthiest men in Saudi Arabia.

Bin Laden came from an exceptionally large family. His father was said to have had about fifty children by his several wives (Islam allows men to marry more than one woman at the same time). Bin Laden was the only child of his mother, a Syrian, who was the fourth and final wife of Mohammad bin Laden. Bin Laden's mother had a reputation for being less traditional than Mohammad's other wives, who were all Saudis. According to some sources, Bin Laden was the seventeenth child in the family. His father took steps to keep all his children together as a family. He insisted that the boys meet every day at his house and eat at least one meal together. Mohammad bin Laden insisted that brothers and sisters maintain good relations and mutual respect.

The bin Ladens were a conservative (traditional) family that observed the teachings of Islam, although they do not appear to have been more committed to religion than most other families in their time and place. Mohammad bin Laden insisted that his children follow strict rules, including the social code of Islam as practiced in Saudi Arabia. The children

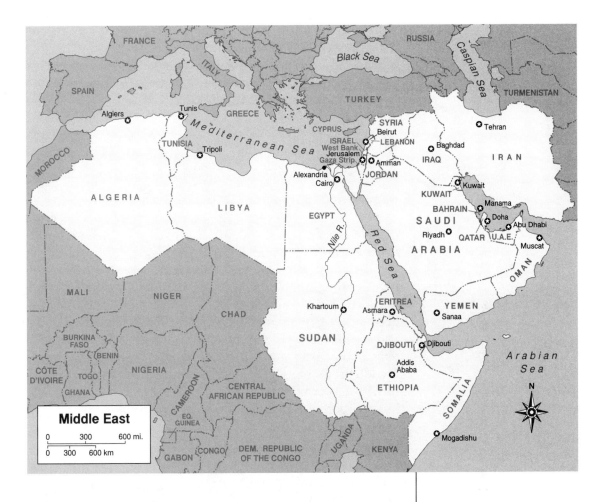

Middle East

0   300   600 mi.

0   300   600 km

were required to follow a regular daily program that included religious observances. Bin Laden's father often entertained or hosted Islamic scholars visiting Saudi Arabia as part of a hajj. (A hajj is a visit to Mecca, Islam's holiest city. Every Muslim is expected to make the journey at least once in their lifetime.) In 1968 bin Laden's father died in a helicopter crash. Bin Laden inherited a large fortune, estimated at between $80 and $300 million.

Bin Laden was raised and went to school in Jeddah. In 1979 or 1980 (accounts vary), he graduated from King Abdul Aziz University with a degree in public administration. Stories about bin Laden at this time offer different pictures. Some describe a modest young man raised in a conservative Islamic household. Others say that he often visited Western-style nightclubs in Beirut, Lebanon, and had a reputation as a fun-loving man who was a heavy drinker and sometimes got into fights over women. There was nothing to predict that twenty years after graduating from college he would be the object of a global manhunt by the United States.

Russia invades Afghanistan

While bin Laden was attending college in Saudi Arabia, events were taking place in the country of Afghanistan that would significantly affect his life over the next twenty years. In April 1978 army officers in Afghanistan staged a coup d'etat (pronounced coo day-TAH; the takeover of a government by force, usually by the military). The new rulers were communists and began a series of reforms in the remote, mountainous country. (Communism is a political and economic system that does not include the concept of private property; instead, the public—usually represented by the government—owns the goods and the means to produce them in common.) The government redistributed land, gave women new rights, and tried to change the long-standing social structure of the country. The government also became an ally of the Soviet Union (today, Russia and its neighboring countries), the leading communist state in the world and at the time the enemy of the United States.

The reforms were strongly resisted. Leaders of the coup drove out dissatisfied military officers, even as armed tribal members began to attack the shrunken Afghan army. By March 1979 the city of Herat in western Afghanistan was openly rebelling against the government in the capital of Kabul. The Afghan army occupied Herat, while the air force bombed an army division that also was in revolt. Six months later, more than half the Afghan army had deserted or been killed. The Soviet Union looked on these events with dismay. Afghanistan had become its ally in the Cold War (the world-wide struggle for influence between the United States and the Soviet Union, which lasted from 1945 to 1990). As it had done many times in other countries, the Soviet Union decided to send in its army to defend the communist government.

In December 1979 Russian troops invaded Afghanistan. While previous Russian invasions of countries like Hungary (in 1956) and Czechoslovakia (1968) had met weak resistance that soon died out, resistance in Afghanistan gained in strength.

Afghanistan had a long history of resisting foreign conquerors, with armed tribesmen using Afghanistan's rugged mountain ranges to their advantage. But religion became an even greater element. Where the Russians and the communist Afghans they put into power were atheists (they believed that there was no God), most Afghans were Muslims, followers of Islam. The resistance to Russian occupation soon turned into a religious crusade in which Muslims were resisting nonreligious Russians.

Holy war

The fight between Afghanistan and the Soviet Union seemed one-sided. Russia was one of two superpowers in the world in 1979 (the United States was the other), while Afghanistan was desperately poor. But the Afghans were not alone.

The United States, always on the lookout for attempts to expand Soviet influence, began providing money and weapons to the rebelling Afghans. This was done secretly by the Central Intelligence Agency (CIA) to

What Is a Jihad?

"Jihad" is an Arabic word meaning "to try." In Islam, jihad is considered a religious obligation, and Muslims who are involved in a jihad are called *mujahideen* (holy warriors). It is an important concept in Islam, and especially to Osama bin Laden, who regarded his terrorist activities as part of a jihad. In Islam, the word jihad can carry several different meanings.

On one level a jihad can be personal—the act of trying to observe the teachings of Islam in one's personal life, as well as promoting justice and Islamic teachings. Jihad is also referred to in the Koran (Islam's holy book) as a holy war, either to defend Islam against attack by nonbelievers or to use military force to expand Islamic influence and convert nonbelievers. For Muslims, spreading the word of Islam is a duty that knows no national boundaries.

avoid an open conflict with Russia. (This kind of underground conflict was typical of the Cold War.) In the Middle East, wealthy Muslim countries like Saudi Arabia saw the invasion as an attack on Islam. They were willing to contribute money—and eventually people—to help the Afghans resist the Russian occupation.

Among the people outside Afghanistan who were drawn to this cause was bin Laden. In 1980, shortly after the Russian invasion, bin Laden visited Pakistan, where leaders of the Afghan resistance had found a safe place to hide. His family name and personal wealth gave bin Laden access to leaders in the struggle against the Russians, and he soon became

Osama as Holy Warrior?

After the September 11, 2001, attacks on the World Trade Center and the Pentagon, the television usually showed Osama bin Laden carrying a military rifle, or with one at his side. The meaning was clear: he was a fighter.

But during the jihad against the Russians in Afghanistan, bin Laden's exact role was not as obvious. In an interview with the U.S. television program *Frontline,* former Central Intelligence Agency (CIA) official Milton Bearden, who was active in Afghanistan in the 1980s, said in an interview: "You can find nobody who is familiar with the situation in Pakistan and Afghanistan in those years that would say bin Laden played any role other than the fund-raiser. . . . He possibly was engaged in a battle in 1987 . . . [but] regardless of how many pictures someone can cough up showing bin Laden with a walkie-talkie or bin Laden with a Kalashnikov [military rifle] . . . it's the whole Osama bin Laden mythology. It's almost part entertainment."

Some reporters who were in Afghanistan in the 1980s said bin Laden was known as "the Saudi Prince" who visited Afghan or Arab fighters in the hospital dressed in elegant custom-made English boots and fine woolen pants under a traditional Saudi robe, handing out nuts and candy. He noted each injured man's name and address and later sent a check to the man's family. Other times, bin Laden was reported running bulldozers and other construction equipment from his father's company to build military tunnels, storage depots, and roads.

Other people who knew bin Laden insist that he was involved in military activity, fighting in five or six major battles against Russian troops. More than once, bin Laden was said to have come close to being killed.

As with many parts of bin Laden's story, it is difficult to sort out fact from fiction, or even intentional lies.

caught up in the cause himself. For bin Laden the main issue was more religious than political.

Bin Laden's involvement in Afghanistan grew gradually. He returned to Saudi Arabia and started raising money to help finance the Afghan resistance. He returned to Pakistan occasionally over the next two years to deliver money and materials. He brought a few employees of his father's construction company to help. In 1982 bin Laden went to Afghanistan, getting closer to the fighting and occasionally joining battles himself. He encouraged other Saudi Arabians to join him in the fight. In 1984 he set up a residence in Peshawar, Pakistan, a city near the border of Afghanistan. There, Arabs who had volunteered to fight in the Afghan resistance could be assigned to a fighting unit inside Afghanistan. For these Arabs, the battle in Afghanistan was a jihad, or holy war. Muslims engaged in a holy war are called *mujahideen* (holy warriors).

Two years later, in 1986, bin Laden set up his own camps inside Afghanistan. He eventually had six, mostly staffed by Arabs recruited to help the Afghans drive out the Russians. Bin Laden recruited experienced military men from Syria and Egypt and fighters from Saudi Arabia, Kuwait, Algeria, Egypt, and Yemen. Western officials estimated that he attracted between thirty thousand and forty thousand soldiers, most of them from Saudi Arabia. These soldiers became known as "Arab Afghans" and fought battles against Russian units entirely with fellow Arabs recruited for the holy war.

Bin Laden's involvement in the war created a need for improved organization, to assign newcomers and to let the families of fighters know about their status. In 1988 bin Laden created a formal organization and called it "the base," or Al Qaeda (pronounced al KAY-duh), which served as a central organization for Arabs who had volunteered to fight on behalf of the Islamic government in Afghanistan.

The Persian Gulf War (1990–91)

In 1989 the Soviet Union gave up trying to conquer Afghanistan and pulled out its troops. The communist government it supported collapsed, and local tribal leaders began fighting among themselves for power. But once the Russians were gone, bin Laden's job was done, and he returned to Saudi Arabia. He began working in his family's businesses. But his experience in Afghanistan had left an impression, and he started to criticize the Saudi government. He announced plans to start a new holy war in South Yemen (which at the time had a pro-communist government), and gave speeches warning that Iraq's leader, Saddam Hussein (1937–), planned to invade the small country of Kuwait. This made the Saudi government, which was friendly toward Iraq and did not want trouble with South Yemen, unhappy. Saudi Arabia's ruling family tends not to tolerate disagreement, especially from a member of the country's business elite. Bin Laden was ordered to stop making speeches and to remain in Saudi Arabia. Members of the government and his family urged him to be quiet, and for a while bin Laden concentrated on his business affairs and his family. He had four wives, the maximum allowed in Islam, and ten children.

In 1990 Hussein did invade Kuwait, which lay between Iraq to the north and Saudi Arabia to the south. Bin Laden approached the Saudi government and offered to recruit some of the fighters from Afghanistan to help defend Saudi Arabia against any possible threat from Iraq. He still had the records of the Al Qaeda organization he had built to organize his efforts in Afghanistan. While the Saudi government considered his offer, another piece of news reached bin Laden: American troops were being sent to Saudi Arabia. Bin Laden was enraged. To him, fresh from driving infidel (non-Muslim) troops out of Afghanistan, another set of infidels had been invited to enter the holiest country in Islam. People who knew bin Laden at the time recalled that he was shocked and depressed at the idea of having American troops anywhere near Mecca and Medina.

Bin Laden's reaction was to persuade religious leaders to issue a *fatwa* (an Islamic religious decree) stating that it was the religious duty of Muslims to train to defend Saudi Arabia. Bin Laden then reopened his old training camps in Afghanistan, attracting about four thousand volunteers ready to fight in Saudi Arabia. In the end, however, the Gulf War was largely conducted by the United States, aided by European allies and the government forces of Saudi Arabia. There was no role for bin Laden's fighters. Instead, bin Laden was ordered not to leave the city of Jeddah; the Saudi government did not trust a citizen who acted independently without orders.

Sudan

Bin Laden felt that he was under arrest in Jeddah. Although he had been ordered not to travel abroad, with the aid of his brother and a friendly member of the ruling family, he managed to leave Saudi Arabia and went to Afghanistan in 1991. His situation was now difficult. He had left his own country against government orders. (He would soon lose his Saudi citizenship.) He feared that other countries in the region, such as Pakistan, might arrest him and send him back to Saudi Arabia.

In late 1991 bin Laden went to Sudan, a largely Muslim country on the east coast of Africa, across the Red Sea from Saudi Arabia. Bin Laden used his inheritance to buy or build new businesses in Sudan. He liked the country's strict Islamic form of government. He owned and worked farms, and reports said that he used his experience in construction to build a road linking the capital of Khartoum to Port Sudan, on the Red Sea. The next five years in Sudan were apparently a mixture of peaceful pursuits and the beginnings of terrorism. According to the U.S. State Department, bin Laden established terrorist training camps in Sudan and paid to bring five hundred Arab veterans of the Afghan war to Sudan, a number that grew over time. As more so-called Afghan Arabs arrived, he gave them jobs in his companies or in his terror training camps. Bin Laden also helped finance about a dozen Islamic terrorist groups in other countries. Al Qaeda became a source of funding and loose coordination for terrorist groups from Asia to North Africa.

These activities continued to disturb the Saudi Arabian government, which warned bin Laden not to do anything that might threaten Saudi Arabia. Reports claim that the Saudis secretly tried to murder bin Laden in Sudan but failed. In 1994 Saudi Arabia took away bin Laden's citizenship and seized his assets in the country. (Bin Laden claimed in a magazine interview that two years later the Saudi government changed its mind and offered to let him back in the country, but he refused. No explanation was offered.) It appeared that the Saudis could do nothing to affect his behavior, even as bin Laden was moving from giving speeches to launching violent attacks on Saudi Arabia and the United States.

Attacking the United States

This period in Sudan also saw the beginning of bin Laden's involvement in terrorism. In Sudan, bin Laden developed close ties to the Islamic Jihad, an Egyptian organization that used terrorism to support what it considered to be a purer form of Islam in Egypt. Al Qaeda began carrying out its own jihad against American interests:

- **December 1992:** A bomb exploded in a hotel in Aden, Yemen, at the southern end of the Arabian peninsula. The hotel was housing several U.S. soldiers at the time. No one was killed.

- **February 26, 1993:** A powerful bomb hidden in a van exploded in the underground parking garage of New York City's World Trade Center. The explosion killed six people and injured more than a thousand. A police investigation soon linked the explosion to Omar Abdel Rahman, an Egyptian who preached Islam in New York City, and to bin Laden's Al Qaeda organization.

- **October 1993:** An attack was launched against U.S. soldiers in Somalia. American troops were in the African country to help relieve a famine. Eighteen Americans died. (This attack became the subject of a book and 2001 film, *Black Hawk Down.*) The United States later bombed a factory in Mogadishu, Somalia, thought to have been owned by bin Laden.

- **February 1994:** Al Qaeda planned to assassinate U.S. President Bill Clinton (1946–). The first plot, intended to kill Clinton in Pakistan in February 1994, fell apart when the president canceled his visit. A second plot to kill him in Manila, the capital of the Philippines, in December 1994 was never carried out, according to claims by U.S. intelligence officials.

- **November 13, 1995:** Bin Laden was accused of supporting a car bomb attack on a Saudi Arabian military training facility in the Saudi capital of Riyadh, which killed seven people (five of them Americans) and injured sixty other people, including about thirty-four Americans. Two bombs exploded around lunchtime at a site where Americans, both civilians and soldiers, trained Saudi soldiers to use weapons sold to Saudi Arabia by the United States. Saudi authorities later executed four men blamed for the attack before American investigators could determine whether the attack was linked to a later bombing aimed at an apartment house used by American soldiers (see Khobar Towers, 1996, on page 86). Saudi officials disclosed few details about those convicted of carrying out the bombing.

In addition to being blamed for attacks in Africa and Saudi Arabia, bin Laden often criticized the government of Saudi Arabia for continuing to allow American troops to be based there, long after the war against Iraq was over. Bin Laden called for changes in the Saudi government, a call that

Bin Laden and Al Qaeda

The exact nature of Osama bin Laden's role in the terrorist attacks on the World Trade Center and the Pentagon became the subject of debate after September 11, 2001. In the battle against Russian troops in Afghanistan during the 1980s, bin Laden's main role appeared to be providing funds and organization. Al Qaeda started as a way to keep track of the thousands of Arabs who volunteered to fight in Afghanistan, rather than as a organization of men taking orders directly from bin Laden.

Once bin Laden returned to Afghanistan in 1996, Al Qaeda took on a similar role in terrorist activities carried out throughout the Middle East. Many reports at the time said bin Laden was linked to or backed terrorist attacks inside Saudi Arabia and plots to assassinate President Bill Clinton of the United States or President Hosni Mubarak (1928–) of Egypt.

No one claimed that bin Laden personally planted any bombs. Instead, Al Qaeda became a loose network of "cells": semi-independent, small groups of a handful of terrorists who planned and carried out their own operations. Whether bin Laden controlled individual cells or simply provided general guidance, money, and his blessing became the subject of debate among antiterrorism experts.

A former U.S. State Department official, David Long, said in an interview with the *New Yorker* magazine that Al Qaeda "is not a terrorist organization in the traditional sense. It's more a clearing house from which other groups [get] funds, training, and logistical support. It . . . constantly changes shape according to the whims of its leadership, and that leadership is Osama bin Laden. It's highly personalized. Bin Laden is a facilitator—a practitioner of the most ancient way of doing things in the Middle East. . . . If you were to kill Osama tomorrow, the Osama organization would disappear, but all the networks would still be there." (A facilitator is someone who helps get things done but does not actually do them.)

Bin Laden, through Al Qaeda, has provided funds to terrorists in Egypt, Algeria, Yemen, Somalia, Saudi Arabia, Chechnya, Kosovo, Kashmir (part of India), Bosnia, Tajikistan, and the Philippines, according to U.S. officials. On this basis, bin Laden is often blamed for attacks by groups over which he has little control. One result is that bin Laden has been built up as the world's super-terrorist by writing checks rather than planting bombs.

Terrorists themselves helped add to the confusion. Terrorist activities are by nature secretive. Those responsible for bombings sometimes claim credit; sometimes people claim credit who had nothing to do with an attack; and sometimes people are blamed without evidence. False or shaky claims can build a group's reputation among people who support its cause.

appealed to some people but not to the governments of Saudi Arabia or the United States.

"Kill the Americans"

In 1996 Sudan ordered bin Laden to leave the country in response to diplomatic pressure from the United States. Bin Laden returned to Afghanistan with his wives, his children, and several hundred Afghan Arab followers. They arrived in the middle of a bitter civil war that followed the collapse of the Russian invasion six years earlier. The civil war pitted regional tribal warlords (leaders of independent military forces) against the central government, and also against an ultraconservative group of religious students called the Taliban. Bin Laden sided with the Taliban and soon provided them with $3 million to finance their fight. One of bin Laden's daughters married the Taliban's leader, Mullah Muhammad Omar, making bin Laden his father-in-law. Bin Laden resumed his activities, recruiting fighters and funding the Taliban. Soon afterward the Taliban seized the capital city of Kabul and imposed a strict version of Islamic law on Afghanistan.

In February 1998 bin Laden and leaders of other radical Islamic organizations declared war on the United States in a statement published in a London-based Arabic newspaper, *al-Quds al-Arabi*. They described the statement as a *fatwa*. The *fatwa* criticized the United States for having troops in Saudi Arabia and for supporting the Jewish state of Israel against Arab states, particularly Iraq. Bin Laden's statement went on to urge "all Muslims . . . to kill the Americans and their allies—civilians and military. . . . We—with God's help—call on every Muslim who believes in God and wishes to be rewarded to comply with God's order to kill the Americans and plunder their money wherever and whenever they find it."

From his safe haven in Afghanistan, Bin Laden began campaigning against U.S. influence in the Middle East, using terrorist tactics to attack American military installations.

Khobar Towers, 1996

About 10 P.M. on June 25, 1996, a fuel truck stopped outside Khobar Towers, an apartment house in Dahran used by American troops stationed in Saudi Arabia. Seconds later, a bomb concealed in the truck exploded. The blast blew off the front of

the building. Nineteen American soldiers died and another five hundred people were injured, about half of them Americans. It was the deadliest attack on American soldiers in the Middle East since 1982, when 241 U.S. Marines died in an attack on their base in Beirut, Lebanon. The attack strained American relations with Saudi Arabia. U.S. investigators were not allowed to question suspects in the case before they were executed for an earlier bombing of a Saudi military facility in Riyadh.

Kenya and Tanzania, 1998

Two years later, on August 7, 1998, the U.S. embassies in two east African countries, Kenya and Tanzania, were attacked almost at the same time. At about 10:30 A.M., bombs exploded outside the embassies in Nairobi, Kenya, and Dar es Salaam, Tanzania. The two bombs killed 224 people—mostly Africans working in or near the buildings, and a dozen Americans—and injured about 5,000. Bin Laden came under suspicion the same day.

A powerful bomb shattered Khobar Towers in Dahran, Saudi Arabia, in 1996. The towers housed U.S. soldiers stationed in Saudi Arabia, to which Osama bin Laden strongly objected. Nineteen American soldiers died and another five hundred people were injured, about half of them Americans. *Photograph reproduced by permission of AP/Wide World Photos.*

About two weeks later President Clinton approved missile attacks on a bin Laden training camp in Afghanistan and a drug factory in Khartoum, Sudan. U.S. officials said at the time they thought the drug factory was owned by bin Laden and was manufacturing poisonous gas for future terrorist attacks. Later, major questions were raised about whether the factory had anything to do with bin Laden or with deadly gases.

Eventually, in May 2001, at a trial in New York City, four men were found guilty of planning the bombings and were sentenced to life in prison. They were described as having connections to bin Laden.

Millennium plot, 2000

On December 14, 1999, just two weeks before the celebrations of the year 2000, the millennium, an Algerian man named Ahmed Ressam (1967–) aroused the suspicions of U.S. Customs inspectors as he drove off a ferry from Canada to the United States. He seemed nervous and was sweating. The inspectors soon discovered why: inside his car were explosives. Eventually officials discovered that he was planning to bomb the Los Angeles airport and that his plan was just one part of a larger "Millennium Plot" sponsored by Al Qaeda and bin Laden. Intelligence officials in the United States said there might have been other targets in the United States in addition to the airport.

Around the same time, officials in Jordan stopped a plan to bomb the Radisson SAS Hotel in Amman and two other locations that Christian tourists often visited. Those attacks were also scheduled to happen during the year 2000 celebrations.

U.S. intelligence officials discovered later that Al Qaeda had planned to bomb a U.S. warship while it was docked in the port of Aden, Yemen. That plan failed because the boat intended to carry explosives up to the USS *The Sullivans* sank because it was overloaded. (An identical plan was carried out successfully ten months later against another U.S. Navy ship, the *Cole*.)

In India a terrorist organization associated with bin Laden, the Harakat ul-Mujahideen, hijacked a plane on December 24, 1999. The hijackers held the plane and its more than 160 passengers and crew hostage in Afghanistan for a week, until the government of India freed a group of jailed militants who wanted independence for the Indian state of Kashmir.

USS *Cole*, 2000

On October 12, 2000, a small powerboat came alongside the USS *Cole*, a U.S. Navy destroyer that was refueling in the harbor of Aden, Yemen. The boat was loaded with a bomb, which exploded, tearing a hole in the side of the navy ship. The bomb went off near the dining hall of the ship. It killed seventeen crewmen and injured thirty-nine others. Yemen police arrested nine people thought to be connected with the attack—the two people who steered the boat were killed in the explosion—and American officials blamed bin Laden and Al Qaeda, although they had no firm evidence of bin Laden's involvement.

The following March an Arabic television broadcast (Al-Jazeera in Qatar) showed bin Laden at the wedding of one of his sons, praising the attack on the *Cole*. "In Aden, the young man on the attacking boat stood up for holy war, and destroyed a destroyer feared by the powerful," he said.

As he spoke, bin Laden had already been charged with planning the embassy bombings in Nairobi and Dar es Salaam. The Taliban government in Kabul had refused demands to hand over bin Laden to the United States for trial.

USS *Cole* with a hole in its side, Aden, Yemen, 2000. The blast killed seventeen American sailors.
Photograph reproduced by permission of AP/Wide World Photos.

A fireball erupts from one of the World Trade Center towers as it is struck by a second of two airplanes in New York, September 11, 2001. *Photograph reproduced by permission of AP/Wide World Photos.*

New York and Washington, D.C., September 11, 2001

On September 11, 2001, bin Laden brought his campaign to the United States itself. Nineteen terrorists associated with Al Qaeda hijacked four passenger jets within ninety minutes of one another. Two jets were leaving Boston, Massachusetts, one was leaving Newark, New Jersey, and one was leaving Washington, D.C. All four were headed to the West Coast, meaning they were fully loaded with jet fuel. The two Boston jets were flown into the World Trade Center in New York City; the one from Washington was crashed into the Pentagon, headquarters of the U.S. armed forces. The fourth jet crashed in Pennsylvania. Tape recordings recovered from this plane showed that passengers had rushed the hijackers; in the struggle, the plane went down. In all, about three thousand people died in the attacks, most of them in New York City, where the World Trade Center towers collapsed.

Nine days later, President Bush, in an address to Congress, blamed Al Qaeda and bin Laden for planning and carrying out the attacks.

The United States demanded that the government in Kabul, Afghanistan, arrest bin Laden and hand him over to the United States. The Taliban refused. On October 7, 2001, U.S. Air Force planes began bombing targets in Afghanistan. Their goal was to attack camps set up by Al Qaeda and to force the Taliban government to hand over bin Laden.

By the middle of November the Taliban had lost control of most of the country. American troops had set up bases inside Afghanistan and were searching for bin Laden and other members of Al Qaeda.

Osama bin Laden after 9/11

After a month of intense bombing, the U.S.-led military campaign drove the Taliban from the Afghan capital of Kabul and its stronghold in the city of Kandahar, leaving Afghanistan without an effective national government. An alliance of Afghans who had opposed the strict Islamic rule forced on the country by the Taliban tried to form a government, and a politician who had been living in exile in the United States, Hamid Kharzai, was installed as a temporary head of government. Bin Laden's attack on the World Trade Center and Pentagon had

"The Evidence We Have"

On September 20, 2001, just nine days after the attacks on the World Trade Center and the Pentagon, President George W. Bush addressed the U.S. Congress and blamed bin Laden for launching the deadly raids. Bush told Congress:

"Americans are asking: Who attacked our country? The evidence we have gathered all points to a collection of loosely affiliated [connected] terrorist organizations known as Al Qaeda. They are the same murderers indicted for bombing American embassies in Tanzania and Kenya, and responsible for bombing the USS *Cole.*

"Al Qaeda is to terror what the mafia is to crime. But its goal is not making money; its goal is remaking the world—and imposing [forcing] its radical beliefs on people everywhere.

"The terrorists practice a fringe form of Islamic extremism that has been rejected by Muslim scholars and the vast majority of Muslim clerics—a fringe movement that perverts the peaceful teachings of Islam. The terrorists' directive commands them to kill Christians and Jews, to kill all Americans, and make no distinction among military and civilians, including women and children.

"This group and its leader—a person named Osama bin Laden—are linked to many other organizations in different countries, including the Egyptian

the opposite effect of what Al Qaeda wanted: American troops were now the strongest force in Afghanistan, and other U.S. forces were still based in Saudi Arabia.

Bin Laden himself appeared twice on an Arabic television station after September 11. Without claiming responsibility for the attacks, he praised the men who carried them out and vowed to fight on against American influence in the Islamic world. In one interview bin Laden was asked whether he was responsible for the attacks of September 11. He replied: "America has made many accusations against us and many other Muslims around the world. Its charge that we are carrying out acts of terrorism is unwarranted [without good reason]. . . . If inciting [encouraging] people to do that is terrorism, and if killing those who kill our sons is terrorism, then let history be witness that we are terrorists."

Islamic Jihad and the Islamic Movement of Uzbekistan. There are thousands of these terrorists in more than sixty countries. They are recruited from their own nations and neighborhoods and brought to camps in places like Afghanistan, where they are trained in the tactics of terror. They are sent back to their homes or sent to hide in countries around the world to plot evil and destruction. . . .

"We will direct every resource at our command—every means of diplomacy, every tool of intelligence, every instrument of law enforcement, every financial influence, and every necessary weapon of war—to the disruption and to the defeat of the global terror network. . . .

"Americans should not expect one battle, but a lengthy campaign, unlike any other we have ever seen. It may include dramatic strikes, visible on TV, and covert operations, secret even in success. We will starve terrorists of funding, turn them one against another, drive them from place to place, until there is no refuge or no rest. And we will pursue nations that provide aid or safe haven to terrorism. Every nation, in every region, now has a decision to make. Either you are with us, or you are with the terrorists. From this day forward, any nation that continues to harbor or support terrorism will be regarded by the United States as a hostile regime."

Perception of Bin Laden in the Islamic world

America's pursuit of bin Laden was just one part of U.S. foreign policy. Support for Arabic governments such as the one in Saudi Arabia (a major source of U.S. oil imports) was another part. In the aftermath of September 11 these two sides came together in an unexpected way. While Americans and most Europeans were horrified by the attacks on New York and Washington, D.C., some people in the Middle East cheered wildly. Television news showed scenes of Palestinians dancing in the streets to celebrate the attacks. Public opinion polls showed many people in the Islamic world doubted that Muslims were responsible for the attacks. In Pakistan, whose military government was an ally of the United States, many young men in the streets wore bin Laden T-shirts and expressed support for Al Qaeda.

Bin Laden had become a public hero to many people in Muslim countries. He appeared to be the one person able and willing to resist the United States, which was viewed by many as the power behind undemocratic, harsh governments. And in a region where religion plays an important role in the daily lives of millions of people, bin Laden represented Muslims conducting a holy war for Islam against the "infidel," the United States.

Bin Laden disappeared from view after the U.S. attacks on Afghanistan, leaving people to wonder whether he had become ill and died, been killed in the bombing, or found a hiding place to plan another attack. But in some ways, it no longer mattered whether bin Laden was dead or alive. If alive, he remained a potential threat to the United States and a hero to some Muslims. If dead, he could become a martyr who could inspire other Muslims to take up his holy war.

For More Information

Books

Bergen, Peter L. *Holy War, Inc.: Inside the Secret World of Osama bin Laden.* Waterville, ME: G.K. Hall, 2002.

Bodansky, Yossef. *Bin Laden: The Man Who Declared War on America.* Rocklin, CA: Forum, 2001.

Jacquard, Roland. *In the Name of Osama bin Laden: Global Terrorism and the bin Laden Brotherhood,* translated by George Holoch. Durham, NC: Duke University Press, 2002.

Landau, Elaine. *Osama bin Laden: A War against the West.* Brookfield, CT: Twenty-First Century Books, 2002.

Reeve, Simon. *The New Jackals: Ramzi Yousef, Osama bin Laden and the Future of Terrorism.* Boston: Northeastern University Press, 1999.

Periodicals

Bin Laden, Osama. "Jihad against Jews and Crusaders." *Al-Quds al-Arabi,* February 23, 1998.

"Public Enemy No. 1: A Son of Privilege, Osama bin Laden Recasts Himself as the Bloody Defender of Islam." *People Weekly,* October 8, 2001, p. 161.

Rosenbaum, Ron. "Degrees of Evil—Some Thoughts on Hitler, bin Laden, and the Hierarchy of Wickedness." *Atlantic Monthly,* February, 2002, p. 63.

Voll, John O. "Bin Laden and the New Age of Global Terrorism." *Middle East Policy,* December 2001, p. 1.

Kathy Boudin

May 19, 1943
New York, New York

Member of the Weather Underground

Kathy Boudin was a member of the radical group founded in the 1960s called the Weathermen (later called the Weather Underground) that wanted to start a violent revolution in the United States. The movement had gained influence as part of two political movements of the 1960s: the civil rights movement and the anti-Vietnam War movement. After many young **radicals** (people who want rapid changes in a society) of the 1960s moved on to other things, Boudin remained active until 1981, when she was arrested and charged with murder for her part in robbing an armored car. The robbery killed three people, including two policemen.

The incident, which brought a twenty-years-to-life jail sentence, made Boudin a symbol of how student radicals of the 1960s turned into revolutionaries, even though most of her companions eventually gave up their extreme politics.

Childhood

Boudin was born in 1943 and grew up in New York City's Greenwich Village. Her father, Leonard Boudin, was a

> "I believed at the time that the robbery would help bring greater equality and freedom to African-Americans, and that this would help bring greater equality and justice to our whole society. But I was wrong."

leading lawyer who specialized in **civil liberties.** He defended many people accused by the government and by Congress of having sympathies with **communism.** (Communism is a system in which the state controls the economy, including factories and businesses. In the 1950s, during the Cold War, when the capitalist United States was vying with the Communist Soviet Union [present-day Russia and neighboring countries] for world power, people with progressive views were often labeled communist.) Leonard Boudin's defense of alleged communists brought the family to the attention of the Federal Bureau of Investigation (FBI). In the mid-1950s Leonard Boudin's passport was taken away on the grounds that he was a communist, despite the fact that no evidence was ever presented. Two federal courts ordered the State Department to restore the passport, but it seriously harmed Leonard Boudin's reputation in an era when fear of communism was everywhere.

Boudin was sent to private schools—The Little Red School House for elementary school and Elisabeth Irwin High School—where her teachers included some people who could not get jobs elsewhere because they were suspected of being sympathetic to communism, if not of being communists themselves.

Boudin was remembered as being intelligent, thoughtful, an outstanding athlete, and an independent thinker (asked to write an essay on any topic, she chose "Why Can't I Play Football with the Boys?"). In the eleventh grade she led classmates to East Harlem in New York to paint and plaster buildings, helping out the low-income African American and Latino residents.

Kathy and her brother, Michael, grew up in a family that had high expectations of both children; their parents believed they would make major contributions to society. The two took slightly different lessons from their father's example. Michael focused on the law and became a leading business lawyer and federal judge. Kathy considered law school but decided instead to work for the rights of African Americans and try to lead a revolution.

College and political radicalism

In 1961 Boudin entered Bryn Mawr College, a respected women's school near Philadelphia, Pennsylvania. It was an odd match. Bryn Mawr was a conservative, traditional place for a liberal New Yorker like Boudin. Each afternoon, for example, women at the school sat down to a formal tea (the school advised them to bring tea sets with them when they enrolled).

At this time, in the early 1960s, Boudin became active in the civil rights movement, the effort to gain equal rights for African Americans during the 1950s and 1960s, which was running at full speed. At Bryn Mawr Boudin attended a scheduled civil rights demonstration but was the only person to show up. That evening at dinner in the school cafeteria, to protest student disinterest in social causes, she stood up and smashed a dinner plate against a wall. "No one stopped eating or said a word," she remembered later. "They didn't even look up from their plates."

In 1963 Boudin was arrested at a civil rights demonstration in Chester, Pennsylvania. This demonstration had a major impact on Boudin. She became involved in an organization called Students for a Democratic Society (SDS), which wanted greater equality for all Americans and planned to use direct action to effect change rather than traditional political campaigning. Picketing was an example of the sort of "direct action" SDS supported.

Another example of direct action was the Economic Research and Action Project (ERAP), an organization sponsored by the SDS in which SDS members moved into poor African American neighborhoods to help residents improve their lives. Boudin joined ERAP in Cleveland, Ohio, after her junior year. Her mother later remembered visiting Boudin and finding rats in the building where her daughter was living.

ERAP pointed to a central problem of SDS. While left-wing (socialist or communist inspired) politics talked about "the workers" rising up against their terrible economic and

The Special Vocabulary of Radical Politics in the 1960s

The world of Kathy Boudin in the late 1960s and early 1970s used a special vocabulary to describe politics. Among the key words and phrases are:

- **Left wing** and **right wing.** People who push liberal or radical measures to solve social problems, usually in order to achieve equality and the well-being of the common people, are described as "left wing." People who prefer to rely on individual action to solve social problems are called "right wing." These two terms cover a wide range of attitudes and policies, including such issues as civil rights, civil liberties, and economic policies. They also cover a range of opinions.

- **Liberal.** In some contexts a "liberal" is on the left wing, while a "conservative" is on the right wing. In another sense, though, "liberal" refers to the idea of using electoral politics (voting) to achieve gradual social and economic change. It is in contrast to a radical.

- **Radical.** A radical believes changes in a nation's political and economic system should come quickly. Radicals may or may not regard themselves as revolutionaries.

- **Revolutionaries.** Revolutionaries seek major, immediate change through a violent uprising. Some revolutionaries believe the poor can improve their lives by taking up arms against the established political and economic powers and seizing property and political control.

social conditions, the SDS itself consisted mostly of middle- and upper-middle-class college students. In the 1960s white people in the working class generally supported the Vietnam War (1955–75, a civil war in Southeast Asia in which the United States military was fighting alongside noncommunist North Vietnamese to rid the southern part of the country of communists) and wanted nothing to do with the left-wing SDS. Through ERAP, the SDS found in African American ghettos (areas in a city where members of a minority group, usually poor, live) the very workers they were hoping to help, not to mention victims of centuries of racism. It seemed that here was what they needed to start a revolution. This view had more to do with the SDS's wishful thinking than with the problems of black Americans who could not get high-paying jobs and whose neighborhoods were filled with crime, drugs, and alcohol abuse.

After graduating from Bryn Mawr in 1965, Boudin was at loose ends. She had applied to Yale Law School and had been turned down. She had enjoyed her time in Cleveland the previous summer and decided to return to the work that gave her a sense of purpose: "learning the realities of class. . . . It was the discovery that there was a whole other world that I was living next to, part of, and didn't really know about," she told a magazine interviewer many years later.

1968

The year 1968 was a painful and dramatic one for the United States. In January communist forces in South Vietnam launched a strong new military campaign that made it seem that the Vietnam War would drag on forever. On April 4, 1968, civil rights leader Martin Luther King Jr. (1929–1968) was assassinated in Memphis, Tennessee, where he had gone to support a strike by city garbage workers. Two months later in Los Angeles, Senator Robert F. Kennedy (1925–1968) was assassinated after winning the California Democratic presidential primary. At the Democratic Party's convention in Chicago, Illinois, in August, rioting broke out as police battled antiwar protesters. A report later described the events in Chicago as a "police riot."

Easily overlooked among all this was the collapse of the ERAP project in Cleveland, which left Boudin at loose ends again. She went to Chicago for the convention, where she was arrested for helping with a project to spread foul-smelling liquid onto a carpet at the Palmer House hotel, where Democratic convention attendees were staying. Boudin said she did not spill any of the liquid herself, but she surrendered to police anyway. "I was somebody who was looking for a way to be a hero," she told a reporter for *Time* in 1984.

The events of 1968 deeply affected some members of the SDS. The assassinations of King and Kennedy and the violence at the Democratic Party convention convinced some radicals that they had to use violence to counter the violence used by the government. The result was the creation, the following year, of the Weathermen (also called the Weather Underground), a small group of former SDS members who decided to form a branch of what they called the "International Liberation Army" inside the United States. Their enemies were class privilege, capitalism, and "American imperialism" (the belief that the United States was trying to force its will on underdeveloped countries like Vietnam).

American political terrorism

Although not a national leader, Boudin was an early member of the Weathermen. Her involvement in America's newest political terrorist organization quickly led her into a series of events that ended twelve years later in a maximum-security prison for women in New York state. The terrorist acts included:

- **October 1969:** To fight back against police violence the previous year, Weathermen tried to organize a new set of riots, called the Days of Rage. The event was a flop—only a handful of demonstrators showed up—and Boudin was arrested for minor vandalism while carrying a Vietcong flag through a park. (The Vietcong were the military forces of North Vietnam, against which the United States was fighting.)

- **March 1970:** In a townhouse in Greenwich Village, several Weathermen were building a bomb that accidentally exploded. Boudin, who was taking a shower when the bomb went off, ran into the street without any clothes on. One other person in the house escaped; the three Weathermen who were working on the bomb died. The house was destroyed. The explosion grabbed national headlines and put Boudin on "wanted" posters for helping assemble explosives intended to attack military facilities. To avoid arrest Boudin disappeared from public view.

- **March 1970–1981:** For a decade Boudin avoided capture by the FBI and local police. She has described her time as a fugitive as uneventful. She lived briefly in Mexico and then went with Mexican migrant workers to pick grapes in California. Later she had a job in a hospital in Massachusetts.

During the 1970s the Weathermen were blamed for at least two dozen terrorist bomb attacks, including ones at the National Guard in Washington, D.C.; the police headquarters in New York City; and the U.S. Capitol building. Either by luck or by design, no one was killed in any of these bombings. Boudin has said she was not involved in the bombings (although her fingerprints were found in a San Francisco house used as a "bomb factory," according to police). Also during the 1970s Boudin wrote a book titled *Prairie Fire,* making a case that American history is one of imperialism, and she appeared in a documentary, *Underground,* by filmmaker Emile de Antonio (1919–1989).

The war in Vietnam finally ended in 1975, and with it went SDS and its offshoots. The group had not had any real influence for a long time, but the end of the war seemed to remove its last reason for existence. Its leaders abandoned the group and, for the most part, began to pursue more mainstream careers.

But Boudin was still a fugitive. She considered surrendering to authorities but decided against it. Instead, Boudin supported herself with a series of menial jobs, such as cleaning houses. She later told *Time* magazine: "The very status of being underground was an identity for me. It was a moral statement. . . . I was making a difference in no way, so then I elevated [raised] to great importance the fact that I was underground."

While working as a house cleaner, Boudin read about the Underground Railroad—the pre-Civil War system of whites who offered hiding places and aid to slaves escaping to freedom in Canada—and decided that something more meaningful than living underground would be helping African Americans.

Black Liberation Army

In 1978 Boudin moved back to the East Coast from Ohio and joined a tiny organization called the May 19th Communist Organization, which was thought to have fewer than a dozen members. Their main goal was to hook up with the Black Liberation Army (BLA). The BLA was a group that had spun off from the Black Panthers, a black revolutionary movement founded in 1966. By the time Boudin became associated with it, the BLA had allied with another African American group called the Family. The Family appeared to be part gangsters and part political terrorists. Some critics thought the Family was mostly about robbing armored trucks to raise money, with a thin coating of political theory to make it seem more respectable.

The BLA, in combining crime with politics, had started something new. Members of the BLA argued that robbing banks

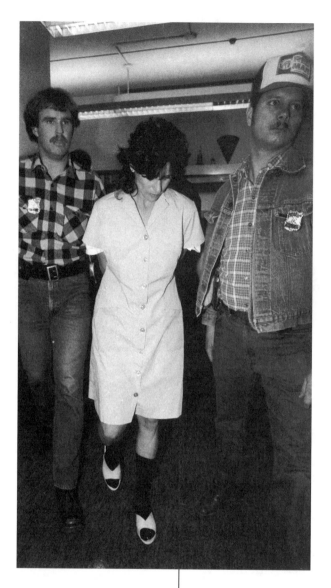

Kathy Boudin began life as the privileged daughter of a New York civil liberties attorney. At age 38, she was charged with murder in the death of a policeman and two armored truck guards. *Photograph reproduced by permission of AP/Wide World Photos.*

was an acceptable activity for an organization fighting a war against society. The BLA also was known for attacking policemen in African American neighborhoods, killing some of them.

The big dance

Boudin's role in the Family was to serve as a respectable white woman who might attract less notice than a black woman. One of her main tasks was to help members of the terrorist group obtain false identities. Working as a retail clerk, she would photocopy driver's licenses from customers who were paying by check. With personal details from the driver's license, Family members could apply for a "replacement" for their "lost" license without having to show additional identification. The new driver's licenses were then used to rent cars or vans the gang needed to stage armored car robberies, which was the Family's specialty. Gradually, Boudin was becoming a gangster.

On October 20, 1981, the Family planned to use a red Chevy van to rob an armored truck in Nyack, New York, a suburb north of New York City. Boudin's job was to ride in a U-Haul truck rented for the occasion. Other members of the gang planned to rob the armored truck, meet up with the U-Haul, and then hide in the truck while Boudin and her long-standing boyfriend (and father of her son), David Gilbert, drove the U-Haul back to New York City. They thought that police would be looking for black men driving a red car, and that a white couple driving a U-Haul truck would not arouse suspicion.

The robbery did not go well. While the guards were making a pickup of cash, the red van pulled up alongside the Brinks armored truck. One Brinks guard, Peter Paige, was shot to death

during the robbery, which netted the Family $1.6 million in cash. The robbers made their getaway in the red van and drove behind a nearby discount department store to meet the U-Haul.

But there was a catch. A college student living next to the parking lot saw the exchange and called police. The police set up a roadblock at the entrance to the New York State Thruway heading to New York City. Soon they spotted the U-Haul and ordered it to stop. There was momentary confusion: the police were looking for black men, but the U-Haul was driven by a white couple. Could they have stopped the wrong truck?

Police approached the truck, guns drawn. The woman on the driver's side—Boudin—got out, her hands raised, and asked police to put away their weapons. As this was happening, other officers went around to the back of the truck to get a look inside.

Suddenly the truck's rear doors flew open, and the heavily armed robbers started firing at the police. In the shootout, two policemen, Waverly Brown and Edward O'Grady, were killed. Members of the gang tried to flee. As she ran across

Demonstrators protesting the parole review for Kathy Boudin, 2001. Boudin was a passenger in the getaway car for a 1981 Brink's robbery and was supposed to provide cover for the gunmen. She was picked up, unarmed, as she fled the scene. *Photograph reproduced by permission of AP/Wide World Photos.*

the highway, Boudin was grabbed by an off-duty prison guard who had gotten out of his car to see what was happening.

Twelve years after fleeing the wreckage of a Greenwich Village townhouse, Boudin had resurfaced, this time charged with murder.

Guilty

Before her trial was scheduled to start, Boudin pleaded guilty to murder and robbery charges. Although she had not been armed during the robbery, under New York law someone who helps commit a serious crime can be held responsible for any deaths that result from the crime.

Boudin was sentenced to twenty years to life in prison. Held in a high-security prison for women, she helped start education programs for women prisoners, most of whom were poor and black. She also developed an AIDS education program that served as a model for other prisons.

Although she was behind bars, Boudin was in some respects back where she started after graduating from Bryn Mawr in 1965: living among poor African Americans and applying her training and education to improving the lives of the women around her. And just as she once took her identity from living underground, she now gained an identity living in prison.

For More Information

Books

Castellucci, John. *The Big Dance: The Untold Story of Kathy Boudin and the Terrorist Family That Committed the Brink's Robbery Murders.* New York: Dodd, Mead, 1986.

Frankfort, Ellen. *Kathy Boudin and the Dance of Death.* New York: Stein and Day, 1983.

Jacobs, Ron. *The Way the Wind Blew: A History of the Weather Underground.* New York: Verso, 1997.

Periodicals

"A Radical Unexpectedly Recants." *Time,* May 7, 1984, p. 27.

Shapiro, Bruce. "Kathy Boudin's Prison Odyssey." *The Nation,* March 20, 1995, p. 380.

Serrill, Michael S. "Trials on Twin Tracks." *Time,* September 5, 1983, p. 54.

John Brown

Born May 9, 1800
Torrington, Connecticut
Died December 2, 1859
Charlestown, Virginia

Militant abolitionist

John Brown was hanged in 1859 for his role in attacking a government arms warehouse in Harpers Ferry, Virginia (now in West Virginia). The attack was designed to encourage slaves to run away from their masters and gain their freedom. To many people at the time, Brown was a terrorist, a religious fanatic who would not wait for the law to free slaves. To others, he was a hero, willing to sacrifice his life to right a terrible wrong: the enslavement of one people by another in the United States.

To himself, he was a man who took up arms in the cause of righteousness. Brown's passion in life was opposition to slavery, which was worth attacking with guns.

Religion in the wilderness

Brown was born in Torrington, Connecticut, in 1800. His father was a deeply religious man and an **abolitionist** (a person who wants to outlaw slavery), the social issue that would become central in Brown's life. At Brown's birth, in 1800, the United States was less than a generation old. Slavery

"I believe that to have interfered as I have done, as I have always freely admitted I have done in behalf of His despised poor slaves, I did no wrong, but right."

Photograph reproduced by permission of the National Archives and Records Administration.

Words to Know

Abolitionist: a person who wants to outlaw slavery.

Armory: a place where weapons are stored.

Martyr: someone who is killed for a cause.

Militiamen: part-time soldiers who could take up arms in an emergency, somewhat like the National Guard.

Synonymous: having the same meaning.

was legal in many states, although in some states such as Pennsylvania, it had been outlawed. The great westward migration that settled states beyond the Appalachian Mountains was just beginning. Brown became part of that migration at age five, when his family moved to the frontier town of Hudson, Ohio, south of Cleveland. Life on the frontier was difficult. The truths taught in the Brown household were religion and abolition; the law took second place. As a child Brown saw runaway slaves taking shelter in his family's home. For the Brown family, heavenly laws that stated the equality of all men and women were more important than the earthly laws that allowed one human to own another.

As a young man Brown married Dianthe Lusk and started his own family. Eventually, he had twenty children by two wives. Brown tried several jobs but was never very successful at any of them. For a while, he tried earning a living tanning animal hides into leather. He tried farming. He tried dealing in cattle. In 1826 he and his family left Ohio and moved to neighboring Pennsylvania to build a tannery. In his barn he built a secret room to hide runaway slaves.

In 1831 one of Brown's children died, the first in a long string of sorrows and disappointments. Brown fell ill and was unable to keep up his farm. The next year, his first wife died while giving birth. In 1833 he married again, this time to sixteen-year-old Mary Ann Day, who eventually had thirteen children, of whom just six survived to adulthood. In 1836 financial pressures forced Brown to move his family back to Ohio, where he borrowed money to start a business trading cattle and land. But economic hard times forced Brown into bankruptcy. He and his family moved repeatedly as Brown went from one job to the next. Throughout, he and his wife lost one child after another, mostly to disease but also to accidents. In 1844 Brown moved his family to Springfield, Massachusetts, where he became a partner in a wool business.

Abolitionism

Brown had been a lifelong opponent of slavery. Now, in Massachusetts, he got to know many of the leading abolitionists of the era. Massachusetts was the center of the fight against slavery in the 1840s. William Lloyd Garrison (1805–1879) had started his newspaper, *The Liberator,* in Boston in 1831. Sojourner Truth (c. 1797–1883), a former slave from New York and a campaigner for abolition, lived in Springfield for a time. Frederick Douglass (c. 1818–1895), another former slave and a newspaper publisher (*The North Star* and *Frederick Douglass's Paper*), became a close friend of Brown.

Abolitionism began to gain ground in the 1840s. The issue was beginning to split the United States between the pro-slavery South, where slaves were considered an economic necessity to work on cotton plantations (farms), and the North, where industrial manufacturing was beginning to drive the economy and where antislavery beliefs were growing in popularity.

William Lloyd Garrison published a leading anti-slavery newspaper in Boston, Massachusetts. He was responsible for building sentiment in the North against slavery in the United States. *Photograph courtesy of the Library of Congress.*

But Brown was a man of action rather than of politics or speeches. He said that he took his instructions from the Bible, such as "do unto others as you would have them do unto you." He wanted to inspire a slave revolt. In his first meeting with Douglass, in 1847, Brown outlined his plans for such a war. In 1849 Brown started a farm in northern New York state near land that a wealthy abolitionist, Gerrit Smith (1797–1874), had bought to help former slaves get started in a new life. Brown's intention was to serve as "a kind of father" to the African Americans, despite his own problems as a farmer.

1850s: Prelude to the Civil War

In 1850, under pressure from southern legislators, Congress passed the Fugitive Slave Act, designed to help slave owners fight back against abolitionists who were helping their slaves escape. The Act basically said that any escaped slave could be returned to his or her owner, even if that slave was living in a state where slavery had been outlawed. The Act was aimed straight at the activities of the Underground Railroad, a system abolitionists developed to transport and hide runaway slaves in their search for freedom. It put the federal government on the side of slave owners, who felt that escaped slaves were essentially stolen property. In response, Brown helped organize the League of Gileadites, a small group of whites and blacks who promised to take up arms, if necessary, to protect runaway slaves from being taken back South.

Brown also helped start a new political party, the Radical Abolitionists, to support the immediate, total abolition of slavery. It was an era when many different solutions to the problem of slavery were being proposed. One group wanted to send black slaves back to Africa, from where they or their ancestors were brought. Another, the Free-Soil Party, wanted to prevent slavery from being made legal in new territories in the West, but it was willing to accept the existence of slavery in Southern states. The Radical Abolitionists made little progress, and in some respects they seemed to be losing ground.

In 1854 Congress passed another law—the Kansas-Nebraska Act—to deal with the issue of whether new western states joining the Union should allow slavery. Since the Missouri Compromise of 1820, slavery had been banned north of the Mason-Dixon line, which ran along the southern border of Missouri. (As part of the compromise, Missouri was allowed to join the Union as a slave state.) The Kansas-Nebraska Act allowed people living in the territories of what were to become Kansas and Nebraska to vote on whether slavery should be legal in the new states. To abolitionists the law was a major setback; it meant slavery might extend north of the Mason-Dixon line. The act drew militant abolitionists to Kansas to affect the vote. Supporters of slavery also poured into Kansas to sway the vote on slavery.

Brown and five of his sons joined the rush to Kansas, settling in the town of Osawatomie. There, they plunged into the battle over slavery. They went into the neighboring state of Missouri and kidnapped slaves to escort them to Canada and freedom. They also fought pitched battles in Kansas with pro-slavery settlers.

Bleeding Kansas

Kansas in 1855 became the scene of running battles between pro- and antislavery forces. So-called "Border Ruffians" from the slave state of Missouri (who were also known as "Bush-whackers") crossed into Kansas and attacked communities of abolitionists. (Among the Border Ruffians were the brothers Frank [1843–1915] and Jesse James [1847–1882], who later became famous bandits.) Antislavery settlers, such as Brown and his sons, launched attacks on pro-slavery communities. Famously, Brown led a group of antislavery guerrillas who helped defend the town of Lawrence from an attack by pro-slavery fighters. On May 24, 1855, Brown's gang got revenge for another raid by attacking a pro-slavery settlement on Pottawatomie Creek. Brown's raiders pulled five settlers from their cabins and murdered them with swords. The attack caused even more killings and gave rise to the expression "Bleeding Kansas" to describe the virtual civil war in Kansas Territory. (In the end Kansas entered the Union as a free state in January 1861, just weeks before the start of the Civil War [1861–65]).

The murders of the five pro-slavery settlers led to Brown's nickname, "Old Brown of Osawatomie," a name **synonymous** (having the same meaning) with terrorism in the minds of southerners. Brown insisted his raids were justified as a means to end the evils of slavery and said he was following the principles of the Bible. In the East many abolitionists had become discouraged with their slow progress in trying to outlaw slavery. They believed that direct action, like Brown's, was the only way to succeed. When Brown left Kansas and returned to Massachusetts in 1856, he was hailed as a hero by many abolitionists.

But Brown was not finished. He had a plan to start a slave revolt and he began working to make it happen. He began raising money to finance the purchase of guns that he planned to distribute to slaves in the South from a base in the Blue Ridge Mountains of Virginia. He thought they would rise up against their masters and launch a revolt that would end slavery throughout the United States. By 1858 Brown thought he had raised enough money and was almost ready to put his plan into action. But then he learned that one of his followers was possibly considering betraying the plan to authorities, so he went into hiding.

John Brown and Frederick Douglass

John Brown was close friends with many leaders of the antislavery movement in the 1850s. Others who did not know him personally supported his actions, both in Kansas and later in Virginia. He financed his raids in Kansas, for example, with contributions from abolitionists in the East.

Frederick Douglass was a particularly close friend. Douglass was a former slave who escaped to the North and then received an education in England. He was well spoken and published an abolitionist newspaper, *The North Star,* in Rochester, New York. He had supported Brown's move to Kansas to fight slavery, and before launching his attack in Harpers Ferry, Brown tried to persuade Douglass to join him. But Douglass thought the raid had no chance of success and tried to talk Brown into instead setting up a camp and encouraging blacks to run away from their masters. He failed.

John Brown's raid

The next summer, in 1859, Brown rented a farm in western Maryland near the town of Harpers Ferry, Virginia. That was the location of a United States government **armory** (a place where weapons are stored), from which Brown planned to seize arms and hand them out to slaves. But the delay of several months had hurt Brown's plan. Some of the men who were ready to help him the previous year had changed their minds. He tried to persuade Douglass to come along, but Douglass refused. Attacking the armory, Douglass argued, would bring the wrath of the government down on Brown and lead to certain defeat. Instead, he suggested setting up camp in the Blue Ridge Mountains and fighting a guerrilla war. But Brown was not convinced.

In early July 1859 Brown and about twenty followers quietly moved into the area around Harpers Ferry. Brown, using the name Isaac Smith, rented a farm about 4 miles (6.4 kilometers) from the town. There, he was seen farming, but he was also inspecting the surrounding territory. He said he was looking for land to buy, and that he might start mining in the area. His actual purpose was to learn the area in preparation for his

raid. In the meantime, three other members of his group were collecting guns and ammunition in nearby Chambersburg, Pennsylvania. The weapons, originally meant for his raids in Kansas, were gradually smuggled into his camp in Maryland.

On October 16, 1859, Brown moved his guns and ammunition to a schoolhouse closer to Harpers Ferry. He included extra arms to be used by the slaves whom he believed would hear of the raid and immediately come to help. At 11 P.M. Brown set off with nineteen of his followers—fourteen whites and five blacks—and crossed the Potomac River from Maryland into Virginia. They crossed at Harpers Ferry and quickly overpowered guards at a railroad bridge owned by the Baltimore & Ohio Railroad. From there they moved to seize the armory and a rifle factory near the town.

The raiders put guards at the armory and factory and on street corners in Harpers Ferry. Brown took up watch inside the thick walls of the armory.

John Brown in his prison cell. His 1859 raid on a federal armory at Harpers Ferry, Virginia, was the culmination of a life spent fighting slavery. Denounced as a terrorist in the South, Brown was hailed as a hero in the North for his direct action designed to inspire a slave revolt. *Illustration reproduced by permission of The Library of Congress.*

Next Brown sent six of his men to seize as hostages some of the leading citizens of Harpers Ferry, with instructions to urge black slaves to rebel and join them at the armory. The raiding party broke into the house of Colonel L. W. Washington, 5 miles away, at 1:30 A.M. on October 17, 1859, and took the colonel and four servants hostage. At 3 A.M., the raiders seized another citizen, Mr. Allstadt, and six of his servants. The raiders gave guns to the black servants and walked through the rain back to Harpers Ferry. As dawn came other citizens appeared on the street and were herded into the armory. Altogether, Brown and his men seized about sixty hostages. They then settled back to wait for slaves in the area to come join them.

Here the plan began to fall apart. The slaves, having had no previous word of the plan, did not come. News of the hostage taking spread rapidly, and citizens took up arms and rushed to Harpers Ferry. By 11 A.M. on October 17, groups of **militiamen** had descended on the town. (Militiamen were part-time soldiers who could take up arms in an emergency, somewhat like the National Guard.) They forced Brown's men to retreat inside the armory. From there the abolitionist raiders fired on any white men who appeared on the street. By sunset more troops had arrived, including a group of U.S. Marines commanded by Colonel Robert E. Lee (1807–1870), who later became commander of the Confederate armies of the South during the Civil War. Lee waited until daylight on October 18 to attack Brown's raiders.

Soon after daylight, Lee demanded that Brown surrender. When Brown refused, Lee used a ladder as a battering ram to break down the armory's doors. Some shots were fired, but the raid was finished a few minutes later. The marines used swords (to avoid accidentally injuring the hostages), and Brown was wounded. Both of his sons who took part in the raid were killed, along with eight others. A few others escaped; the rest, including Brown, were captured. Brown was taken to Charlestown, Virginia, to stand trial.

Terrorism on trial

Brown and his fellow captives were accused of treason (acting against the government) and murder. Their trial began on October 20, 1859, and lasted a month. Brown and his colleagues were convicted of both crimes. Their appeal of the death sentence was denied, and his execution was set for December 2, 1859. Before he was sentenced, Brown was allowed to make a statement to the court. His words today, recounted in a biography of Brown by Stephen B. Oates, stand as a classic defense of the terrorist: breaking the law for a greater good:

> I see a book kissed which I suppose to be the Bible, or at least the New Testament, which teaches me that all things whatsoever I would that men should do unto me, I should do even so to them. It teaches me further to remember them that are in bonds as bound with them. I endeavored [tried] to act up to that instruction. I say that I am yet too young to understand that God is any respecter of persons. I believe that to have interfered as I have done, as I have always freely admitted I have done in behalf of His despised [hated] poor, I did no wrong, but right. Now if it is deemed necessary that I should forfeit my life for the furtherance of the ends of justice and mingle my blood further with the blood of my children and with the blood of millions in this slave country whose rights are disregarded by wicked, cruel and unjust enactments, I say, let it be done.

Brown was executed at about noon on December 2, 1859. In the South it was widely believed justice had been done. In the northern states, however, church bells rang in mourning or protest. Church services and public meetings were held to celebrate Brown's deeds, and he came to be viewed as a **martyr** for abolitionism. (A martyr is someone who is killed for a cause.) Philosopher Henry David Thoreau (1817–1862) praised Brown as a heroic man of action who gave life to the spirit of Christianity. In a speech defending Brown, Thoreau said:

> The more conscientious preachers, the Bible men, they who talk about principle, and doing to others as you would that they should do unto you,—how could they fail to recognize him, by far the greatest preacher of them all, with the Bible in his life and in his acts, the embodiment [living example] of principle, who actually carried out the golden rule?

His name became part of a northern soldiers' marching song during the Civil War, sung to the tune of "The Battle Hymn of the Republic":

> John Brown's body lies a-mouldering in the grave,
> John Brown's body lies a-mouldering in the grave,
> But his soul goes marching on.
>
> Chorus:
> Glory, glory, hallelujah,
> Glory, glory, hallelujah,
> His soul goes marching on.

John Brown, terrorist, lit a spark of public indignation over slavery. His raid also enraged the southern, slaveholding states. The two opposite reactions heightened emotions and helped lead to the outbreak of war between the states.

John Brown's legacy

Almost 150 years after his execution Brown remains a controversial figure. On one side are those who argue that however noble his goal may have been, violence was the wrong method to use. Who was Brown to take up arms against a democratically elected government, even if that government accepted slavery?

On the other side are those who, like Thoreau, argue that Brown was one of the few who saw clearly that destroying slavery was more important than obeying an unjust law. If the law would not free the slaves peacefully—which, in the end, it would not—then violence was justified, just as Brown said from the gallows in 1859.

For More Information

Books

Hinton, Richard J. *John Brown and His Men*. New York: Arno Press, 1968.

Oates, Stephen B. *To Purge This Land with Blood: A Biography of John Brown*. Amherst: University of Massachusetts Press, 1984.

Quarles, Benjamin. *Allies for Freedom: Blacks and John Brown*. New York: Oxford University Press, 1974.

Thoreau, Henry David. *A Plea for Captain John Brown; Read to the Citizens of Concord, Massachusetts, on Sunday Evening, October Thirteenth, Eighteen Fifty-nine*. Boston: D.R. Godine, 1969.

Periodicals

Oates, Stephen B. "God's Angry Man." *American History Illustrated,* January, 1986, p. 10.

Ward, Geoffrey C. "Terror, Practical or Impractical." *American Heritage,* September 1995, p. 14.

Carlos the Jackal
(Ilich Ramirez Sanchez)

October 12, 1949
Caracas, Venezuela

"Terrorist for hire"

In 1949 in Caracas, Venezuela, when it came time for José Altagracia Ramirez Navas to choose a name for his first son, he went through the usual Spanish names and decided against all of them. Navas was determined that his son should bear the name of one of his personal heroes, and so he called him Ilich, after the Russian revolutionary Vladimir Ilich Ulyanov (1870–1924), better known as Lenin. Perhaps baby Ilich's fate was sealed on the day of his naming, for he grew up to bedevil governments and play the part of terrorist for hire. Ironically, the terrorist organization that trained him in adulthood gave him a common Spanish name: Carlos.

Sanchez's father, a wealthy lawyer who nevertheless considered himself a committed communist, taught young Ilich about his left-wing beliefs and told stories of South American revolutionaries. (Communism is a political and economic system in which there is no form of private property; instead the people—represented by the government—owns all goods and all their means of production. In politics the left wing consists of people who push liberal or radical measures to solve social problems, usually in order to achieve equality and the well-being of

These ordinary people injured in a terrorist bombing have great power. Much influence. It manifests itself in what is called public opinion. They may not care about the Palestinians. They certainly don't care about some members of the Red Army [a Japanese terrorist group]. But throw a grenade among them and they care very much.

Photograph reproduced by permission of AP/Wide World Photos.

115

the common people.) Sanchez attended the Fermin Toro School in Caracas, which had a reputation for left-wing teaching. While there he joined the Venezuelan Communist Youth organization and took part in violent antigovernment demonstrations.

At age seventeen Sanchez went to London, England, to continue his education. He gained a reputation as a lazy student and a "party boy." It would stay with him for the next thirty years.

Off to Moscow

Sanchez's father arranged for his son to attend Patrice Lumumba University in Moscow, in the Soviet Union (present-day Russia and neighboring countries), named after a revolutionary leader in the Congo. It had a reputation as a training ground for communist leaders in underdeveloped countries. It was an open secret that the KGB, the Russian spy agency, closely watched foreign students, looking for potential spies or agents.

At Lumumba, Sanchez made friends with some Palestinian students and quickly began to sympathize with their cause. (Palestinian Arabs were involved in a struggle to take back their land from the state of Israel, which had been founded in 1948 on Palestinian land, driving many Palestinians from their homes.) From them he heard of the rebel Palestinian leader named Wadi Haddad, who headed the Popular Front for the Liberation of Palestine (PFLP). Its mission was to carry out acts of violence against the state of Israel, particularly hijacking airplanes. In Haddad's view, any person or property connected with Israel, whether in the Middle East or Europe, was a fair target.

In the summer of 1970 Sanchez made his way to Jordan, where he hoped to receive training in guerrilla warfare (learning tactics, such as using the element of surprise, to defeat a much larger force) at a camp run by the PFLP. It was the first step on a path that would make Sanchez a household name throughout Western Europe and the United States for more than a decade as one of the world's most wanted terrorists. But it was not under his given name that he became famous. When he arrived at the Palestinian guerrilla training camp, he was assigned the code name Carlos.

The Palestinian Cause

The nation of Israel was founded in 1948 in the area that had been the Jewish homeland in biblical times. In the early twentieth century, though, it was called the Palestine Mandate and was ruled by Britain, which had taken control of the area from Turkey after World War I (1914–18). Before World War I Palestine was part of the Ottoman (Turkish) Empire.

After the Holocaust, during which more than six million Jews were murdered by Nazi Germany during World War II (1939–45), the United States and European governments agreed that the Jewish people needed a nation of their own. They decided the new Jewish homeland should be located in Palestine. However, the Palestinian Arabs living there claimed the territory for themselves.

On the day Israel was founded, armies from several neighboring Arab countries attacked, determined to stop Jews from taking control of the land. But neither that war, nor several others that followed, managed to defeat the Israelis.

Frustrated by their failures to defeat Israel, in the 1970s and 1980s many Palestinians turned to terrorist tactics. These included aircraft hijackings, bombings, and assassinations. Their targets were not only in Israel but also Israeli and Jewish interests in many European countries. Eventually, Carlos the Jackal extended the target list to nearly everyone, even if there were no obvious connection to Israel.

No other region in the world has experienced as many terrorist attacks.

Carlos: Secret agent

A month after his arrival, while "Carlos" was still in training, the PFLP hijacked four planes at once and then hijacked a fifth plane to gain the release of a PFLP hijacker who had been captured during the first hijackings. This disturbed Jordan's King Hussein (1935–1999), who was afraid Israel would target his country in revenge for the hijackings. Hussein ordered his army to drive the Palestinians out of his country, and in the bitter battle between the Palestinians and the Jordanians that was later called "Black September," Carlos got his first taste of war. The fighting ended with a bloody defeat for the Palestinians. Carlos also had gained a reputation as a fearless soldier and had come to the attention of the man he most wanted to impress: Wadi Haddad of the PFLP.

Carlos the Jackal: Timeline of Events

- **December 1973:** Tries to murder British department store executive Joseph Sieff in London.

- **January 1974:** Sets bombs at Israeli bank in London and at newspaper offices and a radio station in Paris, France.

- **December 1974–January 1975:** Efforts to hijack or shoot down Israeli El Al planes in Paris stopped by police; Carlos escapes.

- **June 1975:** Questioned by police; kills two policemen and escapes to Beirut, Lebanon. Becomes object of a massive police manhunt.

- **December 1975:** Takes oil ministers hostage at Organization of Petroleum Exporting Countries (OPEC) in Vienna, Austria; flies to North Africa. Ministers are ransomed; Carlos escapes with the money.

- **February 1976:** Thrown out of the Popular Front for the Liberation of Palestine (PFLP); becomes a freelance terrorist.

- **December 1977:** Meets Saddam Hussein, the dictator of Iraq; begins building a terrorist gang.

- **January 1982:** Fires rockets at a nuclear power plant in France, without effect.

- **February–April 1982:** Wife arrested in France. Bombing campaign to achieve her release. French authorities refuse and sentence her to four years in prison.

Carlos continues to attack French targets, without success.

- **August 25, 1983:** After a year's truce arranged by Syria at the request of France, bombs French targets in West Berlin, West Germany.

- **December 31, 1983:** Claims credit for bombing two trains in France in revenge for a French air strike against a terrorist training camp in Lebanon the previous month.

- **Early 1984:** U.S. negotiations with Eastern European communist governments result in gradual closing of these countries to terrorists. Carlos is shunned by most Palestinian organizations.

- **May 1985:** Wife released from prison in France for good behavior. Couple moves to Syria on promise of future employment as a terrorist.

- **August 1986–September 1991:** Syria says his services are not needed after all but offers to protect him if he remains inactive. Syria throws him out after learning he has been working for Saddam Hussein. Carlos moves to Jordan.

- **Sometime in 1993:** Granted asylum in Khartoum, Sudan.

- **August 1994:** Captured in Khartoum by French agents, returned to France. Tried for murder of two policemen in 1975; sentenced to life in prison.

Carlos returned to London in early 1971. He once again took up the life of a wealthy playboy, attending cocktail parties and juggling several girlfriends. Behind this front, Carlos was working part time as an agent for the PFLP. He arranged "safe houses" where PFLP agents could hide in London and helped plan an unsuccessful assassination attempt against Jordan's ambassador to Britain in revenge for Black September.

In July 1973 Carlos flew to Beirut, Lebanon, and told Haddad he wanted to work full time as an undercover agent for the PFLP. Haddad agreed.

A full-time terrorist

To prove his loyalty and abilities Carlos was asked to murder a leading Jewish businessman in London: Joseph Sieff, head of the Marks and Spencer department store chain and a major contributor to Israeli causes. On December 30, 1973, Carlos broke into Sieff's London townhouse and shot him almost point-blank in the face. Sieff survived: the first bullet lodged in his jaw and Carlos's gun then jammed. A month later Carlos threw a bomb inside the Israeli Hapoalim Bank in London; the bomb did not work as well as it was supposed to and did only minor damage.

Despite these failures, the pace quickened. The PFLP moved Carlos to Paris, where he planted bombs outside newspaper offices and a radio station thought to be sympathetic to Israel. In September 1974 Japanese Red Army terrorists took the French ambassador to the Netherlands hostage, hoping to force France to release an imprisoned terrorist from a French jail. Carlos and the PFLP helped plan and execute the operation, but it was botched at the start: the Japanese terrorists got lost and their rented car broke down. The result was a standoff in Amsterdam. Carlos, already back in Paris, was determined to solve the situation. He threw a hand grenade into a crowded Parisian café, killing two people and injuring thirty-four. He told the media there would be more attacks unless the Amsterdam terrorists' demands were met. Two days later France freed the terrorist in exchange for the ambassador.

Firing rockets at the airport

Three months later, in December 1974, the PFLP ordered Carlos to hijack an El Al Israeli plane to prevent a possible peace deal between the Palestinians and Israel. It proved to be a frustrating assignment. At first Carlos's plan was ruined when El Al employees went on strike, keeping the planes on the ground. A month later Carlos led a team that tried to shoot down an El Al plane at Orly Field in Paris with a rocket launcher, but the rockets missed. Four days later Carlos and his colleagues tried a third time, but a security guard spotted them taking aim and opened fire with a submachine gun.

The terrorists fled through the passenger terminal, firing wildly. They took ten hostages and shut themselves inside a restroom. After hours of negotiations, the terrorists were given a plane to fly them to Baghdad, Iraq. But Carlos was not with them; he had escaped and flown to London.

Six months later, in June 1975, Michel Moukharbal, head of PFLP operations in Europe and Carlos's direct boss, was held and questioned by Lebanese police in Beirut. Documents linking him to terrorist activities were found in his briefcase. Moukharbal was eventually released and allowed to fly to Paris. There, followed by undercover police, he visited Carlos, and police photographed the two of them together.

Two French policemen killed

A short time later French police visited an apartment on Rue Toullier (Toullier Street) that belonged to one of Carlos's girlfriends and began questioning him. He managed to conceal a gun inside his pants, and when Moukharbal was brought in to identify him, Carlos pulled out the gun and started firing. Two policemen and Moukharbal were killed, and a third policeman was wounded. Carlos became the object of one of the biggest manhunts in French history, one that soon spread to London.

As the police investigation of the shoot-out on Rue Toullier proceeded, Carlos received a lot of coverage in the press: a mysterious Latin American working for the Palestinians, a series of girlfriends in London and Paris, apartments, safe houses, suitcases with false passports and weapons, shoot-outs with the police. It was the stuff of fiction, and he was given a new name from a novel about an assassin that was found in his London apartment: *The Day of the Jackal* by Frederick Forsythe. From then on, he was known in newspapers as

Carlos the Jackal, the most famous terrorist in the world.

Carlos's most spectacular operation: Attack on OPEC

Carlos managed to escape Paris, traveling first to London and then to Beirut, where he was greeted as a hero by the PFLP. Haddad assigned him to a new operation: an attack on the Vienna, Austria, headquarters of the Organization of Petroleum Exporting Countries (OPEC) during a conference in December 1975. The terrorists planned to hold the oil ministers who were attending the conference hostage, except for the oil ministers of Saudi Arabia and Iran, who were sympathetic to western democracies, who were to be killed.

On Sunday, December 21, 1975, the terrorists walked calmly into OPEC headquarters and started shooting. Three people were killed in the attack. The terrorists invaded the OPEC conference room and took the oil ministers hostage while police surrounded the building. Carlos demanded that a message be read over radio and television expressing support for the Palestinian cause and that a bus be provided to take him and his men to the airport, where a plane was to be waiting to take the terrorists and their hostages to their destination.

At 6:22 P.M., their first demand was met: Carlos's statement was broadcast on radio and TV. The Austrian cabinet met in an emergency session and agreed to meet the terrorists' other demands on the condition that OPEC employees—but not the oil ministers—be released. At 6:40 the following morning, the terror-

Carlos and Communism

Was Carlos an agent for the Soviet Union (today, Russia and its neighboring countries)? His early years, including his attendance at Patrice Lumumba University in Moscow, convinced many journalists that the hand of the KGB (the Soviet spy agency and secret police) was behind Carlos's hijackings and kidnappings.

The question of Soviet involvement in terrorism during the 1970s and 1980s was part of the Cold War, the long struggle between the United States and the Soviet Union for worldwide influence that lasted from 1945 to 1990. Labeling a terrorist like Carlos as an agent of the Soviet Union fit neatly into the anti-Soviet propaganda that Western governments were spreading. Carlos denied he was working for the Soviets; anticommunists saw his denial as yet another lie by a communist agent.

Although he sometimes hid in countries of Eastern Europe that were controlled by the Soviets, Carlos did not travel in the Soviet satellites after he became a terrorist. These countries were often sympathetic to the Palestinian cause, even without the Soviet government in Moscow directing them to be.

ists were taken to the airport by bus; Carlos was clearly visible in the front window, waving at the passersby. At the airport the Austrian interior minister shook hands with Carlos, a gesture that was widely criticized afterward. At 9 A.M., the plane took off for Algiers in Algeria, a country in North Africa.

The foreign minister of Algeria greeted Carlos warmly in Algiers, and Carlos agreed to release thirty of the hostages. The plane was refueled and left for Tripoli, Libya. There, Libyan authorities demanded that the Libyan hostages on the plane be released, and after a brief standoff Carlos gave in. The plane then returned to Algiers, where authorities negotiated a $50 million ransom payment for release of the OPEC ministers, and Carlos and his men were allowed to go free.

The drama had captured the world's attention, and it appeared to be a victory for Carlos and the PFLP. But to Haddad, the operation had not ended satisfactorily: he had specifically ordered that the oil ministers of Saudi Arabia and Iran be executed, yet they were allowed to live.

Carlos flew to Aden, the capital of South Yemen, where Haddad had called a meeting to review the attack. At the end of the meeting, Haddad threw Carlos out of the PFLP, accusing him of acting like "a star."

After his biggest strike ever, Carlos was a terrorist without a cause. He was also the object of an enormous international manhunt, making it more difficult for him to travel.

Unemployed terrorist: Have bomb, will travel

Rejected by the PFLP, Carlos decided to go into business, hiring himself out as a terrorist to whoever was willing to pay him. For nearly two years Carlos went from one hideout to another, including Yugoslavia, where he was briefly arrested at the request of Germany. He then went to Syria, Iraq, and South Yemen. In December 1977 he met Saddam Hussein (1937–), the dictator of Iraq, who offered his support.

Three months later, in March 1978, Carlos's old boss Haddad died. Carlos thought this created an opening in the Middle East for a new terrorist organization. He recruited some PFLP terrorists as well as Europeans from Switzerland and West Germany. Among these was Magdalena Kopp, who married

Carlos in 1979. Carlos called his new group the Organization of Arab Armed Struggle.

Four years passed before the group staged its first action: a rocket attack in January 1982 at a nuclear power plant under construction in France. The rockets failed to break through the plant's dome. The next month Kopp was arrested in France while on a mission to bomb the offices of an Arabic magazine that had criticized the Syrian government.

Car bomb explosions such as this one in Paris in 1982 were a signature tactic of Carlos the Jackal. *Photograph reproduced by permission of AP/Wide World Photos.*

When Carlos heard that his wife had been arrested, he launched a bombing campaign to free her. This time France refused to give in, and Carlos's wife was sentenced to four years in jail. The attacks had another effect, however: they angered French President François Mitterand (1916–1996), who formed a new counterterrorism unit to go after terrorists.

Unable to capture Carlos, France persuaded Syria to limit Carlos's activities, and a year passed without more attacks. The peace ended on August 25, 1983, when a large explosion went off at Maison de France in West Berlin, destroying a French consulate, culture center, offices, and a restaurant. One person was killed and twenty-two others were injured. Carlos wrote to the West German interior minister, claiming responsibility.

The welcome mat is pulled back

Early in 1984 there was a development that Carlos could not have foreseen or controlled: the United States launched successful diplomatic talks with countries of Eastern Europe that had protected Carlos and other Middle Eastern terrorists. The subject of terrorists came up during these talks, and gradually Eastern Europe began closing its doors to Carlos, starting with East Germany and followed by Romania and Czechoslovakia.

In response Carlos traveled to Aden to attend an emergency summit meeting with other Palestinians, but there he discovered he was no longer accepted as part of their movement. Carlos was on his own.

In 1985 Kopp was released from prison, and the couple began looking for a nation that would take them in. They went from country to country: Lebanon, Hungary, Libya, Cuba. Everywhere, the welcome mat had been taken in. Finally, Syria offered to protect Carlos in exchange for his services, but after a year the country ordered Carlos to stop his activities. At age thirty-nine, Carlos was in early retirement.

In 1990 Iraq invaded Kuwait, which sparked the Persian Gulf War (1990–91). Western intelligence agencies learned that Saddam Hussein had hired Carlos to lead a terrorist campaign against the United States. This news upset Syria, which opposed Iraq's invasion of Kuwait. Syria drove Carlos out of the country in 1991, and he went to Jordan.

By this point, not only his career as a terrorist but also his family was collapsing. Carlos separated from his wife and married another woman. For two years Carlos searched for a country that would admit him permanently. Finally he and his new wife were allowed to move to Khartoum, the capital of Sudan in eastern Africa. There he took up his old life of socializing and partying at nightclubs.

The kidnapper is kidnapped

But Carlos was still being tracked by French intelligence agents. French authorities in Paris began negotiating with the government of Sudan to expel Carlos. France offered to sponsor economic development loans to Sudan, to help pay Sudan's foreign debts, in exchange for Carlos. Sudan's leader, Sheik Hassan al-Turabi, was shown a videotape of Carlos at a party; the terrorist's behavior and use of alcohol offended the Muslim al-Turabi, who agreed not to interfere in Carlos's capture.

In August 1994 Sudanese police lured Carlos out of a hospital, where he was recovering from minor surgery, and into an apartment near al-Turabi's home. At 3 A.M. the next morning, Carlos was awakened by a group of men pinning him to his bed. He was handcuffed and bundled into a car for the trip to the airport, where an executive jet was waiting to fly him to France.

In France Carlos was charged with the murder of two police agents in 1979. In December 1997, after a long and dramatic trial, the international terrorist was convicted and sentenced to life in prison.

Carlos the Jackal arriving in a Paris courtroom, 2000.
Photograph reproduced by permission of AP/Wide World Photos.

Carlos disappeared from public view once he was in prison, but after hijacked planes destroyed the World Trade Center in New York and damaged the Pentagon near Washington, D.C., on September 11, 2001, Carlos told a French newspaper that he was "relieved" by the attacks. He said he wished good luck to **Osama bin Laden** (c. 1957–; see entry), who was accused of planning the attacks.

Also in 2001, Carlos's lawyer, Isabelle Coutant-Peyre, announced that she planned to marry her client, despite very slim chances that they could ever live together since Carlos was sentenced to life in prison without the possibility of parole.

Carlos the Jackal: A classic terrorist

The life of Ilich Ramirez Sanchez in some ways is straight out of a spy novel: a mysterious, cold-blooded killer who liked to show off for TV cameras, feared and hated by authorities throughout Europe and North America, seemingly undefeatable. He was on the front pages of newspapers for a decade, almost making him a celebrity.

But Carlos was blamed for eighty violent deaths. He did not hesitate to attack civilians. His commitment to the Palestinian cause seemed to melt away when he was offered a ransom for the oil ministers he had taken hostage. Rather than trying to avoid notice, he seemed to enjoy the headlines linking him with murder and destruction.

In the end Carlos was sent to prison. His organization, the PFLP, faded from the scene without achieving its political goals. All that was left was a nickname drawn from a novel: the Jackal.

For More Information

Books

Dobson, Christopher, and Ronald Payne. *The Carlos Complex: A Study in Terror*. New York: Putnam, 1977.

Follain, John. *Jackal: The Complete Story of the Legendary Terrorist, Carlos the Jackal*. New York: Arcade Publishers, 1998.

Smith, Colin. *Carlos: Portrait of a Terrorist*. New York: Holt, Rinehart and Winston, 1977.

Yallop, David A. *Tracking the Jackal: The Search for Carlos, the World's Most Wanted Man*. New York: Random House, 1993.

Periodicals

Holland, Max, and Kai Bird. "Columbia: The Carlos Connection." *Nation*, June 22, 1985, p. 759.

Markovits, Andrei S. "The Minister and the Terrorist." *Foreign Affairs*, November/December, 2001, p. 132.

Smolowe, Jill. "Carlos Caged: The Capture of the Infamous Jackal Exposes a Past of Clumsy Terrorist Acts, High Living and Tall Tales." *Time*, August 29, 1994, p. 53.

Michael Collins

October 16, 1890
Clonakilty, Ireland
August 22, 1922
Beal na Blath, Ireland

Leader of the Irish independence movement

> "Think, what have I got for Ireland? Something she has wanted this past 700 years. Will anyone be satisfied in the bargain? Will anyone? I tell you this, I have signed my death warrant."

T he story of Irish independence from Great Britain covers more than a century of fighting and bloodshed. During and after World War I (1914–18), Michael Collins was a military leader of the pro-independence forces that eventually took control of the island nation. During the final battles, which raged from 1916 to 1922, Collins played a number of key roles: military strategist, finance minister, and treaty negotiator.

But, eventually, Collins agreed to a treaty short of full-fledged independence. His decision enraged some supporters of Irish independence, and in 1922 Collins was assassinated by supporters of the same cause to which he had devoted his life.

Collins's life showed how terrorism—or **guerrilla** attacks, depending on one's point of view—can play a role in **nationalist** movements.

An Irish childhood

Collins, born in 1890, lived a pleasant rural Irish childhood near the little town of Sam's Cross in County Cork in Ireland. He lived on a 60-acre farm owned by his father, Michael

Photograph reproduced by permission of Archive Photos, Inc.

John Collins, who had not married until he was fifty-nine years old (and was seventy-five when Collins was born). Ireland in 1890 was ruled by Britain, when the British Empire was at the height of its worldwide power and influence. It was first invaded by the Normans (from France) in the twelfth century and had become part of the British Empire in 1801. The nineteenth century had been an eventful time in Irish history. More than a million people died from starvation or disease and at least another million left the country during the great potato famine that lasted from 1845 to 1849. Irish independence fighters had been active on and off for a hundred years.

Collins grew up hearing patriotic stories and songs—as well as stories about terrorist attacks on the government in London, England, twenty years earlier—while sitting around the kitchen table in his family's farmhouse. Members of his family had long had ties to the cause of Irish nationalism, and his uncle could remember Irish patriots of the eighteenth century.

In 1896 Collins's father suffered a heart attack and died a few months later. On his deathbed, his father pointed at Collins and declared: "Mind that child. He'll be a great man yet and will do great things for Ireland."

Collins attended his local school, in which one teacher taught all the children from ages five to eleven. The headmaster (principal) there, Denis Lyons, was a member of the Irish Republican Brotherhood (IRB), an organization that wanted independence for Ireland as a republic. The village blacksmith, James Santry, who worked near the school, also influenced Collins. He remembered later that Lyons and Santry first instilled in him pride of being Irish. There was irony in this because the national school system had been set up by the government specifically to prevent children from being taught Irish nationalist sentiments.

At the age of eleven Collins went to a nearby school to study for the civil service examination—a test that people who

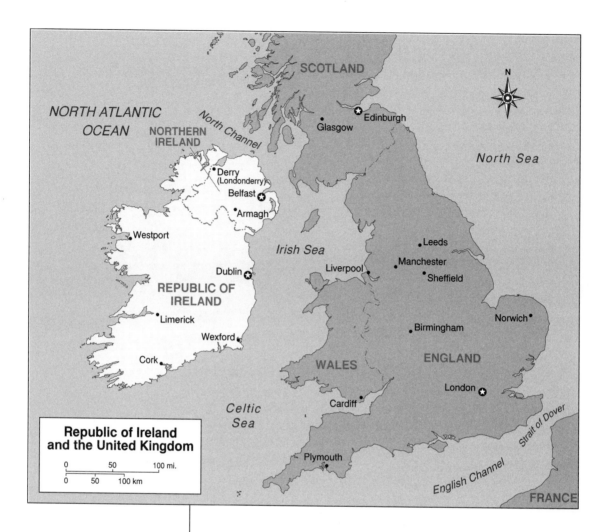

The Republic of Ireland (the Irish Free State) and Northern Ireland in relation to England, Scotland, and Wales.

wanted to work for the government had to pass—and lived with an older sister in the small town of Clonakilty, where Collins had been born and where his sister's husband owned the local newspaper. Young Collins was occasionally assigned to cover a wedding or a sports match.

London

In 1906 Collins moved to London. It was common at that time for young men to leave Ireland for England, where there were better jobs available. There he began working at the Post Office Savings Bank. He spent most of his free time with a close friend from home, Jack Hurley, and lived mainly with other young men who had come to London from Ireland. Collins became a leader of the Gaelic Athletic Association in London, a group that played Gaelic football.

Three years later, in 1909, Collins joined the IRB. The IRB was part of a larger movement called the Fenians, which had been organized in the 1850s to fight for Irish independence. It was named after an ancient band of knights said to have roamed Ireland in the third century B.C.E. The Fenians believed in using violence to achieve independence. The IRB also was active in North America among Irish immigrants. It tried to organize an invasion of British-ruled Canada in 1867, rescued prisoners from western Australia in 1876, and built a submarine to attack the powerful British Royal Navy in 1881.

In London Collins became increasingly involved in the Irish independence movement. He had studied the background of unsuccessful uprisings in Ireland and concluded that lack of organization was to blame. Collins decided that he would be the one to fix that problem.

Easter, 1916

Collins returned to Ireland from Britain in early 1916. His plan was to take part in a revolt to declare Irish independence. Although Collins had decided that disorganization had been the death of Irish independence in the past, Easter, 1916, proved to be no better an uprising.

The plan had been to seize control of the center of Dublin and to defend it against English forces posted outside the city. Collins was assigned to help the chief military strategist of the uprising, Joseph Mary Plunkett (1887–1916). Plunkett was oddly unqualified for the job: he had no military experience of any kind and was largely ruled by his romantic imagination. About fifty of the Irish Volunteers—most of whom, like Collins, had returned home to Ireland from London—were camped around the house of Plunkett's sister, not far from Dublin. There, while waiting for the uprising, Collins could be heard reciting a speech by an earlier Irish rebel, Robert Emmet, who had led a failed uprising in 1802.

On the eve of the uprising, one of the leaders, Roger Casement, had been sent to pick up arms from a German submarine (the Germans were helping the Irish rebels in order to

On Monday, April 24, 1916, Irish nationalists staged an uprising in Dublin designed to drive the British out of Ireland and achieve Irish independence. The uprising failed after a few days, but it set the stage for a terrorist campaign and the eventual creation of the Irish Free State. *Photograph reproduced by permission of the Corbis Corporation.*

strike a blow against Britain, their enemy in World War I). But Casement was arrested, and the arms were never delivered. A leader of the Irish Volunteers became disgusted and insisted that the uprising be called off. He even put an advertisement in the *Sunday Independent* newspaper announcing that maneuvers had been canceled for the weekend. Other leaders decided to put off the attack by twenty-four hours, until Monday morning.

On Monday morning Collins put on a military uniform—as did most of the Irish Volunteers, although not all the uniforms were the same—and set off for the center of Dublin. At 11 A.M. a group of fifty-seven rebels got on the tram (train) into Dublin, sitting among the other passengers, who complained when they were bumped by the Volunteers' rifles. The commander of the operation ordered the conductor to skip all the stops until the O'Connell Bridge, which they were to guard to keep British soldiers from coming into the city. More complaints were heard from the passengers as the tram rushed past their normal stops.

The rebels gathered in the center of Dublin and marched on the General Post Office. Some people on the street did not realize anything unusual was happening until the marchers got to the building and gave the order to charge. On the ground floor, Collins took delight in smashing the windows and blocking them, the better to defend the building. But apart from a group of British soldiers on horseback that came down the street, no counterattack was made.

It was not until Thursday that the British attacked, and then it was not as the rebels had imagined. Instead of storming the General Post Office, the British army parked some heavy artillery a few blocks away and started firing shells. The next day, incendiary shells (designed to start fires) started coming into the General Post Office, setting the building on fire. By Saturday, the rebels had surrendered. The uprising was over.

Despite the silly beginnings, the deaths were real: 450 people died, and more than 2,600 were injured.

Having been in Dublin for only a few months, Collins was arrested and sent on a cattle boat to Britain. The rebellion had been put down, but the Irish revolution had started.

Turning defeat into victory

The British reaction to the rebellion was swift and harsh. The leaders were rounded up, and fifteen of them were executed, acts that generated more sympathy for the rebel cause than the Easter Rising had.

The prisoners not judged to be leaders of the uprising were sent to a prison camp in Wales, a principality of Great Britain, east of Ireland and west of England, where they were largely free to conduct military training exercises, hold athletic contests, and talk about what went wrong in Dublin. It was here that Collins got his nickname, "The Big Fella." The name did not come so much from his physical size—he was not quite 6 feet tall—but from a manner that offended some people. He seemed overly impressed with his own importance and to have a bullying manner. He was highly competitive about everything and hated to lose.

During the time the rebels were in prison, they developed friendships that lasted long after they were released. In the camps, Collins emerged as an energetic and organized leader.

But after their anger over the Easter Rising had settled, the British authorities realized they were creating a much bigger problem for themselves in the form of sympathy for the rebels. Before Christmas 1916 Britain released many of the prisoners, Collins among them.

Back in Ireland, Collins plunged into organizing Irish nationalists. Working as the employment secretary of the Irish National Aid and Volunteer Dependents Fund—an outgrowth of his political work—Collins tried to revive the Volunteer movement from which fighters had come. But he quickly realized that a new nationalist political movement, Sinn Féin, was more likely to win popular acceptance. Collins began recruiting for Sinn Féin.

Sinn Féin did well in the polls; one of their winning candidates was still being held prisoner because of the Easter Rising. Worried about public reaction, the British quickly released all the remaining prisoners.

Getting organized

The period following the Easter Rising of 1916 was one of confusion and conflict among supporters of Irish independence. Some were willing to settle for "**home rule**," with the Irish in charge of affairs in Ireland, but leaving the British in charge of international affairs. Others would settle for nothing short of full independence, like the United States achieved after 1776. A third idea was to form two nations—Britain and Ireland—under a single monarch, an arrangement adopted from the Austro-Hungarian empire. New efforts were made to organize armed groups to fight for independence. By 1917 some Irish nationalists thought the cause of Ireland should be put before an international conference that was expected to settle World War I.

Among the new generation of leaders of the movement were Collins and another veteran of the Easter Rising, Eamon de Valera (1882–1975), who was about to become the president of Sinn Féin. De Valera was also elected to head the Irish Volunteers, which served as Sinn Féin's armed wing. Eventually he would become president of the Republic of Ireland.

In 1918 Collins was named director of organization of the Irish Volunteers as well as adjutant general, in charge of training and discipline. Although Ireland was not an independent nation and did not have its own army, the Irish Volunteers began to take on the appearance of a regular armed force. As Collins traveled throughout Ireland, organizing the Irish Volunteers, he was being watched by police. In the spring of 1918 Collins was about to become an underground terrorist.

Independence . . . sort of

In the spring of 1917 the British government had once again played into the hands of the nationalists by proposing to extend the military draft from England to Ireland, to make up for losses in World War I. Opposition to the draft was immediate and helped to bring together Irish politicians previously at odds on the subject of independence. So upset did some feel over the proposed draft that assassination squads were sent to London to shoot at members of the British cabinet. But before these plans could be put into action, the British decided to put off introducing the Irish draft.

In Ireland, U.S. citizen Eamon De Valera was arrested twice for participating in the Easter Rising of 1916. The first time he was sentenced to life imprisonment but was released under a general amnesty in 1917. The second time he escaped and went to the United States, where he raised funds for Irish independence.
Photograph courtesy of the Library of Congress.

Despite the setback of the Easter Rising, the Irish independence movement continued to gain strength. In some respects, British efforts to squash the movement only helped it. In May 1918 the British arrested many of the leaders of Sinn Féin for their continuing campaign against British rule. The arrests caused a popular uproar. In the meantime, more radical (extreme) Sinn Féin members like Collins, who had avoided arrest, took control of the party while the more moderate leaders sat in jail.

In July the British government banned all public meetings, even football games, without a permit. Collins promptly began organizing games without permits and held almost two thousand political rallies, also without permits. Ireland seemed to be sliding toward mass disobedience.

In December 1918 British Prime Minister David Lloyd George (1863–1945) called national elections for Parliament (the British governing body) just a month after fighting in World War I ended. In Ireland, Sinn Féin put up candidates throughout the country. With many Sinn Féin leaders still in prison, Collins played a central role in organizing the election.

Collins was also running for office, and in his standard election speech he asked voters to endorse the idea that Ireland should be a fully independent country. He told voters that any solution that deprived the people of Ireland of full control over both internal and external affairs would not be acceptable— although in time, something less than full independence was accepted.

The results of the voting were strongly in favor of independence. The Sinn Féin candidates won 73 out of 105 seats. Clearly the majority in Ireland favored independence. In January 1919 two dozen of the newly elected members of Parliament met in Dublin and declared they were in favor of "an independent Irish republic." They decided not to attend English Parliament. The feelings expressed during the Easter Rising now had the power of a popular vote behind them.

On the same day the members-elect said they were going to establish their own Irish government, two policemen were ambushed and killed while accompanying a load of explosives to a quarry in Soloheadbeg, Ireland. It was not Collins's doing, but he was blamed for it. It seemed to be the first blow for Irish independence. In fact it was locally planned; Collins had been in England, figuring out the details of an operation to free the leaders of Sinn Féin from jail.

Underground

Supporters of an independent Ireland now had to make it happen; Britain was not about to accept the loss of Ireland without a fight.

Collins became director of intelligence (espionage or spying) for the Irish Volunteers. Intelligence was a point of pride for the British, who became embarrassed when they were outdone by the Irish in the struggle for independence. Collins organized his intelligence with an aim of going to war against Britain, but not fighting a conventional battle but a guerrilla war of surprise attacks. He was not always in agreement with other leaders of the independence movement on the tactics to use against the British.

When the rebel Irish organized their own republican government on April 1, 1919, Collins also was named minister of finance. He was only twenty-nine years old and lacked experience in money matters. But he did have a following in the independence movement, and he had proved himself effective in the tasks he was given, including arranging for the newly recognized Irish prime minister, De Valera, to be freed from jail.

Two months after the formal Irish declaration of independence, De Valera sailed for the United States to raise funds. He stayed away from Ireland for eighteen months. In the meantime, Collins and another independence fighter, Cathal Brugha, were left in charge of fighting the British for Irish independence.

As a first step the Irish Volunteers swore loyalty to the new Irish Parliament, called the Dáil éireann in the Gaelic language. Their name also changed. Instead of the Irish Volunteers, they became the Irish Republican Army (IRA).

In September the British outlawed the new IRA, the Sinn Féin, and the Dáil. Collins went underground (into hiding), concentrating on fighting a guerrilla war for Irish independence.

Terrorist?

From the standpoint of English authorities, Collins had become a terrorist. From the viewpoint of those in Ireland who favored independence, he was an underground guerrilla fighter and hero. From either point of view, he was highly effective.

Collins had already successfully recruited spies from the Irish Constabulary, which patrolled the countryside, and the Dublin police, which were responsible for the country's largest cities. Spies within these organizations helped keep Collins informed of planned moves by the police anywhere in the country.

Collins also organized a special group within the IRA, called "the Squad." Its purpose was to murder British agents. As intended, the possibility of being suddenly killed served to terrorize people connected with the British government in Ireland. The police offered a 10,000-pound reward for Collins's capture. But British intelligence lacked a good photograph of Collins, so their target could freely bicycle through Dublin without being caught.

Britain also brought in a special police force to deal with the IRA. They were called "Black and Tans" after the colors of their uniforms. They soon gained a reputation for being ruthless and vicious in their pursuit of the rebels. The IRA responded in kind, and the battle for the independence of Ireland saw horrifying acts committed on both sides.

British authorities also recruited a group of undercover agents who had been active in Egypt; they were soon called the Cairo Gang. Realizing the threat that these officers posed, Collins obtained the names of the agents by October 1920. On November 21, 1920, Collins sent execution squads to various hotels and rooming houses in Dublin. Nineteen members of the Cairo Gang were killed.

The Black and Tans struck back quickly. The same afternoon the IRA attacked the Cairo Gang, the Black and Tans drove armored cars into a Dublin park where a Gaelic football game was taking place and shot fourteen people. November 21, 1920, would become known as Bloody Sunday.

The following month De Valera returned from his long fund-raising tour in the United States. Collins, who had always been an impatient man, quickly became annoyed with De Valera, who was more inclined to think things over carefully. Collins's brash style, in turn, irritated De Valera.

Opening negotiations

In May 1921 another round of Parliamentary elections was held. Again Sinn Féin swept Ireland. It became clear to the British government that popular feelings in Ireland ran toward independence. In June 1921 Prime Minister George invited De Valera, as the head of Sinn Féin, to come to London to discuss peace and the establishment of a new republic. De Valera agreed, and a truce between the two sides was set for July 11, 1921. Peace talks were scheduled for the autumn, but there was a surprise. Instead of De Valera, Collins and Arthur Griffith (a founder of Sinn Féin) were chosen to represent the new Republic of Ireland.

Talks began on October 10 and progressed slowly for nearly two months. Finally, on December 6, 1921, the British prime minister insisted: either sign an agreement or call off the talks and resume fighting. Collins and Griffith agreed, but not happily. "I have signed my death warrant," Collins remarked as he signed the treaty at 2:10 A.M.

The reason was not hard to understand: Collins had agreed to something less than full independence for Ireland. Britain had agreed only to grant Ireland a status somewhat like Canada or Australia: free to rule itself at home, but still part of the British Empire. Collins felt it was the best he could achieve under the circumstances. Some people back home felt differently.

Some historians believe that De Valera had purposely placed Collins in a difficult situation. Realizing that he could not achieve in negotiations all that was wanted—the British were not going to give in to all the Irish demands—De Valera gave a no-win task to Collins, whom he did not especially like, and who might pose a political challenge to De Valera later on.

In the streets of Dublin, 1921, republicans protest the hanging of IRA volunteers by the British government. *Photograph courtesy of the Gamma Liaison Network.*

The Free State . . . and civil war

When Collins returned with the treaty, De Valera rejected it and resigned as head of the new Irish government. Despite this, the Dáil approved the treaty on January 14, 1922, establishing the mostly Catholic twenty-six counties of southern Ireland as the Irish Free State, with the status of a dominion of Britain. (The six largely Protestant counties of the North remained under British rule.)

The treaty split the Irish Parliament into two camps: pro- and anti-treaty. In the absence of De Valera, Collins became chairman of the provisional government, which took over from the former British administration. It was Collins who formally took control over Dublin Castle, the symbolic center of British government in Ireland for more than 750 years.

In April 1922 some units of the IRA seized control of the Four Courts building in Dublin, and a week later troops loyal to the new Irish Free State attacked them. A civil war had started. Ironically, Collins, who had been one of the most militant fighters for Irish independence, was fighting his former colleagues over the issue.

Some of Collins's closest friends were killed in fighting the IRA troops in and around Dublin in the summer of 1922. Elsewhere in Ireland, troops of Collins's provisional government fought to regain control of towns that had been taken by the Republicans (IRA).

On August 22, 1922, Collins was on an inspection tour in the area of Cork, at a spot named Beal na Blath (in Gaelic, "The Mouth of Flowers") not too far from where he was born, when Republicans attacked his party.

Collins was killed immediately by a gunshot wound to the head.

For More Information

Books

Coogan, Tim Pat. *Michael Collins: The Man Who Made Ireland*. Boulder, CO: Roberts Rinehart Publishers, 1996.

Dwyer, T. Ryle. *Big Fellow, Long Fellow: A Joint Biography of Collins and De Valera*. New York: St. Martin's Press, 1999.

Mackay, James A. *Michael Collins: A Life*. North Pomfret, VT: Mainstream Publishing, 1997.

O'Connor, Frank. *The Big Fellow*. New York: Picador USA, 1998.

Periodicals

Daly, Steve. "The Fighting Irish: Liam Neeson and Director Neil Jordan Waged a 12-year Battle of Their Own to Bring the Story of the Controversial Irish Revolutionary Michael Collins to the Screen—and the Rest Is History." *Entertainment Weekly,* October 18, 1996, p. 22.

Abimael Guzman (Comrade Gonzalo)

December 3, 1934
Mollendo, Peru

Philosophy professor and leader of the Shining Path

"As for terrorism, they claim we're terrorists. I would like to give the following answer so that everyone can think about it: has it or has it not been Yankee imperialism and particularly [U.S. President Ronald] Reagan who has branded all revolutionary movements as terrorists, yes or no?"

From 1980 to 1992, Abimael Guzman, a philosophy professor, terrorized Peru as head of the Shining Path, one of the world's most violent terrorist organizations. About thirty thousand people died in a long string of bombings and raids staged by the organization, which claimed to follow the philosophy of China's revolutionary communist leader Mao Zedong (also spelled Tse-tung; 1893–1976). Guzman was finally arrested in September 1992, after which the level of violence attributed to Shining Path dropped sharply, although Peru's government was not able to put an end to the Shining Path entirely.

Origins of a revolutionary

Guzman was born in 1934 near the small Peruvian town of Mollendo. His father and mother did not marry, and Guzman grew up in his mother's small house down the street from his father, who was a wealthy merchant.

When Guzman was five years old, his mother died and he went to live with an uncle. A few years later, he went to live with his father, his father's wife, and several half brothers. Soon the entire family moved to the town of Arequipa, in southern Peru. There he attended a private Catholic school. Guzman was an excellent student—he graduated near the top of his high school class—and at age nineteen he enrolled in the University of Arequipa.

Guzman studied philosophy and the law. He became especially interested in the writings of social philosopher Karl Marx (1818–1883), the father of communism. (Communism is an economic theory that does not include the concept of private property; instead, the people—represented by the the government—owns all goods and means of production.) Marx led Guzman to the writings of Vladimir Lenin (1870–1924), the leader of the Russian communist revolution; Joseph Stalin (1879–1953), the dictator who ruled over the Soviet Union (today, Russia and its neighboring countries) for almost thirty years; and Mao Zedong, leader of the Chinese Communist Party. Although Guzman eventually led one of the most violent communist terrorist organizations in the world, he always maintained the image of philosopher and writer. He was never shown wearing a military uniform, but he was often shown carrying a book.

Guzman did, however, take on the revolutionary name Comrade Gonzalo. Some of his followers called him Doctor Puka Inti, meaning "Red Sun" in the Quechua language of native Peruvian Indians. Others called him Shampoo because, in the words of one follower, "he washes your head [thoughts]."

As a university student Guzman was strongly influenced by two men. One was a philosophy professor, Rodriguez Rivas, who was the center of a group of philosophy students who followed the German philosopher Immanuel Kant (1724–1804) and the rule of "Reason." Guzman edited a magazine published by a group of Rivas's followers. Its main thrust was how to change the world, and mankind, by applying reason, regardless of how impractical the actions taken might be.

The other influence on Guzman was Carlos de la Riva, a painter and a communist. He convinced Guzman that in the 1960s, Chinese communists under Mao Zedong, who were in the midst of the Cultural Revolution in China that left millions of Mao's "opponents" dead, had inherited the true spirit of communism.

His career begins

Guzman graduated from the University of Arequipa in 1962 and was hired as a philosophy professor at the Universidad Nacional San Cristobal de Huamanga. When Guzman left Arequipa for his new position in the town of Ayacucho, he was already well on the road to being a revolutionary.

Guzman's new university focused on technology in hopes that it could train people in an exceptionally poor and backward part of Peru to create greater economic growth. To accomplish this goal, well-paid professors were brought to the university, which was in a poor town of decaying, partially abandoned churches and (unable to read or write) Indians.

Guzman began organizing the many young communist students into groups to protest against the government. As Guzman succeeded in attracting poor young Peruvians to the Communist Party, which they embraced as an answer to the desperate poverty in Peru, he also worked to get them admitted as students at the university.

As the 1960s progressed, Guzman became an important figure on the campus. Even the sons of the university's president, who disliked the communist professor, were Guzman followers. Guzman was often surrounded by his students, many of whom came from poor Indian families.

In 1964 Guzman married Augusta La Torre, the daughter of the local communist leader. They had no children.

Also in 1964, Peru's Communist Party divided into two factions. One supported the Soviet (Russian) Communist Party; the other supported the Chinese Communist Party of Mao Zedong. The split in Peru reflected a similar division between Russia and China in the mid-1960s. In Peru, Guzman emerged as the leader of the pro-China faction.

The following year an armed revolt, inspired by the success of Cuban communists, broke out in several parts of Peru, including Ayacucho. But Guzman resisted pressure to lead his followers in support. His resistance reflected the growing split between Communist Cuba, which sided with the Soviet Union, and Communist China. The Peruvian authorities threatened to arrest him—to them, all communists seemed alike, whether they were allied with Cuba or with China—so Guzman left the country and went to China.

Guzman's stay in China had a major impact on him. He learned the theory of how to fight a "people's war," a kind of guerrilla revolution. These underground (secret) terrorist tactics had been used successfully by Mao and his Chinese Communist Party in its fight against the Nationalist Chinese in the 1940s.

"Serious revolutionary work"

By 1967 Guzman had returned to Peru, prepared for "serious revolutionary work," as he told his young followers in Ayacucho. His immediate challenge was to take charge of Peru's communists, many of whom were still attracted to the Cuban ideal that had served as an example for young revolutionaries throughout Latin America.

The main difference between the Chinese communist approach and the Cuban communist approach to gaining control of governments was the role of military action versus political action. The Cuban model was based on using small, mobile guerrilla groups to attack the military. Eventually, according to the plan, military victories in the countryside would lead to control of the cities and the country. The Chinese model was based on the idea that political organization had to come first, with military attacks coming later. While the Cuban model was to overwhelm the government's military forces in a series of battles and achieve military victory in the capital, the Chinese model called for gradually taking over the country by gaining the support of the population.

Guzman was a follower of the Chinese model. The Argentine-born Cuban revolutionary Ernesto "Che" Guevara (1928–1967) was a follower of the Cuban model. Guevara was killed fighting a Cuban-style revolution in Bolivia. Guzman used his death as an example of the hopelessness of Guevara's approach.

The year 1968 saw an unexpected development. Peru's military forces, sensing that revolution was about to sweep the country, overthrew the elected civilian president. But instead of clamping down on communists, the Peruvian military launched major reforms and freed jailed guerrillas. Communist Cuba and the pro-Russian Peruvian Communist Party applauded. But Guzman and the pro-Chinese faction of Peru's Communist Party fought the new military government.

The next year, as students in Ayacucho protested a government decision that ended free high school education for students who did not have passing grades, Guzman's faction supported the student demonstrators. The demonstrations became violent and forced the military government to back down. Guzman was arrested briefly. While in jail, he broke with the leader of Peru's Communist Party and set up his own organization upon his release. To mark the difference between the two groups, outsiders began referring to one as Red Banner and to Guzman's group as Shining Path. But as this split was taking place, the military government opened diplomatic relations with China. Soon the two countries were on good terms. China's enthusiasm for a violent political revolution in Peru began to fall, leaving Guzman without a foreign ally.

Despite this setback, Guzman pushed ahead with his version of a people's war and a Chinese-style cultural revolution. The Cultural Revolution was a Chinese political movement in the 1960s that tried to stamp out all signs of capitalism in Chinese culture. (Capitalism is an economic system in which factories and other businesses are owned and controlled by private individuals. It is the opposite of communism, in which property is owned by the people as a whole and, in theory, is distributed to them equally by the government.) Other left-wing (communist-leaning) groups joined together against the Shining Path. By 1976 these groups had gained enough influence to force Guzman to leave the university. Although he had lost his base of operations, Guzman continued to pursue a Chinese-style communist revolution in the countryside. Meanwhile, in China, Mao died and Deng Xiaoping (1904–1997) rose to power, reversing many of Mao's more extreme reforms and opening the way for private businesses in China's economy.

Let the revolution begin

Although they had had close ties to the Chinese communists for a dozen years, Guzman's followers in 1980 criticized the Chinese leadership and struck out on their own to promote their vision of a communist revolution in Peru.

By this point they had only one communist ally in the world: the leader of the tiny European country of Albania, Enver Hoxha (1908–1985). But, eventually, even he sided with the Red Banner faction of Peru's Communist Party.

This loss of his last ally did not discourage Guzman. The Shining Path became more radical (extreme) than ever, constantly purging (forcing out) members whose beliefs were considered suspect. The party committed itself to follow what it called the "Guiding Thought of Comrade Gonzalo."

In January 1979, Guzman was arrested while in the capital of Lima. But the party hired a respected lawyer and persuaded at least one army general to support his release. He was let out of jail and disappeared, emerging only during the 1980s to lead one of the world's most violent and deadliest revolts.

In the first known photo of Shining Path guerrillas, soldiers pose with rifles in hand, Ayacucho, Peru, 1984. *Photograph reproduced by permission of the Corbis Corporation.*

The deadly revolt of the Shining Path

In the spring of 1980, Shining Path began its armed revolution. The organization was largely without friends or allies, even among other communists. Its tactics ranged from violent political demonstrations to more traditional guerrilla attacks against army installations. A favorite strategy of Shining Path was assassinating civilian government officials. This wiped out

Peruvian President Alberto Fujimori swore to crush the Shining Path movement. Under Fujimori's rule, Guzman was tried and convicted of treason and the influence of Shining Path quickly diminished. *Photograph reproduced by permission of AP/Wide World Photos.*

the central government's power in many rural areas, where the Shining Path became the only ruling force.

Guzman never pretended his revolution would be easy. He had long warned his followers to be prepared to cross a "river of blood" to achieve victory. He began to claim an even larger role for himself. New recruits to his party swore loyalty to Comrade Gonzalo, who was described as "chief of the Communist Party of Peru and of World Revolution."

Rural villages that resisted the Shining Path paid a high price. In April 1983, for example, Shining Path guerrillas rounded up villagers in the Andean town of Lucanamarca and murdered almost seventy people. "We made them understand that they were confronting [facing] a different kind of people's fighters," Guzman said of the massacre in a 1990 *New Republic* interview.

For more than a decade, Shining Path fought its revolution with little or no regard for the number of people it killed. In a dozen years, about thirty thousand Peruvians died, many at the hands of Shining Path raiders. By 1986 Shining Path controlled areas on either side of a line running north-south through the Andes Mountains. The organization also spread its influence into Peru's coastal areas and even into the capital of Lima.

In 1987 the organization moved into Peru's main cocaine-producing area, about 500 miles (805 kilometers) southeast of Lima, which brought Shining Path into conflict with drug traffickers, American anti-narcotics workers, and Peruvian military and police authorities. Shining Path welcomed conflict with the United States. If it could transform its communist revolution into a war of resistance against the capitalist United States, the organization said, "90 percent of the population would follow us."

Reaction and arrest

In July 1990 a new president, Alberto Fujimori (1938–), came to power in Peru. At first, little changed. Shining Path continued its brutal campaign. But in May 1992 Fujimori dissolved Peru's congress and its courts. He began ruling the country by decree, backed by the military. The move was highly popular with many Peruvians, who felt the government hadn't done enough to fight the terrorists. Newspaper polls said 80 to 90 percent of the population supported the change. Three years later, in 1995, Fujimori was elected to another term.

Under heavy security, **Shining Path leader Abimael Guzman was caged on a navy ship and transferred from confinement on an island to a new maximum security prison on a navy base in Callao, Peru, 1993.** *Photograph reproduced by permission of AP/Wide World Photos.*

Under strict military rule, the government soon began making progress in its campaign against Shining Path. Regional commanders and party leaders were arrested and its operations were interrupted. The biggest success came in September 1992 when Guzman was arrested, along with six of his leading commanders.

Still operating under military rule, Fujimori's government put Guzman on trial under unusual circumstances. The government prosecutor and the judges all appeared in hooded robes that hid their faces, to prevent Shining Path guerrillas from targeting them for revenge. The entire trial was conducted in secret.

Guzman was convicted of treason (betraying one's country) and sentenced to life in prison. He was sent to an underground cell on an island off the coast of Peru, then transferred to a maximum security prison on a naval base.

Although the Shining Path swore revenge, Guzman's absence was a major blow to the organization. Its numbers and influence soon dropped.

In 1993 Guzman publicly appealed for his guerrilla followers to negotiate a peace agreement with the government. Some thought Guzman had been forced to make the appeal; others thought he was simply admitting defeat. Whichever was the case, the Shining Path refused. Guzman remained in prison, kept in his cell for all but a few hours a day, with no real chance of ever being released.

For More Information

Books

Olsen, William J., editor. *Small Wars*. Thousand Oaks, CA: Sage Periodicals Press, 1995.

Palmer, David Scott, editor. *The Shining Path of Peru*. New York: St. Martin's Press, 1992.

Strong, Simon. *Shining Path: Terror and Revolution in Peru*. New York: Times Books, 1992.

Periodicals

"The Cell at the End of the Path: Peru." *The Economist,* September 19, 1992, p. 50.

Gorriti, Gustavo. "The War of the Philosopher-King." *New Republic,* June 18, 1990, p. 15.

Smolowe, Jill. "His Turn to Lose." *Time,* September 28, 1992, p. 47.

Strong, Simon. "Where the Shining Path Leads." *New York Times Magazine,* May 24, 1992, p. 12.

Werlich, David P. "Peru: The Shadow of the Shining Path." *Current History,* February 1984, p. 78.

George Habash

August 2, 1926
Lydda, Palestine Mandate

Leader of the Popular Front for the Liberation of Palestine

"For decades world opinion has been neither for nor against the Palestinians. It simply ignored us. At least the world is talking about us now."

Through a half century of Palestinian resistance to the nation of Israel, which was established on Palestinian land in 1948, several different kinds of opposition have arisen. One recent kind is militant Islam, represented by **Osama bin Laden** (c. 1957–; see entry), in which **Palestinian nationalism**, the desire to found a new Palestinian nation on the land controlled by Israel, is seen as part of worldwide Muslim resistance to the Jewish state.

George Habash, however, was born a Christian. His opposition to Israel is not based on religious or ethnic grounds. Even as mainstream Palestinian groups moved toward peace with Israel, Habash and his followers in the Popular Front for the Liberation of Palestine (PFLP) remain opposed to negotiating a treaty with Israel.

As leader of the PFLP, Habash was the main Palestinian opponent of Palestine Liberation Organization (PLO) leader **Yasir Arafat** (1929–; see entry). Where Arafat believes the Palestinian Arabs must create their own nationalist opposition to Israel, Habash believes that the entire Arab people must rise up to defeat Israel. Habash supports **pan-Arabism**, the belief that all Arabs should unite in a single nation. The tensions between Israelis and Arabs have sometimes hidden the fact that quarrels among Arabs have resulted in nearly as many terrorist incidents as the Israel-Palestine conflict.

Birth and childhood in Palestine

Habash was born on August 2, 1926, in the city of Lydda, Palestine (now called Lod, a city in Israel). His family, who were well-to-do merchants, were members of the Greek Orthodox Christian Church.

In the 1920s Palestine was governed by Great Britain under a "mandate" granted by the League of Nations (the international organization that came before the United Nations) after the Ottoman Emprie, which had ruled Palestine, was defeated during World War I (1914–18). As Habash was growing up, Arab Palestinians and Zionist Jews were fighting over the future of the land. (**Zionism** is the movement that had as its goal the creation of a Jewish homeland in Palestine.) Palestinian Arabs wanted another Arab state, like the one that had been set up in Lebanon after the war. Jews, including some immigrants from Europe, wanted a Jewish state: Israel. To support their claim on the land, which was held holy by Jews, Christians, and Muslims alike, the Jews pointed to a promise made by Britain's prime minister during World War I, Arthur Balfour (1848–1930). In 1917 Balfour had offered European Zionists land for Israel after the war ended.

In 1948, when Habash was twenty-two, Israel declared its independence. Almost immediately armies from surrounding Arab countries, as well as Arabs living inside the new country, attacked. The new Israeli army successfully defended its country, but the fighting resulted in thousands of Palestinian Arabs being driven from their homes. Habash's family was among them.

Habash moved to Beirut, Lebanon, where he studied at the American University of Beirut and became a pediatrician, a

 Words to Know

Intifada: a popular uprising by Palestinians living under Israeli control.

Palestinian nationalism: the desire to found a new Palestinian nation on the land controlled by Israel.

Pan-Arabism: the idea that all Arabs should unite in a single nation.

Zionism: the movement with the goal of creating a Jewish homeland in Palestine.

doctor who treats children. He opened a child-care clinic, the "Clinic of the People," and a school for the children of Palestinian refugees in Amman, Jordan. He stayed there for five years, until 1957. But pediatrics was not to be his life's work.

Entry into Palestinian politics

While still at the American University, Habash became a follower of Egypt's president, Gamal Abdel Nasser (1918–1970), who dreamed of a single unified Arab country. Habash organized the Arab Nationalist Movement, whose aim was to unite the Arab world against Israel. Unlike the rival Fatah organization led by Arafat, whose goal was to lead the Palestinian Arabs to create a nation of their own, the Arab Nationalist Movement focused on leading all Arabs against Israel.

In 1957 Habash moved to Damascus, Syria, which had become part of the short-lived United Arab Republic, a union of Egypt (led by Nasser) and Syria. The union dissolved four years later, in 1961, and Habash was forced to leave Syria. He moved to Beirut. In 1964 Habash organized Palestinian members of the Arab Nationalist Movement into a new command, with himself in charge. But three years later, the Six Day War (June 1967), in which Israeli troops easily defended itself against the invading armies of surrounding Arab states, including Egypt, was a serious blow to Nasser's ideal of Arab unity.

The result of the Arab loss was the formation of the PFLP in 1967, an organization that became famous over the next decade for a series of spectacular terrorist attacks on Israeli targets. In the PFLP's founding statement, Habash declared that "the only language which the enemy understands is that of revolutionary violence." It was necessary, he said, that the PFLP should turn "the occupied territories [captured by Israel in the 1967 war] into an inferno whose fires consume the usurpers [people who seize something by force]."

Terrorism in earnest

In addition to opposing Israel, the PFLP also turned its anger on Arab governments that supported negotiating a peace treaty with Israel. Habash's organization fought both Israel and these Arab states to avoid a peace treaty with Israel.

The first terrorist attack by the PFLP came in 1968, when its agents seized an El Al (Israel's national airline) jet on a flight from Rome, Italy, to Tel Aviv, Israel, and forced it to land in Algiers, Algeria. There, in exchange for the passengers, the hijackers demanded freedom for sixteen Palestinians jailed by Israel. It took a month, but eventually Israel gave in.

The El Al hijacking put the PFLP in the spotlight. Terrorist groups in Europe, such as the **Baader-Meinhof Gang** in Germany and the **Red Brigades** in Italy, formed alliances with the PFLP. The KGB (the spy agency of the Soviet Union) also took favorable notice of the PFLP. So did a Venezuelan-born radical named Ilich Ramirez Sanchez, who soon joined the PFLP and became one of its leading terrorists: **Carlos the Jackal** (see entries on Baader and Ensslin; Fusako Shigenobu; and Carlos the Jackal).

The hijackings continue

Aircraft hijackings became a specialty of the PFLP. On September 6, 1970, the PFLP attempted to hijack four passenger jets on the same day. The first hijacking, of an El Al Israeli plane, failed when the pilot put the plane into a dive, knocking the hijackers off their feet. One hijacker was shot to death by a security guard, and the other, Leila Khaled, was taken prisoner. The second plane, a Pan American 747, was too big to land at the airstrip in Jordan as planned. It flew instead to the larger airport at Cairo, Egypt, where the passengers were ordered off the plane and the plane was then blown up by the hijackers.

The two other planes hijacked that day were forced to land in Jordan. Yet another plane was hijacked by PFLP sympathizers on a flight from Bombay, India, to London, England, on September 9, 1970, and also forced to land in Jordan. The PFLP said the hijackings were to avenge America's providing military aid to Israel. In exchange for the planes and passengers, the PFLP demanded that several prisoners be released from European jails.

Eventually the passengers and crews were released in exchange for Khaled and several other prisoners, and the planes were blown up on the ground. Although the hijackings were partly successful, Jordan's King Hussein (1935–1999) was furious that the PFLP had staged the incident on Jordanian soil without his permission. The king ordered his army to drive out armed Palestinians from his country in the battle that became known as Black September.

Along with most of the other Palestinian resistance organizations, the PFLP went to southern Lebanon. Habash sent his new Venezuelan recruit, Carlos the Jackal, to London to oversee a series of terrorist incidents under Habash's direction.

In May 1972 the PFLP joined the Japanese Red Army to stage another terrorist attack inside Israel. A group of Japanese, posing as tourists, pulled out guns at the passenger terminal in Lod Airport in Israel and opened fire, killing twenty-six people.

On the international scene, however, Palestinians realized that the terrorist incidents were not helping their cause and were, in fact, turning other countries against them. In 1973 the PLO declared that international attacks (as opposed to attacks on Israel itself) should be abandoned. Although he disliked the PLO, Habash agreed to drop international terrorist incidents. However, his partner in the PFLP, Wadi Haddad, disagreed with the decision. Haddad's part of the PFLP continued to carry out terrorist attacks outside the Middle East.

Change in tactics

After 1973 Habash limited his attacks to targets in Israel, outposts of the government Israel helped set up in southern Lebanon, and Jordan, which was beginning to talk to Israel about a peace agreement.

In 1978 President Anwar el-Sadat (1918–1981) of Egypt signed the Camp David Accords, in which Israel and Egypt agreed to negotiate a peace agreement. For Habash, it was a terrible blow. The homeland of his hero Nasser (who had died of a heart attack in 1970) had become the first Arab state to sign a peace agreement with Israel. The possibility of uniting the Arab world behind the Palestinian cause was shattered by the sight of Sadat shaking hands with Israeli Prime Minister **Menachem Begin** (1913–1992; see entry).

In 1980 Habash suffered a serious stroke that disabled him for several months. Habash never fully regained his influence. Instead, he took on the role of a senior wise man for the

Palestinian cause. (However, he did not formally resign as head of the PFLP until 2000.)

In 1987 the PLO launched the first **Intifada,** a popular uprising by Palestinians living under Israeli control. The PFLP became one of the most active groups in organizing car bombings and assassination attempts against Israeli targets.

The 1993 peace negotiations between Arafat and Prime Minister Yitzhak Rabin (1922–1995) of Israel, which resulted in the peace agreement known as the Oslo Accords, enraged Habash. He spoke out against the agreements and joined other radical Palestinian groups in opposing them. For the first time he allied with two Islamic organizations, Hamas and the Islamic Jihad. It was an unusual friendship, since the Christian Habash had rooted his positions in political philosophy while those of Hamas and the Islamic Jihad are rooted in Islam.

For More Information

Books

Bard, Mitchell, G., editor. *Myths and Facts: A Guide to the Arab-Israeli Conflit.* Chevy Chase, MD: American Israeli Cooperative Enterprise, 2001.

Follain, John. *Jackal.* New York: Arcade Publishing, 1998.

Gee, John. *Unequal Conflict: The Palestinians and Israel.* New York: Olive Branch Press, 1998.

La Guardia, Anton. *War without End: Israelis, Palestinians, and the Struggle for the Promised Land.* New York: Dunne/St. Martin's, 2002.

Mattar, Philip, editor. *Encyclopedia of the Palestinians.* New York: Facts on File, 2000.

Periodicals

"Habash, George." *Current Biography,* March 1988, p. 12.

Hitchens, Christopher. "Minority Report." *The Nation,* December 30, 1991, p. 838.

Rosenzweig, Saul. "A Radical Beyond Yasir Arafat." *New York Times,* July 25, 1982, p. E22.

Soueid, Mahmoud. "Taking Stock" (interview with George Habash), *Journal of Palestine Studies,* Autumn 1998, p. 86.

Theodore "Ted" Kaczynski (The Unabomber)

May 22, 1942
Chicago, Illinois

The Unabomber

"The Industrial Revolution and its consequences have been a disaster for the human race. . . . The continued development of technology will . . . certainly subject human beings to greater indignities and inflict greater damage on the natural world."

O n April 3, 1996, a team of heavily armed federal agents arrested a man outside his one-room cabin in a Montana forest. The arrest ended a seventeen-year hunt for a terrorist known as the Unabomber, who had killed three people with a series of mail bombs. His name was Theodore Kaczynski, a Harvard graduate who had a Ph.D. in mathematics and once taught at the University of California in Berkeley.

A psychiatrist concluded that Kaczynski suffered from paranoid schizophrenia, a severe mental illness that seriously distorted his sense of reality and drove him to a lonely life in the woods—and to a career as America's most wanted terrorist. Kaczynski himself always denied that he was mentally ill.

Growing up

Theodore Kaczynski, called Ted, was born in Chicago, Illinois, on May 22, 1942. His father, Theodore Richard Kaczynski, worked in a sausage factory. His mother, Wanda, at first stayed at home; she later qualified for a teaching license and taught school for a few years. When he was seven, his parents had another son, David. The Kaczynski family lived in a modest neighborhood of working families. The father changed jobs several times, shifting from sausage making to working for companies that cut foam, like the kind used for furniture. For a while, the family lived in Iowa before moving back to a suburb of Chicago.

When Kaczynski was nine months old, he had an allergic reaction and spent five days in the hospital. No one thought much of it at the time, but many years later, his mother wondered whether this separation from his family caused him to become withdrawn and less responsive.

Wanda Kaczynski later remembered that her son tended to play alongside other children, rather than playing with them. She even briefly considered enrolling him in a psychological study on children suffering from **autism.** (Autism is a mental disorder beginning in infancy. Its symptoms include an inability to interact socially, repetitive behavior, withdrawal from reality, and being absorbed in mental activities such as daydreams, fantasies, and delusions.)

Words to Know

Anarchist: a person who holds to the theory that society should be organized around voluntary associations, rather than large government organizations.

Autism: a mental disorder with symptoms including an inability to interact socially, repetitive behavior, withdrawal from reality, and being absorbed in mental activities such as daydreams, fantasies, and delusions.

Genetics: the study of how people and animals inherit their traits, such as eye and hair color.

Hermit: a person who lives alone, away from civilization.

Manifesto: a statement of principles and ideas.

Phoenix: in mythology, a bird that burned to ashes only to be reborn.

Revelation: a sudden realization of a new perception of reality.

Feeling isolated in school

In elementary school, Kaczynski seemed exceptionally bright. His mother had high hopes for her son, and she encouraged him to use a more adult way of speaking than the other children. Kaczynski remembered as an adult that by the time he was eight or nine years old, he did not feel accepted by other children. In the fifth grade, Kaczynski took an intelligence test and scored high enough that the school recommended he skip the sixth grade. Suddenly he was thrown into classes with older children, and he had an even greater sense of being a social outcast. Later in life, he remembered his classmates verbally abusing and teasing him.

Social isolation became a theme in Kaczynski's life. At Evergreen Park Community High School, he did not go out on dates or have close friends. He remembered the growing dislike of the other students. "By the time I left high school, I was definitely regarded as a freak by a large segment of the student body," he told Dr. Sally Johnson. But he did very well in his classes and skipped the eleventh grade as well. The school encouraged him to apply to Harvard University, which accepted him at age sixteen, two years earlier than most college students.

At Harvard, the first signs of mental illness

At Harvard, Kaczynski quickly realized that he was no longer smarter than everyone else. He did not make friends until his second year, and then only a few. Far from his family, Kaczynski's life was lonely until he graduated in June 1962, at the age of twenty. At Harvard he had daydreams about living alone in the woods or becoming a revolutionary and rousing mobs to violence.

After Harvard, Kaczynski entered the University of Michigan as a graduate student in mathematics. He spent five years there, earning master's and doctorate degrees. His academic work received high praise, but his social life was nonexistent. He lived alone in a rooming house. Kaczynski had no girlfriends, a fact that bothered him deeply. He once had fantasies of becoming a woman himself and visited a university health clinic to have the psychological evaluation required before having a sex-change operation. While waiting to see the psychiatrist, he suddenly felt ashamed and left.

Walking away from the clinic, Kaczynski had what seemed like a **revelation**, a sudden realization of a new perception of reality. Kaczynski told Johnson:

> As I walked away from the building afterwards, I felt disgusted about what my uncontrolled sexual cravings had almost led me to do [undergo a sex-change operation], and I felt humiliated, and I violently hated the psychiatrist. Just then there came a major turning point in my life. Like a **phoenix** in mythology, a bird that burned to ashes only to be reborn, I burst from the

ashes of my despair to a glorious new hope. I thought I wanted to kill that psychiatrist because the future looked utterly empty to me. I felt I wouldn't care if I died. And so I said to myself, why not really kill the psychiatrist and anyone else whom I hate? What is important is not the words that ran through my mind but the way I felt about them. What was entirely new was the fact that I really felt I could kill someone. My very hopelessness had liberated [freed] me because I no longer cared about death. I no longer cared about consequences, and I said to myself that I really could break out of my rut in life and do things that were daring, irresponsible or criminal.

Turning a corner

In the space of the short walk from the clinic, Kaczynski decided to go to Canada and live "off the country," alone in the woods. Before his visit to the psychiatrist, he had worried that he might be suffering from a mental illness. But on his walk he decided that his problems were all the fault of his family and the people around him. He began building a complicated explanation for his feelings. He blamed modern technology for his problems. Over time, he focused on **genetics** (the study of how people and animals inherit their traits, such as eye and hair color) and computers as specific technologies that were out to limit his freedom. He thought advertising was designed to control his mind. He also decided that he had been mistreated at home while he was growing up, although there has never been any outside evidence of this.

Years later, a psychiatrist used these stories as evidence that Kaczynski was suffering from paranoia, a mental condition that causes people to imagine that others are out to harm them. For example, in his rooming house, he sometimes heard people talking downstairs and imagined that there was a visitor for him. When no one knocked on his door, he became convinced the rooming house manager had said something negative about him and driven away his visitor. In fact, there was no evidence of this.

Moving into the woods

After receiving his doctorate degree in mathematics from the University of Michigan, Kaczynski took a job teaching mathematics at the University of California in Berkeley, a highly respected university, in order to save enough money so he could buy land and go live alone in the woods. "I would not fit into the present society in any case," he wrote at the time, "but that is not an intolerable unbearable situation." He continued:

> What makes a situation intolerable is the fact that in all probability, the values that I detest [hate] will soon be achieved through science, an utterly complete and permanent victory throughout the whole world, with a total extrication [removal] of everything I value. Through super human computers and mind control there simply will be no place for a rebellious person to hide, and my kind of people will vanish forever from the earth. It's not merely the fact that I cannot fit into society that has induced [led] me to rebel as violently as I have, it is the fact that I can see society made possible by science inexorably [impossible to avoid] imposing on me.

Kaczynski taught at Berkeley from September 1967 until June 1969, and then quit. It was the end of his academic career. He spent the next two years looking for land in Canada, Alaska, and finally Montana. There, he bought 1.5 acres about 4 miles (6.4 kilometers) outside the small town of Lincoln, Montana. With a little help from his brother David, Kaczynski built a one-room cabin measuring about 10 feet by 12 feet (about 2 meters by 3 meters). The cabin had no electricity, no telephone, and no indoor plumbing. He got drinking water from a nearby creek. It was to be his home for the next sixteen years.

In Montana, Kaczynski lived a dual life. To his neighbors, he was a **hermit**, a person who lives alone, away from civilization. He owned a car for a while, and later a pickup truck, but usually he used a bicycle or walked into town, and took a bus whenever he traveled. He received money from his parents and occasionally took a short-term job; he needed about $400 a year to live. He grew a vegetable garden, gathered plants from the nearby woods, and hunted game for food. He used the town's library, where he was friendly with the librarian and sometimes did chores. Residents of Lincoln got to know him and accepted his desire to live alone in the woods.

Emergence of the Unabomber

But there was another side to the hermit: a terrorist who planted bombs or sent them through the mail. The attacks were irregular; sometimes years would pass between

one bomb and the next. Over time, the bombs became more complicated and deadlier.

The first attack came on May 25, 1978, when a package was found in a parking lot at the University of Chicago. The package was addressed to a professor in Troy, New York, and the return address indicated it was from Professor Buckley Crist of Northwestern University in the nearby suburb of Evanston, Illinois. It was odd that a package from a professor at Northwestern addressed to someone at Rensselaer Polytechnic Institute should have landed in a parking lot at a third school. Nevertheless, the package was sent to Crist, who became suspicious and called the campus police. A campus patrolman, Terry Marker, started to open the parcel, which exploded, injuring Marker's left hand. Other bombs followed:

- **May 1979:** John Harris, a student at Northwestern, was injured when he opened a package left in a common room at Northwestern.

The cabin of Theodore Kaczynski sat at the end of a private road, hidden in a wooded setting in Lincoln, Montana. The home, on 1.4 acres, was only 10 by 12 feet, with no electricity or plumbing. *Photograph reproduced by permission of AP/Wide World Photos.*

- **November 1979:** A bomb being carried as air mail exploded in the cargo hold of an American Airlines flight from Chicago to Washington, D.C. Smoke from the bomb forced the plane to make an emergency landing at Dallas, Texas. The bomb was in a wooden box, leading a U.S. Postal Service inspector to conclude that wooden boxes were the "signature" of the bomber.

- **June 1980:** Percy Wood, the president of United Airlines, was injured by a bomb hidden in a hollowed-out book. Following this attack, the Federal Bureau of Investigation (FBI) named its investigation "Unabomb"—standing for UNiversities and Airline BOMBings.

- **October 1981:** A bomb was found at the University of Utah, similar to other attacks. This bomb was disarmed without hurting anyone.

- **May 1982:** A bomb was delivered to the office of Professor Patrick C. Fischer at Vanderbilt University in Nashville, Tennessee. His secretary, Janet Smith, was injured while opening the parcel.

- **July 1982:** Professor Diogenes Angelakos at the University of California at Berkeley noticed a strange device in the faculty lounge used by engineering and computer professors. When he moved it, it exploded, seriously injuring Angelakos.

- **May 1985:** Three years after the previous attack, also at Berkeley, a graduate student and Air Force pilot named John Hauser noticed a three-ring binder lying in a computer lab. When he opened the binder, it exploded, seriously injuring him.

- **June 1985:** A Boeing Aircraft office in Auburn, Washington, received a bomb, but it was disarmed without anyone being injured.

- **November 1985:** A professor at Kaczynski's old school, the University of Michigan, received a bomb disguised as a book. One of the professor's assistants was seriously injured in the explosion, and the professor's hearing was damaged.

- **December 1985:** The Unabomber claimed his first fatality when Hugh Scrutton, owner of the RenTech Computer Company in Sacramento, California, went to move a block of wood with nails sticking out of it, which was lying in his parking lot. When he picked up the block, it exploded. A nail pierced Scrutton's heart, killing him.

- **February 20, 1987:** A secretary at a computer company in Salt Lake City, Utah, noticed a man wearing a hooded sweatshirt and aviator-style sunglasses putting something on the ground. A short while later, an executive with the company kicked aside a block of wood with nails in it, similar to the device found in Oakland. The block exploded, seriously injuring Gary Wright. But for the first time, investigators had a lead: the secretary's description of the man. Perhaps because he had been spotted, or perhaps for some other reason, the Unabomber stopped his campaign for the next six years.

- **June 1993:** Two bombs were mailed within a day or two of each other. One was delivered to Charles Epstein, a geneticist (a scientist who studies genetics) in San Francisco, California, who was severely injured when he opened it. The other went to David Gelernter, a professor of computer science at Yale University, in New Haven, Connecticut, who was also seriously injured.

- **December 1994:** The Unabomber addressed a bomb to Thomas Mosser, an advertising executive in North Caldwell, New Jersey, whose name had been connected in a newspaper story to a major oil spill in Alaska. The powerful bomb exploded with full force, killing Mosser instantly.

- **April 1995:** A bomb addressed to an official at the California Forestry Association—a group that represents companies in the business of cutting trees for lumber—killed Gilbert Murray instantly when it was opened. The bomb had actually been sent to the man Murray had recently replaced at the association.

Hugh Scrutton was the first person killed by a bomb planted by Theodore Kaczynski. Scrutton owned a computer store in Oakland, California. The Unabomber planted a bomb disguised as a block of wood with nails sticking out. *Photograph reproduced by permission of AP/Wide World Photos.*

The Unabomber and Mental Illness

Dr. Sally Johnson, the psychiatrist who examined Theodore Kaczynski in January 1998, concluded that he suffered from "paranoid schizophrenia" and "paranoid personality disorder, with avoidant and antisocial features." He was mentally ill, but not "insane" from a legal viewpoint.

What is "insane from a legal viewpoint"?

The law says that a person who does not know the difference between right and wrong cannot be held responsible for his or her actions. Dr. Johnson concluded that the Unabomber knew that what he was doing was wrong but went ahead with his bombing campaign anyway. Kaczynski suffered from a mental illness, but he was still able to stand trial for his crimes.

What is paranoid schizophrenia?

Schizophrenia (pronounced skits-uh-FREE-nee-uh) is a severe disturbance of the brain's functioning that can sometimes be treated with drugs. Some experts have compared schizophrenia to a broken telephone system, in which calls are routed to the wrong number. Normally, the brain receives information from the eyes and ears (incoming phone calls) and responds with appropriate emotions and actions (replies to the incoming calls). In the case of someone suffering from schizophrenia, the reactions do not match the incoming data. There are different ways this can affect patients, which is why schizophrenia is divided into a number of different types.

Paranoid schizophrenia, which Kaczynski was diagnosed with, means the patient imagines people's words and actions are intended to be harmful. People with this mental illness may believe that people, including complete strangers, are plotting against them or controlling their thoughts in some way (though a secret radio broadcast, for example).

People suffering from schizophrenia often experience depression, a feeling that everything is hopeless. Depression can lead people to decide that they are unlovable or that they have ruined a relationship. It can also cause people to withdraw from contact with others.

Schizophrenia most often begins between the ages of fifteen and thirty. It may develop gradually or suddenly. Patients often experience a crisis episode, which can completely disable them for a short period of time, but behave normally

Beginning of the end for the Unabomber

But well before the last two bombs, investigators had a strong clue provided by the Unabomber himself. At the same

at other times. Some sufferers have only an occasional episode; others may develop chronic schizophrenia, in which the altered thought processes are constant.

Although doctors cannot cure schizophrenia, drugs can help some symptoms. Occasionally symptoms go away on their own. After age forty the symptoms often become less frequent and less severe, making life easier for people suffering from schizophrenia.

What is a personality disorder?

Personality describes the general way a person acts and reacts, especially in social situations. Some people seem to be generally happy, or serious, or friendly. Those are traits of their personality. A personality disorder describes a set of traits that make it more difficult for a person to succeed or be happy in everyday life. A personality disorder is not just an occasional bad mood or outburst. It refers to fairly constant behavior that goes outside the range of what most people experience and that causes problems in a person's daily life and relationships with other people.

Personality disorders can range from mild to severe, and their impact on a person's life can be just inconvenient or very serious. There are several types of personality disorders, each with different characteristics. A paranoid personality disorder, such as Kaczynski is said to have, describes someone who is very distrustful of others and suspicious of their motives. People with this disorder tend to avoid close relationships and constantly search for hidden meanings in what others say or do. They tend to carry grudges for a long time.

An avoidant personality disorder refers to someone who worries about what will happen in social situations and tries to avoid them. An antisocial personality disorder refers to people who do not have a conscience about their actions. People with this disorder are aggressive and more concerned with their needs than with the needs of others.

These characteristics that Dr. Johnson found in Kaczynski are not unique to terrorists. They can be seen in many people. On the other hand, the Unabomber case raises a question about the degree to which psychological problems contribute to terrorism, as opposed to political principles or religious ideals.

time he mailed the bombs to Epstein and Gelernter, the Unabomber sent a letter to the *New York Times* newspaper claiming that the bombs came from an anarchist group (one that

The Washington Post

TUESDAY, SEPTEMBER 19, 1995

Sections

House Plan Would
Federal Thrif

118TH YEAR   No. 288

Unabomber Manuscript Is Published

'Public Safety Reasons'
Cited in Joint Decision
By Post, N.Y. Times

By Howard Kurtz
Washington Post Staff Writer

After weighing the question for nearly three months, The Washington Post and New York Times have agreed to publish in today's Post a 35,000-word manuscript submitted by the Unabomber, the serial mail bomber who has promised to halt his deadly attacks if either newspaper ran his lengthy critique of industrial society.

Donald E. Graham, The Post's publisher, and Arthur O. Sulzberger Jr., publisher of the New York Times, said they jointly decided to publish the document "for public safety reasons" after

This text was sent last June to The New York Times and The Washington Post by the person who calls himself "FC," identified by the FBI as the Unabomber, whom authorities have implicated in three murders and 16 bombings. The author threatened to send a bomb to an unspecified destination "with intent to kill" unless one of the newspapers published this manuscript. The Attorney General and the Director of the FBI recommended publication. An article about the decision to publish the document appears on the front page of today's paper.

A SUPPLEMENT TO THE WASHINGTON POST

INDUSTRIAL SOCIETY AND ITS FUTURE

INTRODUCTION

1. The Industrial Revolution and its consequences have been a disaster for the human race. They have greatly increased the life-expectancy of those of us who live in "advanced" countries, but they have destabilized society, have made life unfulfilling, have subjected human beings to indignities, have led to widespread psychological suffering (in the Third World to ...

9. The two psychological tendencies that underlie modern leftism we call "feelings of inferiority" and "oversocialization." Feelings of inferiority are characteristic of modern leftism as a whole, while oversocialization is characteristic only of a certain segment of modern leftism; but this segment is highly influential.

his own needs. The leftist is antagonistic to the concept of competition because, deep inside, he feels like a loser.

17. Art forms that appeal to modern leftish intellectuals tend to focus on sordidness, defeat and despair, or else they take an orgiastic tone, throwing off rational control as if there were no hope of accomplishing anything through rational calculation and all that was left was to immerse oneself in the sensations of the moment.

18. Modern leftish philosophers tend to dismiss reason, science, objective reality and to insist that everything is culturally relative. It is true that one can ask serious questions about the foundations of scientific knowledge and about how, if at all, the concept of objective reality can be defined. But it is obvious that modern leftish philosophers are not simply cool-headed logicians systematically analyzing the foundations of knowledge. The...

example, we are
anyone, yet alw
somebody at se
either he admi
Some people ar
that the attempt t
morally impose t
them. In order to
they continually
selves about their
find moral explana
and moral origin. W
moral origin. We t
cialist" to describe
36. Oversocializ
defeatism, guilt, etc
important means to
socializes children
feel ashamed of beh
is contrary to societ
this is overdone, or
is especially a

At the request of U.S. Attorney General Janet Reno and the FBI, the *Washington Post* ran the unedited, 35,000-word Unabomber manifesto in the hope of ending the seventeen-year letter bomb campaign. *Photograph reproduced by permission of Liaison/Getty Images.*

wanted to do away with government) named the Freedom Club (or FC, initials that had been etched on most of the bombs sent by the Unabomber). The letter threatened to continue even bigger bombing attacks, unless the *New York Times* agreed to publish the group's **manifesto**, its statement of principles and ideas. Similar letters were sent to the *San Francisco Examiner* and *Penthouse* magazine. The Unabomber promised to stop his campaign if his views were published.

After talking to the FBI, on September 19, 1995, the *New York Times* and the *Washington Post* decided to share the cost of publishing the manifesto. It appeared as an eight-page special insert in the *Post*. The long essay declared that the Industrial Revolution (the period of technological change that began in England in the second half of the eighteenth century) and development of computer technology had been a disaster for mankind. About his bombing, Kaczynski wrote in his manifesto: "In order to get our message before the public with some chance of making a lasting impression, we had to kill people." The

"Unabomber Manifesto" was an extension of the theories that Kaczynski had begun developing to explain his mental illness at the University of Michigan. Many people thought the long essay was rambling and repetitive, but it did provide one critical clue.

The FBI had supported printing the manifesto in hopes that someone who read it would recognize the Unabomber's writing style. One reader noticed a particular phrase: "you can't eat your cake and have it too." Usually this expression is stated the other way around: "You can't have your cake and eat it too." David Kaczynski remembered that his mother had said it just the way the Unabomber wrote it, and he called the FBI.

After weeks of investigation and detailed planning, on April 3, 1996, the Unabomber task force surrounded Kaczynski's little cabin in Montana and arrested him. Inside the cabin were diaries and a written autobiography that confirmed they had found the Unabomber.

Trial and sentence

Kaczynski was formally charged with sending the bombs that killed three people. If found guilty, Kaczynski could have been sentenced to death. His trial was scheduled to begin in November 1997. The months leading up to the trial were filled with legal motions by Kaczynski's lawyers challenging the government's right to use evidence collected in Montana. His lawyers knew that the evidence was fatal to Kaczynski's case. These efforts were only partially successful.

Kaczynski's trial began on November 12, 1997, and was almost immediately thrown into chaos by the conflict between Kaczynski and his lawyers. His attorneys insisted on using an insanity defense (telling the court that Kaczynski was not responsible for his actions because he is insane), but Kaczynski refused to submit to psychological testing. His lawyers told him that pleading insanity was his best chance of avoiding a death sentence; Kaczynski did not want to be described as a madman. He asked U.S. District Judge Garland Burrell to assign him a new lawyer, which the judge refused. Then Kaczynski asked to serve as his own lawyer. The judge agreed to consider this request, but only if Kaczynski agreed to a psychiatric examination to prove that he was able to represent himself. Kaczynski agreed.

Kaczynski was examined by Dr. Sally Johnson, a psychiatrist who worked with the federal prison system. She interviewed Kaczynski at length, examined his diaries and other writings, and interviewed his family and other people who had known him. Her lengthy report provided a detailed picture of the Unabomber's life. She concluded that Kaczynski suffered from paranoid schizophrenia and several other personality disorders (see box on pages 166–67), but nevertheless decided that he was competent to stand trial.

On January 22, 1998, Kaczynski suddenly pleaded guilty to all the charges against him. He had made a deal with the prosecution: he pleaded guilty in exchange for being sentenced to life in prison instead of being executed. Formal sentencing took place on May 4, 1998. Kaczynski was ordered to serve four consecutive life sentences (meaning one after the other) in a highly secure prison in Colorado, with no chance of being paroled, or released early from his sentence.

For More Information

Books

Douglas, John, and Mark Olshaker. *Unabomber: On the Trail of America's Most-Wanted Serial Killer.* New York: Pocket Books, 1996.

Graysmith, Robert. *Unabomber: A Desire to Kill.* New York: Berkley Books, 1998.

Mello, Michael. *The United States of America versus Theodore Kaczynski: Ethics, Power, and the Invention of the Unabomber.* New York: Context Books, 1999.

Waits, Chris. *Unabomber: The Secret Life of Ted Kaczynski.* Helena, MT: *Helena Independent Record: Montana Magazine,* 1999.

Periodicals

Chase, Alston. "Harvard and the Making of the Unabomber." *Atlantic Monthly,* June 2000, p. 41.

Finnegan, William. "Defending the Unabomber." *New Yorker,* March 16, 1998, p. 52.

Scarf, Maggie. "The Mind of the Unabomber: Narcissism and its Discontents." *New Republic,* June 10, 1996, p. 20.

James Kopp

August 2, 1954
Pasadena, California

Antiabortion protester

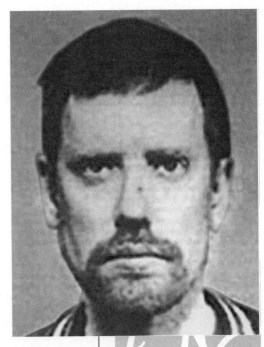

In the autumn of 1998, Dr. Barnett Slepian had just returned from a prayer service for his dead father and was standing in the kitchen of his home in Amherst, New York, a suburb of Buffalo. A bullet smashed through the window and hit him in the back, killing him.

Within three days, police were looking for a well-known antiabortion protester named James Kopp, who had the nickname "Atomic Dog" among other antiabortion activists. Police said that Kopp's car, a 1987 black Chevrolet Cavalier, had been seen in Dr. Slepian's neighborhood; it was found in a parking lot at the Newark, New Jersey, airport a few days later. Later, investigators found a rifle buried near the murder scene as well as hairs that matched Kopp's.

Despite these police accusations and charges by Canadian officials in connection with the shootings of other **abortion** providers, others in the antiabortion movement insisted that Kopp could not be a murderer. They described him as a devout Catholic, committed to nonviolence, whose bad eyesight meant he could not fire a rifle accurately.

"I am innocent. I want my innocence recognized as soon as possible."

Photograph reproduced by permission of AP/Wide World Photos.

171

Words to Know

Abortion: the act of ending a pregnancy by removing the fertilized egg from a woman's uterus.

Anthrax: an infectious disease that can be fatal unless a person gets treatment soon after he or she has been exposed.

Atheist: a person who believes there is no God.

Fetus: a developing unborn baby in the mother's uterus.

Infanticide: baby killing.

Leukemia: an often fatal disease affecting the blood, which causes an abnormal increase in the number of white blood cells.

Schizophrenia: a severe disturbance of the brain's functioning that can sometimes be treated with drugs.

The story of Kopp's pursuit and arrest highlighted the development of the antiabortion movement over the previous decade. It had consistently lost legal challenges to abortion (the medical termination of a pregnancy that antiabortion advocates view as a form of **infanticide**, or baby killing) and became more desperate in its efforts to stop abortions from being performed. With Kopp, that desperation may have eventually led to murder.

Terrorism and abortion

Abortion has long been a highly emotional topic. For people who believe abortion should be legal, it is about a woman's right to control her own body. For people who want it outlawed, it is about the sacredness of life and preventing "baby killing." It is an issue that has been fought bitterly in the courts, in elections, and in the streets.

Once outlawed almost everywhere in the United States, abortion gradually became legal in all states. In 1973, in a case called *Roe v. Wade,* the U.S. Supreme Court upheld the right of women to obtain abortions on demand. That decision, and the fact that public opinion had gradually shifted to support the right to an abortion, forced abortion opponents into the role of protesters. (Despite court decisions declaring abortion to be legal, some religious organizations—especially the Roman Catholic Church—have always considered abortion immoral and wrong.)

Various means of opposing abortion developed over the two decades following the *Roe v. Wade* decision and eventually came to include violence as a means of discouraging doctors from performing abortions and pregnant women from having abortions. Terrorist tactics used in the name of antiabortionism have included bombing clinics, sending envelopes containing white powder that was claimed to be **anthrax** (an infectious disease that can be fatal unless a person gets treatment soon after he or she has been exposed), and murdering abortion providers.

Middle-class origins

Born in Pasadena, California, in 1954, Kopp was the son of a corporate lawyer and a licensed nurse. He grew up in the suburbs of Marin County, north of San Francisco. His father, Charles Kopp, was a former lieutenant in the U.S. Marine Corps, seemingly gentle and straight-laced, but also prone to heavy drinking and strict discipline. For college, Kopp chose the University of California at Santa Cruz, a campus that was only a couple of hours from his parents' home. There, he lived in an off-campus apartment with his girlfriend. After graduating in 1976, he enrolled at California State University at Fullerton and earned a master's degree in biology in 1982.

Kopp considered several careers. He thought of following his father's footsteps and becoming a lawyer, or a doctor. But eventually he turned to religion. In the 1980s Kopp underwent a series of experiences that challenged his orderly childhood. His sister Mary, who suffered from **schizophrenia** (a severe disturbance of the brain's functioning that can sometimes be treated with drugs) and **leukemia** (an often fatal disease affecting the blood, which causes an abnormal increase in the number of white blood cells), died at age twenty-one. Kopp then discovered that for years his father had been having an affair with a woman in Dallas, Texas, who thought he was divorced. Within a year, his parents divorced and his father married his lover. Kopp found out about his father's remarriage through an announcement delivered in the mail. A year after the wedding, Kopp's father suffered a stroke.

Adopting a religious life

Even before the divorce, abortion had been a topic of discussion in the Kopp family. Kopp, his sister Anne, and his mother, Nancy, argued that abortion was murder. Kopp's twin brother Walt, his sister Mary, and their father thought a woman had the right to choose whether to bear a child. The argument within the family reflected a division along religious

The Nuremberg Files

The Nuremberg Files was a Web site established by Neil Horsley, an extreme opponent of abortion, on the Internet. It consisted of "wanted posters" of abortion providers, along with gory photographs of aborted fetuses.

More threateningly, the database listed the home and office addresses of abortion providers, along with other personal information. Some names appeared with lines drawn through them: these are people who have been murdered, apparently by abortion foes.

The Nuremberg Files came under intense criticism and was forced off the Internet several times. American Internet service providers refused to rent space to the site. It was eventually moved to a computer located in South Africa. In the spring of 2001, a U.S. Appeals Court ruled that the database had a right to exist under the First Amendment to the Constitution (which guarantees freedom of speech). The Appeals Court also overturned a lower-court ruling that ordered the database's maintainers to pay more than $100 million to Planned Parenthood, an organization that provided women with birth control methods, including abortion, and other groups that it had targeted.

beliefs: Kopp, his mother, and Anne were devout Christians, while Mary was an **atheist** (a person who believes there is no God) and Walt gave money to an organization that helped finance birth control, including abortion.

But perhaps the biggest blow to Kopp was dealt by his girlfriend Jennifer. According to his father's second wife, Jennifer became pregnant and had an abortion before breaking up with Kopp. It was a terrible blow, partly because, as the father, he felt he should have been consulted, according to his stepmother.

Kopp had long been a Christian, like his mother. Faced with the need to make a career choice after earning his master's degree in biology, he decided to pursue religion more seriously. The subject of abortion was to play a central role. Not only had Kopp's personal life been deeply affected by the subject, but the mid-1980s was a period when the national debate over abortion was beginning to heat up.

The abortion debate

Abortion is the act of ending a pregnancy. Normally, a male sperm cell combines with an egg in a woman's uterus (sometimes called a womb) to begin the process of creating a new human being. The process starts with a single fertilized egg, which then begins dividing over and over again and forming organs. Nine months later, what started as a single cell has grown into a **fetus** that emerges from the uterus as a living baby. An abortion interrupts this process by removing the fertilized egg, which is called by different names as the pregnancy advances.

The debate over abortion is whether a woman should be allowed to have the fertilized egg removed from her uterus. Defenders of abortion believe each woman should be able to decide whether she wants to have a child. Opponents of abortion believe that a new human being has been created as soon as a woman's egg is fertilized by the man's sperm, and that from that moment, the fertilized egg deserves the same protection as any other person. This is often called the "moment of conception" in the debate over abortion.

The underlying question is: at what point does a fetus become a human being? Opinions differ. Some believe that a new human exists from the moment of fertilization; some, at the other end of the range, believe life does not begin until a baby is born. Many people believe it takes place somewhere between the two extremes.

To those like Kopp, who believe that life begins at conception, an abortion is the same as murdering a tiny, helpless human being. Anyone who would help in this process is guilty of murdering a baby, a phrase that can create a strong emotional reaction.

The path of an abortion opponent

In 1984 Kopp helped found a "pregnancy crisis center" in San Francisco. There, young women could come in and be tested to determine whether they were pregnant, and to receive counseling if they were. The counseling included showing them photographs of aborted fetuses to discourage them from getting abortions. It was a common technique for abortion opponents, but it seemed to some people that at some level Kopp just wanted to talk to women like his former girlfriend to keep them from getting an abortion.

Two years later Kopp got in touch with an antiabortion activist named Joan Andrews, who had been sent to jail in Florida for entering an abortion clinic and destroying the equipment used to perform abortions. Andrews had been sentenced to an unusually long term—five years in prison—and was held in solitary confinement for forty days as punishment for not cooperating with prison authorities.

Kopp traveled to Pensacola, Florida, in 1986. There he joined a group of activists trying to rouse public opinion against abortion by staging demonstrations and blocking the entrances to abortion clinics. Kopp was arrested for using a truck to block access to an abortion clinic. It was a time in the national debate over abortion when activists like Kopp were trying to attract support by breaking the law.

Collectively, these activists were known as the Rescue Movement, meaning they intended to "rescue" fetuses in danger of being aborted. The activists in this movement disagreed on what tactics to use. Some believed in using only nonviolent tactics. Others—Kopp among them—blocked the entrances to abortion clinics or chained themselves to the doors. A few activists went as far as bombing abortion clinics.

During this period, Kopp's own views were apparently still developing. Although he had been raised as a Protestant, in the mid-1980s he converted to Roman Catholicism. In 1986 he spent six months living in a facility near Yankee Stadium in the Bronx in New York operated by the Missionaries of Charity, a religious order founded by Roman Catholic nun Mother Teresa (1910–1997). There, he started work at 4:30 A.M. to help feed the homeless and drug addicts, and then spent hours in meditation. He owned just three changes of clothes, which he washed in a bucket (the religious order banned the use of appliances).

By the time he left the Missionaries of Charity, Kopp's life was thoroughly linked to the battle against legal abortion.

Operation Rescue

In 1988 Kopp joined a group called Operation Rescue, with headquarters in Binghamton, New York, a faded industrial city northwest of New York City. The organization took its inspiration from a passage in the Bible, Proverbs 24:11: "Rescue those who are being taken away to death; hold back those who are stumbling to the slaughter." Its goal was to "rescue" fetuses from abortion by blocking abortion clinics.

Kopp worked with Catholic churches to organize protests at abortion clinics, and he specialized in designing the locks and chains used by activists in their efforts to block access to the clinics. Demonstrators used Kopp's designs to chain themselves to the doors, forcing police to spend hours cutting them off and effectively closing the facilities for an entire day. Kopp was given the nickname "Atomic Dog" by the other people in the movement.

But despite the efforts of Operation Rescue and similar groups, abortion opponents steadily lost ground in the courts. They also lost ground in the court of public opinion, as more people in the country supported legal abortion. These setbacks seemed simply to add to their determination.

Although Operation Rescue officially preached nonviolence, some abortion opponents were beginning to turn to violence to stop what they saw as acts of murder.

Lambs of Christ

In 1988 a virtual army of antiabortionists turned out to protest at the Democratic Party's convention in Atlanta, Georgia. Police arrested more than a thousand of them for trying to disrupt the political convention. Protesters were later quoted as saying the Atlanta turnout had a feeling similar to the civil rights protests during the 1960s, during which Americans of all walks of life demonstrated for the equal rights of African Americans: a rising tide of people on the right side of an issue that was gaining strength. Expectations were high that the aging Supreme Court justices who supported abortion rights would retire and be replaced by Republican-nominated judges who, conservative and traditional, would reverse the Court's position on abortion. Among the protesters jailed in Atlanta, there was a sense of camaraderie, a spirit of good fellowship among people engaged in the same cause. And in this group, Kopp was considered a respected and experienced veteran of the movement.

One outcome of the Atlanta protest was the founding of a new antiabortion group, the Lambs of Christ, by Reverend Norman Weslin, a former military officer turned clergyman. In some respects, Weslin resembled Kopp's father: a strict man who did not welcome disagreement or argument. He insisted that members of the Lambs "submit themselves totally and completely to the Lamb concept, which places a shepherd in charge. And that shepherd calls all the shots." On another occasion, Weslin told a journalist: "Unless you understand that this is a colossal war between Jesus Christ and Satan, you don't understand what we are doing."

Dr. Barnett Slepian, a doctor who performed abortions, was shot through his kitchen window in New York, 1998. Slepian had been receiving death threats from antiabortion activists since the 1980s. *Photograph reproduced by permission of AP/Wide World Photos.*

In 1990 Kopp took part in a "lock and block" protest in Burlington, Vermont, as a member of the Lambs of Christ. He was sentenced to spend fifty-one days in jail by Judge Matthew Katz, along with about one hundred other protesters. Later, Katz's name appeared on an Internet Web site called the Nuremberg Files that targeted abortion providers and other people who supported a woman's right to an abortion (see box on page 174).

Afterward, Kopp began living in a farmhouse near St. Albans, Vermont, owned by a fellow antiabortion activist, Anthony Kenny. Kopp registered two cars at Kenny's house, including a 1987 Chevrolet Cavalier.

In June 1992 the antiabortion movement suffered a serious blow. Conservative, Republican-appointed Supreme Court justices joined the more liberal (progressive) judges on the Court in upholding a woman's right to an abortion. The sense of victory that the protesters at the 1988 Atlanta protest had enjoyed was shattered. To make matters worse for the movement, at about the same time the federal government began going after abortion protesters in court, including the leader of Operation Rescue. Fearful of being forced to pay enormous fines, many of the more militant antiabortionists dropped out. So, too, did public support by well-known figures like conservative Christian leader Jerry Falwell (1933–), some of whom feared becoming involved in government actions against abortion foes.

Underground

Many antiabortion activists reacted to the legal setback in the Supreme Court and the government's prosecutions by dropping out of the movement and returning to a more ordinary life. But not Kopp.

Along with a small group of others, he tried to continue the crusade. He took his activities to Europe and the Philippines. There is evidence that he associated with another antiabortion group, Missionaries to the Preborn, whose address he gave on a Wisconsin driver's license application. Some members of the Missionaries have supported the use of firearms to stop abortion providers.

In 1992 Kopp's father died of a heart attack. Two years later, his mother also died. She had been the person to whom Kopp was closest and an important source of financial support. The same year Nancy Kopp died, the Freedom of Access to Clinic Entrances Act became law, guaranteeing women access to abortion clinics. It was a direct blow against Kopp's tactics, and it threatened him with federal prosecution if he continued his work.

James Kopp, charged with the 1998 murder of New York doctor Barnett Slepian, arriving at a French courthouse in 2001. *Photograph reproduced by permission of AP/Wide World Photos.*

Even before the act passed, however, evidence was emerging that the antiabortion movement was beginning to embrace violence. At a 1993 demonstration in Pensacola, one protester pulled out a gun and murdered a doctor at the clinic. Later in 1993, another protester shot and wounded a doctor in Wichita, Kansas. In 1994, a protester killed another abortion doctor in Pensacola, who had replaced the physician murdered the year before. In Brookline, Massachusetts, a man armed with an automatic rifle killed two workers and wounded five others at two abortion clinics in December 1994.

The campaign also moved to Canada. In November 1994, a abortion doctor in Vancouver, British Columbia, was shot in the leg with a rifle fired through a window of his house. In 1995 another doctor was shot and wounded in Ancaster, Ontario, and in 1997 a Winnipeg doctor was shot in the chest, seriously injuring him.

On October 23, 1998, Slepian was murdered while standing in his kitchen. A sniper with a rifle shot the doctor through his kitchen window, the same technique that had been used four years earlier in Vancouver.

Three days later, the police began hunting for Kopp.

For two and a half years, the trail seemed to grow cold. Then, suddenly, on March 2, 2001, French police swooped down on the post office in the small French town of Dinan and arrested a man who had just picked up an envelope sent to him from New York. It was James Kopp, and the French police were acting at the request of the Federal Bureau of Investigation (FBI).

The FBI said it had traced Kopp to Ireland, where he had lived after fleeing the United States. Authorities had monitored Internet activity, including messages sent to Kopp from a man and woman in Brooklyn, New York, who had supported him and were preparing to provide Kopp with shelter upon his return.

Kopp remained in custody in France for over a year. French authorities would not extradite Kopp, or send him back to the United States, as long as he faced the prospect of capital punishment, or being put to death, as a result of being accused of killing Dr. Barnett Slepian. Finally, federal and state authorities agreed to charge Kopp with crimes that did not carry the death penalty, and he was flown to the United States under arrest in June 2002. He was charged with the federal crime of using deadly force to interfere with the right to abortion, and with the state crime of second degree murder.

For More Information

Books

Risen, James, and Judy L. Thomas. *Wrath of Angels: The American Abortion War.* New York: Basic Books, 1998.

Solinger, Rickie, editor. *Abortion Wars: A Half-Century of Struggle, 1950–2000.* Berkeley, CA: University of California Press, 1998.

Terry, Randall A. *Operation Rescue.* Springdale, PA: Whitaker House, 1988.

Tribe, Laurence H. *Abortion: The Clash of Absolutes.* New York: Norton, 1990.

Periodicals

"Captured: After a Two-year Overseas Manhunt, Police in France Seize a Suspect in the Sniper Murder of a Buffalo, New York, Doctor Targeted by Antiabortion Radicals." *People Weekly,* April 16, 2001, p. 62.

Offley, Will. "The Furtive Alliance between the Catholic Church and the Advocates of Anti-Abortion Terrorism." *Canadian Dimension,* November, 2000, p. 35.

Samuels, David. "The Making of a Fugitive." *New York Times Magazine,* March 21, 1999, p. 46.

Timothy McVeigh

**April 23, 1968
Pendleton, New York
June 11, 2001
Terre Haute, Indiana**

The Oklahoma City bomber

"It's a very tragic thing."

On the morning of April 19, 1995, a bomb hidden in a rented truck exploded outside the Alfred P. Murrah Federal Building in Oklahoma City, Oklahoma. The explosion killed 168 people, including 19 children who attended a day-care center on the second floor. At the time it was the deadliest single terrorist attack in American history.

The bomb had been left by a young man named Timothy McVeigh. McVeigh planned the bombing with the help of two friends as an act of revenge for a government raid on a religious group's headquarters in Waco, Texas. Six years later, on June 11, 2001, McVeigh was executed for the crime.

Growing up

McVeigh was born in the small town of Pendleton, New York, near the old manufacturing city of Buffalo, on April 23, 1968. His father worked at a General Motors radiator factory in nearby Lockport, New York; his mother worked for a travel agency. McVeigh had an older sister; later, he would have a younger sister. His father was a solid worker who lived quietly. His mother was lively and longed for a more exciting life. In 1978 his parents separated. The two girls went to live with their mother; McVeigh chose to live with his father. "I don't want Dad to be alone," he said, according to his biography, *American Terrorist*.

In high school, McVeigh did not make much of an impression. He went out for the football and track teams, but quit. He did not have a girlfriend and did not date. Thin and quiet, he was almost an invisible man. After graduating from high school, he went to a two-year business college, but he soon dropped that, too. He had a job at a Burger King and drove an old, beat-up car.

McVeigh was fascinated with guns. The year after graduating from high school, he got a pistol permit and took a job as a guard with an armored car company. Over time, he bought several guns. Two years after high school, in 1988, he and a friend bought 10 acres of rural land to use as a shooting range.

You're in the army now

The same year, McVeigh enlisted in the U.S. Army. After basic training, he was assigned to the army's 1st Infantry Division, based in Fort Riley, Kansas. In the army, McVeigh was somewhat successful. He moved up the ranks, from private to corporal, sergeant, and then platoon leader. At the end of his first term in the army, he re-enlisted and then applied to join the elite Special Forces.

While in the military McVeigh also read *The Turner Diaries*, a novel about a secret underground army in the United States dedicated to, among other things, the worldwide destruction of the Jewish people. The army seized power by dropping atomic bombs on several East Coast cities. *The Turner Diaries* was written by a man named William Pierce (writing under the name Andrew Macdonald), who had long been associated with the neo-Nazi National Alliance and other far-right extremist groups. Some fans saw the book as a blueprint for a Nazi-like future for the United States. (The Nazis was a political party headed by Adolf Hitler that controlled Germany in the years prior to and during World War II. During the war the Nazis attempted to wipe out the Jews of Europe, and killed an estimated six million before the war ended in 1945.) McVeigh apparently liked the book well enough to recommend it to his friends.

Before McVeigh could begin his Special Forces training, the United States was drawn into the Persian Gulf War (1990–91) after Iraq invaded the tiny Middle Eastern country of Kuwait. McVeigh's unit was sent to Saudi Arabia in early 1991, and he saw some combat in the war. His performance was good enough for him to leave the Middle East early to begin his Special Forces assessment at Fort Bragg, North Carolina. But once there, McVeigh quickly realized that he was not in good enough physical condition for the course. He failed one test—carrying a 45-pound (20.5-kilogram) backpack on a ninety-minute march—and after two days he dropped out. With his military future looking less bright, he applied for an early discharge and left the army in 1991.

Back where he started

In early 1992 McVeigh went back to his father's house in Pendleton, New York, where he got another job as a security guard. At age twenty-four, he was right back where he had been after high school.

The year 1992 was a significant one for people who took *The Turner Diaries* seriously. In Ruby Ridge, Idaho, federal marshals tried to arrest Randy Weaver, a white supremacist who believes that white people are superior to members of other races. Weaver had been accused of selling weapons illegally. An agent of the federal Bureau of Alcohol, Tobacco and Firearms (ATF) shot and killed Weaver's fourteen-year-old son and later killed his wife while she was standing in the doorway of their cabin holding their baby. (The baby was not harmed.) The incident enraged the militia movement, various armed citizen groups who have banded together to oppose what they believe to be too much government control over their personal lives. They viewed the seige at Ruby Ridge as a government conspiracy to take away people's firearms.

The next year, 1993, ATF agents laid siege to the compound of a religious sect, the Branch Davidians, in Waco, Texas. The siege ended with a fire that killed eighty members

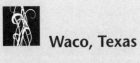

Waco, Texas

On April 19, 1993, the Federal Bureau of Investigations (FBI) attacked the compound of a religious sect called the Branch Davidians near Waco, Texas. The compound had been under siege for fifty-one days following an unsuccessful attempt by federal agents to arrest its leader. The attack on the compound quickly went wrong. A fire started, and the building burned to the ground. Inside, eighty people died, including twenty-one children.

The Branch Davidians traced their roots to the late 1920s. Their leader, David Koresh (1959–1993), believed he was fated to be the next messiah (savior) and lead his people to paradise after the end of the world. Koresh had developed his theories about the end of the world from the Book of Revelation, the last book of the New Testament of the Bible. He and his followers lived near Waco in a large structure filled with guns that they were going to use to defend themselves during the coming apocalypse, a battle at the end of the world.

In May 1992, a driver for the United Parcel Service told authorities he had seen hand grenades spill out of a box he was delivering to the Branch Davidian compound. Six months later, the federal Bureau of Alcohol, Tobacco and Firearms (ATF) got a warrant for the arrest of Koresh, which they tried to carry out on Sunday, February 28, 1993. But Koresh was prepared, and when the agents came to the compound where he lived, a gunfight broke out. Four ATF agents and six members of the Branch Davidians died, and government agents began a long standoff.

After weeks of unsuccessful negotiations, on April 19 the FBI attacked the house, using armored tanks to spray tear gas inside. A fire started and the building burned to the ground. It is unclear whether Branch Davidians set the fire or whether it was caused by the FBI's raid.

The deadly outcome of the siege instantly sparked outrage among many people, particularly extremist groups. Critics believed the raid was evidence the government was trying to take away Americans' constitutional right to bear firearms.

Among the many people who went to see the compound during the siege was Timothy McVeigh, who staged his attack on a federal office building on the second anniversary of the FBI raid.

of the sect (see box). The Waco incident was viewed by some people as further evidence of a government plot to take away their firearms and force a dictatorship on the United States. McVeigh was one of them.

Wandering time bomb

McVeigh had already quit his armored truck job and left his father's house in January 1993. He lived out of his car while traveling the country, sometimes visiting two old army buddies: Terry Nichols in Decker, Michigan, and Michael Fortier in Kingman, Arizona. He also visited the site of the siege at the Branch Davidian compound near Waco, Texas. McVeigh worked a series of jobs and tried to make money by selling weapons at local gun shows.

Although the government raid on the Branch Davidians apparently had deeply upset him, McVeigh did not join any of the militant groups found throughout the West, including Arizona and Michigan. But he did begin planning revenge for the government raid at Waco. McVeigh came to see himself as a warrior against what he believed was a growing government plot to take away people's freedoms. The date April 19 took on a special importance for McVeigh. Not only was it the date of the Waco fire, but it was also the date that Revolutionary War patriots had their first shoot-out with the British army in Lexington and Concord, Massachusetts: April 19, 1775.

McVeigh's disappointment with his life after the army, his growing extremist political views, and his obsession with firearms made him a walking time bomb—a bomb that went off on April 19, 1995.

April 19, 1995

In early spring 1995 McVeigh persuaded Nichols to help him put together a fertilizer bomb. A large quantity of fertilizer, combined with diesel fuel, can be turned into a deadly bomb, and the materials are easy to find, especially in rural areas.

McVeigh rented a large Ryder truck, loaded about 7,000 pounds (3,182 kilograms) of the lethal fertilizer–fuel oil mixture in the back, and drove it to Oklahoma City. On the morning of April 19, he parked the truck outside the large Alfred P. Murrah Federal Building in downtown Oklahoma City, where various government agencies had offices. Inside on the second floor, just above where the truck was parked, was a day-care center.

A few minutes after 9 A.M., the truck bomb exploded. The explosion shattered the building, completely destroying one-third of it. The front of the building fell away, exposing offices inside. Several floors of the building collapsed, leaving a mound of rubble. Shattered glass from the bomb's blast injured people blocks away from the site.

"May I see your license and registration?"

Ninety minutes after the blast, an Oklahoma Patrol officer near Perry, Oklahoma, noticed a 1977 yellow Mercury Grand Marquis without license plates. The patrolman pulled over the car, whose driver got out to talk to the officer. The driver said he had just bought the car and did not have license plates or other documentation. Then the patrolman noticed that the young man was carrying a pistol. The officer drew his own gun and arrested the driver.

The driver was twenty-seven-year-old Timothy McVeigh. The patrolman took McVeigh to the nearby Noble County Jail and charged him with unlawfully carrying a weapon, carrying a loaded gun in a car, failure to have current license plates, and failure to have proof of car insurance.

As McVeigh waited in jail for a bail hearing on his traffic violations, the FBI identified the rented truck from the wreckage and quickly interviewed the person who had rented it out. The FBI investigation led to a motel, where an employee recognized an artist's sketch as a man registered as Timothy McVeigh. When the FBI punched that name into a law enforcement computer system, they discovered that a man by that name was currently sitting in the Noble County Jail. McVeigh was about to be released on bail on April 21 when word came in that he was a suspect in the Oklahoma City bombing.

McVeigh on trial

McVeigh's trial was moved from Oklahoma City to Denver, Colorado, on the grounds that potential jurors in Oklahoma City would not be able to give him a fair trial.

The government presented 141 witnesses against McVeigh. Among those testifying were his sister Jennifer and his two friends Michael and Lori Fortier. The Fortiers testified that McVeigh had shared with them his plans to bomb the

Mementos hang on the fence that surrounds the destroyed Murrah Federal Building in Oklahoma City, Oklahoma. A posted newspaper announces Timothy McVeigh's death sentence, 1998. *Photograph reproduced by permission of AP/Wide World Photos.*

Murrah building in the mistaken belief that the ATF had offices there. Lori Fortier said at the trial: "We turned the news on early that morning . . . and we seen what happened . . . we saw that the building had been blown up, and I knew right away that it was Tim."

The jury reached its verdict after three days of deliberations: McVeigh was guilty. The federal judge sentenced him to die by lethal injection.

In a separate trial, Nichols was found guilty as an accessory to the crime and was sentenced to life in prison with no hope of parole. Michael Fortier, who also helped in the planning but who testified against McVeigh, was sentenced to twelve years in prison for his failure to warn the police about the upcoming attack.

On June 11, 2001, McVeigh—who had dropped his legal appeals—was executed in a federal prison in Terre Haute, Indiana.

For More Information

Books

Michel, Lou. *American Terrorist: Timothy McVeigh and the Tragedy at Oklahoma City.* New York: Avon Books, 2002.

Padilla, Lana, and Ron Delpit. *By Blood Betrayed: My Life with Terry Nichols and Timothy McVeigh.* New York: HarperPaperbacks, 1995.

Serrano, Richard A. *One of Ours: Timothy McVeigh and the Oklahoma City Bombing.* New York: Norton, 1998.

Stickney, Brandon M. *All-American Monster: The Unauthorized Biography of Timothy McVeigh.* New York: Prometheus Books, 1996.

Periodicals

Fletcher, George P. "Unsound Constitution: Oklahoma City and the Founding Fathers." *New Republic,* June 23, 1997, p. 14.

Green, Michael. "Shadow Warriors: Suspected Bomber Timothy McVeigh Was Nourished in a Bizarre World of Soldiers and Survivalists." *People Weekly,* May 8, 1995, p. 58.

Hackworth, David H., and Peter Annin. "The Suspect Speaks Out." *Newsweek,* July 3, 1995, p. 22.

George J. Mitchell

August 20, 1933
Waterville, Maine

U.S. Senator from Maine and mediator

"Tonight we can say to the men of violence all across Northern Ireland, those whose tools are bombs and bullets: Your way is not the right way."

George J. Mitchell brought long experience as a negotiator in the U.S. Senate to the thorny problem of terrorist violence in Northern Ireland. The same patience and skill that he used to persuade sharply divided politicians to agree on new legislation proved useful in the entirely different environment of terrorism.

The two diplomatic challenges Mitchell took on—the war between Catholics and Protestants in Northern Ireland and the conflict between Israelis and Palestinians—had both been in progress for generations. Both had seen the use of terrorism as a leading weapon aimed against civilians in order to achieve political objectives. And both included intertwined ethnic and religious divisions that had defied resolution of the conflicts.

In the case of Northern Ireland, George J. Mitchell made a breakthrough. He persuaded both sides to observe a cease-fire and to begin negotiating a peaceful political resolution. In the case of the Israeli-Palestinian conflict, where Mitchell's assignment had a more limited scope—he headed an international commission established to write a report with recommendations on ways to create a peaceful settlement—his success also had a much more limited scope. Neither the Israelis nor the Palestinians enacted the recommendations before a new wave of terrorist violence and government crackdowns made peace seem more elusive than ever.

Childhood and youth

For a man who operated at the peak of power in Washington, D.C., as the Senate Majority Leader, George J. Mitchell came from modest circumstances. He was born in 1933, at the depth of the Great Depression, the son of George Mitchell and Mary Saad Mitchell. His father was a laborer; his mother a factory worker. His father's family had come from Ireland; his mother's ancestors were from Lebanon. Mitchell grew up and went to public school in Waterville, a small town in central Maine.

Mitchell graduated from Bowdoin College (1954), served in the Counter Intelligence Corps of the Army for two years, and graduated from Georgetown University's law school in Washington, D.C., in 1960. He remained in Washington, working as a lawyer for the U.S. Justice Department's Anti-trust Division, prosecuting companies that violated federal laws prohibiting monopolies or anti-competitive business practices. After two years, he took another job: executive assistant to Maine's Senator Edmund Muskie. It was a key turning point in Mitchell's career, which up to that point had been remarkable only insofar as the son of working class parents had already achieved success thanks to education.

Political career

Mitchell's job with Senator Muskie took him back to Maine, and put him in touch with leading Democrats throughout the state. In the next few years, Mitchell filled a succession of political posts, including:

- 1966–68, state chairman for the Maine Democratic Party, a part-time position while Mitchell worked for a private law firm.
- 1968, deputy director for Senator Muskie's unsuccessful vice presidential campaign with Senator Hubert Humphrey.

- 1969–77, Democratic national committeeman (representing Maine at the Democratic Party's national committee).

- 1972, Deputy director for Senator Muskie's campaign for the Democratic presidential nomination.

- 1977–79, U.S. attorney for the state of Maine, selected by President Jimmy Carter.

- 1979–80, U.S. District Court judge.

In 1980, Senator Muskie became U.S. Secretary of State, and George Mitchell was appointed to fill the last two years of Muskie's term as senator. In 1982, Mitchell was elected to the Senate in his own right, and was twice reelected.

As a senator from Maine, Mitchell was particularly active in environmental and health care legislation—including the first major acid rain bill, reauthorization of the Clean Air Act, and federal funding to help clean up toxic waste, as well as the Americans with Disabilities Act and the Clinton administration's effort to provide universal health care. Mitchell was elected as the leader of the Democratic senators in 1989, and served as the majority leader until his retirement.

Peacemaker

In early spring 1994, Mitchell announced that he would not run for another term in November of that year. Shortly thereafter, Justice Harry Blackmun of the U.S. Supreme Court announced he planned to retire, and President Bill Clinton (1946–) offered to nominate Mitchell to be a judge of the court. Mitchell declined, however, intent on working to pass the President's universal health care initiative, with the goal of providing health insurance to all Americans. The effort ultimately failed.

Mitchell left government service in 1995 to practice law and serve on the board of directors of several leading corporations. But a year after he left the Senate, President Clinton asked him to undertake a daunting task: to help negotiate a peaceful settlement of the decades-long religious and political conflict in Northern Ireland. Mitchell was named a special advisor to Clinton and the Secretary of State, and in this role he wrote a report proposing steps to end conflict in Northern Ireland.

Accomplishments as a Senator

As a senator, and as the leader of the Democrats in the Senate, George Mitchell became closely associated with protecting the environment, among other causes. Highlights of laws that Mitchell championed during fourteen years as a senator include:

- Superfund, establishing a fund that helped pay for damages resulting from factories releasing dangerous chemicals into the environment.

- Campaign Finance Reform, an ongoing effort to reduce the influence of wealthy corporate and private contributors to political campaigns.

- Criminal Law Reforms (1984), a major overhaul of federal criminal law. Mitchell served as a strong liberal voice in the Senate; he particularly worked to bar the government from using evidence obtained illegally in trials.

- Clean Water Act of 1987, which overrode President Ronald Reagan's veto (rejection) of a law that would require federal action to maintain clean water.

- Minimum Wage Act 1989, raising the minimum legal wage for the poorest workers.

- North American Wetlands Conservation Act of 1989, preserving lakes, ponds, streams, and rivers used by migrating birds.

- Clean Air Act of 1990, aimed at reducing air pollution and at cleaning up environmental damage caused by acid rain, among other sources.

- Child Care and Development Act, in which the federal government would help to pay for day care facilities offered by state governments to working parents.

- Civil Rights Bill of 1991, extending federal civil rights protection to victims of all forms of harassment and discrimination, whether based on race, gender, religion, or physical disability.

- Brady Bill, establishing the first federal waiting period to buy a gun.

- Universal Health Care, an unsuccessful attempt sponsored by President Bill Clinton to obtain federal funding to provide health care to all Americans.

Mitchell's job was to help three warring sides get together: the Irish Republican Army (IRA) and it's political party, Sinn Féin, representing Northern Ireland's minority Roman Catholics who wanted to unite with the Irish Republic in the south and break away from Britian; the British government, which had been trying to maintain peace over more

George Mitchell, center, acknowledges the applause of fellow recipients of the John F. Kennedy Profile in Courage Award in Boston, Massachusetts, December 7, 1998. Eight political leaders from Northern Ireland joined Mitchell in the honor, including Gerry Adams, right, and John Hume, left. Liz O'Donnell and Paul Murphy are standing. *Photograph reproduced by permission of the Associated Press.*

than two decades of constant terrorist violence; and the Unionists, Protestants in Northern Ireland who insisted on maintaining the province's relationship as a part of Britain, rather than join the Irish Republic.

Mitchell's task was made doubly difficult because the conflict between the two communities in Northern Ireland combined religion with economics and politics. The Catholics in Northern Ireland felt they had long been the victims of job and economic discrimination by Protestants in Northern Ireland. (Northern Ireland, composed of the northern six counties of Ireland, is also known as Ulster.) The Protestants feared that if Ulster were to unite with the Irish Republic, the Protestants would then become a minority, subject to the same discrimination that the Catholics said they had suffered.

Overshadowing these issues were many years of terrorist attacks by both sides that had created strong resentments and a desire on the part of some for revenge. Mitchell began his negotiations in an atmosphere in which mutual trust was nonexistent.

Despite these odds, in January 1996 Mitchell called on both sides to agree to a cease-fire and to disarm gradually. Two years later, in April 1998, the IRA, the Northern Ireland Protestants, and the British government and the Irish Republic (brought into the negotiations as well, since unification of Northern and southern Ireland was long an issue in the conflict) signed an agreement that was put up for a public vote the following month. In that vote, over 70 percent of the voters in Northern Ireland endorsed the Mitchell peace agreement, as did over 90 percent of the voters in the Irish Republic.

Mitchell received the U.S. Presidential Medal of Freedom, the country's highest honor for a civilian, as well as many awards for his work in Ireland.

On to the Middle East

Having succeeded in bringing closure to a conflict that had lasted for most of the twentieth century, Mitchell was asked by President Clinton in mid-2000 to turn his attention to the conflict in the Middle East, between Israel and the Palestinians.

Israel had been founded in 1948 as a homeland for Jews, who had been targeted by the German military during World War II (1939–45). An estimated six million Jews were killed during that time, known as the Holocaust, and the United Nations, originally formed as an international peace-keeping body, hoped the state would provide a safe haven for Jews. Israel was carved out of Palestinian-claimed land, however, and with the creation of the country and in a series of wars following, hundreds of thousands of Palestinians had been driven from their homes and forced to find refuge in other Arab countries. The Israeli-Palestinan conflict has resulted in bloody terrorist attacks for decades.

Mitchell's role in the Middle East was somewhat more limited than his role in Northern Ireland. In the Middle East he was the chairman of a fact-finding committee whose job was to examine the conflict between Israel and the Palestinians. The committee released its report in May 2001, calling on Israel and the Palestinians to take concrete steps to restart peace talks.

The report urged the Palestinians to "make clear through concrete action to Palestinians and Israelis alike that terrorism is reprehensible and unacceptable" and asked them to promise to try to prevent terrorist acts and punish terrorists.

On the Israeli side, the report called on Israel to stop new settlements from being built on land won by Israel in the 1967 Six Day War.

Despite the prestige of George Mitchell, there was no immediate move by neither Israel nor the Palestinians to adopt the steps recommended in his committee's report. Instead, violence between the two sides continued to escalate.

After issuing the report, Mitchell left public life and pursued a career as a lawyer and businessman.

For More Information

Books

Mitchell, George J. *Making Peace*. New York: Knopf, 1999.

Mitchell, George J. *Not for America Alone: The Triumph of Democracy and the Fall of Communism*. New York: Kodansha International, 1997.

Mitchell, George J. *World on Fire: Saving an Endangered Earth*. New York: Charles Scribner's Sons, 1991.

Periodicals

"Dinner with George: How a Bit of Personal Diplomacy Helped Get the Good Friday Peace Agreement Back on Track." *Time International*, November 29, 1999, p. 20.

"Mitchell, George John," *Current Biography*, April 1989, p. 40.

"Peace Comes Dropping Slow: Hopes for the Deadlocked Negotiations Are Now Focused on Former U.S. Senator George Mitchell." *Time International*, September 13, 1999, p. 22

"Yes to a Ceasefire, No to a Halt on Settlements: Israel and the Palestinians: Ceasefires and Settlers in the Middle East." *The Economist*, May 26, 2001, p. 1.

Abu Nidal
(Sabri al Banna)

May 1937
Jaffa, Palestine Mandate
August 18, 2002
Baghdad, Iraq

Founder of the Abu Nidal Organization

S abri al Banna, the man better known as Abu Nidal, was considered the most dangerous terrorist in the world during the 1970s, much as **Osama bin Laden** (c. 1957–; see entry) would be known thirty years later. He turned his guns and bombs against both Israeli and Palestinian targets. He was as concerned with making sure that Palestinian leaders did not sign a peace agreement with Israel as he was with fighting Israel directly.

Abu Nidal became known as a "gun for hire," working for a variety of governments. Eventually he became unwelcome in most Arab countries and faded from public view.

Born into wealth

Al Banna's life is such a mystery that his exact date of birth is unclear. He was one of two dozen children born to his father, Khalil al Banna, a wealthy businessman and farmer who owned 6,000 acres of land near the city of Jaffa, on the Mediterranean coast of Palestine (now Israel). He was born in a twenty-room house facing the Mediterranean Sea. His mother, a Syrian woman, was his father's eighth wife. Accord-

"In the entire world there are no solutions by peaceful means. If you read Arabic history you will see that no peaceful method has ever brought about a solution for our problems."

Photograph reproduced by permission of the Corbis Corporation.

ing to some sources, al Banna's mother was a family maid at a summer house in Syria when his father married her. After his father died in 1945, when al Banna was eight years old, he and his mother were scorned by the rest of the family. His mother was eventually ordered to leave the house.

Al Banna was sent to private schools, but his education was soon interrupted by the conflict between Arabs and Jews. When al Banna was born, Jaffa was part of the territory called the Palestine Mandate. It had been part of the Turkish Ottoman Empire for centuries, but after World War I (1914–18) Great Britain took over the area until its future could be sorted out. Arabs wanted to create a new country, Palestine. Jews, who had been immigrating to Palestine for several decades as part of a movement called **Zionism**, wanted to establish a Jewish state, Israel, on the lands that had been the Jewish homeland in biblical times. Violence between the two groups broke out from time to time during the 1930s.

Life disrupted

Two months after al Banna started the fourth grade, in 1947, the United Nations General Assembly voted to divide Palestine into two countries, a Jewish one and an Arab one. This decision sparked more intense fighting as the two sides struggled to gain control of territory, and it brought al Banna's education to an end. His family decided to leave their house until the fighting was over. But the fighting did not end until the state of Israel was founded in May 1948, and by then it was impossible for the al Bannas to return to Jaffa. By the time al Banna was eleven, his family had joined thousands of other Palestinian Arab refugees and were living in a refugee camp in the Gaza Strip, a piece of land governed by Egypt.

Becoming a refugee came at a critical time in al Banna's life. Some writers have speculated that bitterness over the loss of his home lies at the heart of his later life as a terrorist. As an adult, however, al Banna did not openly discuss his personal life or motives.

Eventually, the al Banna family moved to the city of Nablus, on the West Bank of the Jordan River in Jordan, and went into business as merchants. As with so much of al Banna's life, details of the years from age twelve to eighteen are not clear. Some sources say that he graduated from high school in 1955 and studied engineering at Cairo University in Egypt for two years. Others say he never returned to school full-time after the fourth grade and spent his teenage years working at odd jobs or as an electrician's assistant.

According to most sources, while living in Nablus, al Banna joined the Ba'ath Party in his late teens. The Ba'athists, who sought to unify all Arabs into one nation that did not respect the right of Israel to exist (see box on page 200), soon came into conflict with Jordan's King Hussein (1935–1999). Hussein used his army to arrest Ba'ath leaders and close the party's newspaper. Al Banna left Jordan (some sources say he was arrested along with other Ba'athists) and moved to Riyadh, the capital of Saudi Arabia, where he worked as an electrician's assistant.

Al Banna becomes Abu Nidal

While working in Riyadh, al Banna became active in the fight against Israel among Palestinian exiles. He founded his own small group—called the Palestinian Secret Organization—to fight for Palestinian independence. He also took a wife, a Palestinian from a leading family that, like his own, had been forced to leave their home after Israel was founded in 1948.

The year 1967, when al Banna turned thirty, was a major turning point for him. In June Israel launched the Six Day War, a lightning strike against Arab forces that extended its territory into Syria and Egypt, as well as the West Bank of the Jordan and the Gaza Strip. Al Banna's political activities came to the attention of the very conservative (traditional) Saudi Arabian government, which threw him out of the country. Unable to return to Nablus, which was now located in Israeli-occupied territory, al Banna moved to Amman, the capital of Jordan. He left the Ba'ath Party and joined the largest and most successful Palestinian resistance group, al-Fatah, led by **Yasir Arafat** (1929–; see entry).

The Ba'ath Party

In his late teens, Sabri al Banna became involved with the Ba'ath movement, an Arab social and political movement that eventually took power in Syria and Iraq (although in different forms). The Ba'ath movement was an important part of al Banna's life. It helps explain why he carried out terrorist attacks for several different Arab governments.

The Ba'ath movement was founded in Damascus, Syria, in the 1940s. It wanted a "rebirth" (the word "ba'ath" means "resurrection" or "rebirth" in Arabic) of a united Arab nation. Its economic philosophy was socialism, meaning state control of the economy. The socialism of the Ba'ath Party was similar to the "socialism" of German National Socialism (the official name for the Nazis, who controlled Germany during World War II [1939–45]). It was based on the concept of the unity of the Arab people. Communism, by contrast, focuses on the unity of working people of all nationalities. A central belief of the Ba'ath movement has always been re-creating the Arab nation and driving out foreign influences and control. Officially, the party also has stood for unifying the separate Arab states, many of which were established by Britain and France after World War I (1914–18).

Believers in Ba'ath's philosophy seized control of the Syrian government in 1958. But quarrels among the Ba'athists sent some (including the Syrian founders of the movement) into exile in Baghdad, Iraq, in the mid-1960s, setting up a long rivalry between the Ba'ath parties in these two countries.

Despite their differences, the Ba'athists agreed on the concept of a single Arab "nation" that did not accept the existence of a Jewish state—Israel. An important position of the Ba'athists was the rejection of any peace treaties that recognized Israel's right to exist.

In order to support their interests in the region without starting an actual war, Ba'athists in Syria founded an organization called al-Sa'iqa in 1968. Most of its members were Palestinian, but it was almost completely dependent on Syria for money and support. It used terrorist tactics to fight not only for Palestinian interests but also to found a single, unified Arab state. The rival Ba'athists in Iraq set up their own terrorist force, called the Arab Liberation Front, in 1969.

The idea of a single Arab nation helps explain how al Banna was able to serve both Syria and Iraqi interests during the years when his own group (the Abu Nidal Organization) was active.

One of the three Abu Nidal Organization hijackers of EgyptAir Flight 648 appears at the plane's doorway, Malta, 1985. *Photograph reproduced by permission of AP/Wide World Photos.*

Fatah was actively involved in launching guerrilla raids (or terrorist attacks, from the Israeli viewpoint) against Israel. Its members frequently took new names. Al Banna chose "Abu Nidal," which means "father of the struggle" in Arabic. It was the name under which he would become famous.

The leaders of Fatah were often well educated, but despite his lack of formal education, Abu Nidal rose quickly through the ranks. He may have succeeded because he came from a leading and once-wealthy Palestinian family, because he joined Fatah as the founder of his own organization, or simply because of his hard work and loyalty to the cause.

The Abu Nidal Organization

In 1969 Abu Nidal became Fatah's representative in Khartoum, the capital of Sudan in east Africa. Two years later, Arafat appointed Abu Nidal to represent the Palestine Liberation Organization (PLO) in Baghdad, Iraq, where a faction of the Ba'athists, Abu Nidal's old party, was in control.

The Deadly Record of Abu Nidal

Abu Nidal has been blamed for more than ninety terrorist attacks and nine hundred deaths since he left Fatah in 1974. At least half of his attacks were aimed at other Palestinian organizations or their Arab allies. A list of his most infamous attacks includes:

- October 1974: Tried to assassinate Abu Mazim, an official of Fatah. Fatah sentenced Abu Nidal to death as a result.

- September-October 1976: Attacked the Semiramis Hotel in Damascus, Syria, and Syrian embassies in Islamabad, Pakistan, and Rome, Italy. Syria was Iraq's political rival at the time.

- December 1976: Tried to murder Syria's foreign minister, but the attack failed. The following October, made another attempt, this time in Abu Dhabi in the United Arab Emirates; the attack resulted instead in the death of the foreign affairs minister of the United Arab Emirates.

- August 1978: Attacked Palestine Liberation Organization (PLO) offices in Pakistan.

- July 1980: Attacked children in a Jewish school in Antwerp, Belgium, and claimed responsibility for murdering an Israeli diplomat in Brussels, Belgium.

- August 1981: Machine-gun attack on a synagogue (a Jewish house of worship) in Vienna, Austria, killed two and wounded seventeen.

- June 1982: Tried to kill Israel's ambassador to Britain.

- August-September 1982: Tried to kill a diplomat from the United Arab Emirates in Bombay, India, and a Kuwaiti diplomat in Madrid, Spain.

Abu Nidal quickly developed a close working relationship with Iraqi intelligence, using his position as the PLO's representative to build up his own organization. Abu Nidal agreed with the Iraqi position of rejecting any negotiations with Israel, which might imply that Israel had a right to exist.

In September 1973 Abu Nidal organized his first terrorist operation, seizing the embassy of Saudi Arabia in Paris, France, and demanding the release of a Fatah terrorist, Abu Dawud, who was being held prisoner in Jordan. Although Abu Nidal was still Fatah's representative, Fatah had not approved the Paris operation and threw Abu Nidal out of the group the following year.

- October 1982: Attacked a synagogue in Rome, killing one child and injuring ten other people.

- April 1983: Killed a PLO official in Lisbon, Portugal.

- November 1984: Assassinated the British high commissioner in India.

- December 1984: Killed a leading Palestinian supporter of Yasir Arafat in Rome.

- March-April 1985: Attacked the offices of Royal Jordanian Airlines in Rome, injuring three people. The next month, fired a rocket at a Jordanian airliner leaving Athens, Greece. The rocket did not explode but left a hole in the plane's fuselage.

- September 1985: Wounded thirty-eight people in a grenade attack at the Café de Paris in Rome. Hijacked an Egyptian plane to Malta, where sixty people died in a botched rescue attempt by Egyptian forces.

- December 1985: Attacks on airport passenger terminals in Rome and Vienna killed sixteen and wounded many more.

- September 1986: Tried to hijack an American plane, Pan American Flight 73, from Karachi, Pakistan. Less than twenty-four hours later attacked a synagogue in Istanbul, Turkey, killing twenty-two people.

- July 1988: Seized the tourist excursion boat *City of Poros,* killing nine passengers and wounding ninety-eight, from the port of Athens.

- January 1991: Assassinated two PLO officials in Tunis, Tunisia, including Arafat's second-in-command, Abu Iyad.

In response, Abu Nidal founded his own group, which he called the Fatah Revolutionary Council, with financial help from the Iraqi government. He began a long career as one of the deadliest terrorists in the Middle East conflict.

Over the course of nearly twenty years, Abu Nidal operated with a core group of about two hundred agents. Conditions of membership were strict: once a man joined, he was not allowed to quit the group. At first Abu Nidal remained in Baghdad, and his choice of targets sometimes reflected the needs and policies of the Iraqi government.

Abu Nidal's welcome in Iraq wore thin, however, during Iraq's war against Iran (1980–88). Iraq needed supplies and support from the West, and in 1983 Iraq drove out Abu Nidal in order to distance itself from terrorism. The Abu Nidal Organization moved to Syria, which was ruled by a rival faction of the Ba'ath Party.

Abu Nidal stayed in Syria for three years (1983–86), during which time one of his main tasks was to oppose any peace negotiations between the PLO and Israel. In September 1986, Syria came under pressure from Western governments for supporting terrorism. As a result, the Syrian government closed Abu Nidal's training camps, and he left for Libya, whose leader, **Mu'ammar Qaddafi** (1942–; see entry), supported a widespread Arab revolt.

Abu Nidal fades from the spotlight

In 1989 the chief spokesman for Abu Nidal's movement publicly left the organization, along with a large number of other fighters. They accused Abu Nidal of murdering more than one hundred members of the group. The next year, Abu Nidal tried to gain control over Palestinian refugee camps in Lebanon from Arafat, but failed to do so. These two developments, plus reports that Abu Nidal had left Libya suffering from **leukemia** (an often fatal disease affecting the blood, which causes an abnormal increase in the number of white blood cells), greatly reduced his effectiveness.

But by then, another radical seeking to unify the Arab world had taken center stage: Osama bin Laden.

Abu Nidal was reported to have returned to Baghdad, Iraq, for medical treatment, but by the 1990s, his involvement in active terrorism appeared to have ended. As the twenty-first century began, his location, and even whether he was dead or alive, was unknown.

In August 2002, however, news reports said that Abu Nidal had been found dead in Baghdad. Initial reports noted he had several gunshot wounds. The same reports also said he had apparently committed suicide.

In the course of his terrorist career, Abu Nidal had two targets: Israel, and Arab states and organizations that proposed negotiating a peace agreement with Israel. Abu Nidal was a leading supporter of the "rejectionist front," those Arabs totally committed to the destruction of Israel and opposed to any proposal that would recognize Israel's right to exist.

Abu Nidal's unbending position toward Israel earned him many enemies in the Arab world, as well as in Western Europe and the United States. Although it waged a long and bloody fight, by the early 1990s the Abu Nidal Organization had achieved few results (besides a reputation as dangerous) for its efforts. Arafat was then on the verge of winning the Nobel Peace Prize for negotiating a peace settlement with Israel. Abu Nidal himself had been forced to move from one Arab country to the next as governments found it in their best interest to oppose terrorism.

For More Information

Books

Melman, Yossi. *The Master Terrorist: The True Story of Abu Nidal.* New York: Adama Books, 1986.

Nasr, Kameel B. *Arab and Israeli Terrorism: The Causes and Effects of Political Violence, 1936–1993.* Jefferson, NC: McFarland Publishers, 1996.

Seale, Patrick. *Abu Nidal: A Gun for Hire.* New York: Random House, 1992.

Periodicals

Norland, Rod. "The 'Evil Spirit'; for Sheer Viciousness, Abu Nidal Has Few Rivals in the Underworld of Terrorism." *Newsweek,* January 13, 1986, p. 23.

Russell, George. "Master of Mystery and Murder; for the Shadowy Abu Nidal, Terror Is a Way of Life." *Time,* January 13, 1986, p. 31.

Mu'ammar Qaddafi

1942
Near Surt, Libya

Leader of Libya

"Palestine cannot be restored by negative means, not by classes, nor by donations. It can only be attained by the march of the Arab masses, free of fetters, restrictions and narrow regionalism."

T he leader of the North African nation of Libya since 1970, Mu'ammar Qaddafi has long been criticized in the West for supporting terrorist organizations in the Middle East and Europe, as well as for directly ordering terrorist attacks on American targets.

Qaddafi has tried to put into action what he calls the Third Universal Theory, which is a blend of socialist economics, in which the government controls the economy, popular democracy, and Islamic law. He has long opposed the influence of Western nations, including the United States, on less-developed countries.

Born in a tent

Qaddafi was born in 1942—the exact date is not known—in a tent in the desert about 20 miles (32 kilometers) from the coastal town of Surt, Libya. His family made a living herding goats and camels. Bedouin (pronounced BED-oo-in) tribesmen, they led a nomadic (wandering) life and strictly followed the rules of Islam (see box on page 210).

Qaddafi's Bedouin origins shaped his adulthood. Although he left his family to attend high school and later to become an army officer, as the leader of Libya he received guests in a camel-skin tent while wearing Bedouin robes. He also enforced the strict moral codes he learned as a child, as well as the democratic decision-making that is characteristic of Bedouin society.

Italy had invaded Libya in 1911, and thousands of Italians moved there over the next few decades, taking the best land for farms. But Italian control was not secure by the beginning of World War II (1939–45), which saw Italian rule swept aside by American and English forces fighting the allied forces of Germany and Italy. Because Libya had not been an independent country before the war, the United Nations oversaw the territory until 1951, trying to decide what form of government should be put in place and who should be the head of state. Finally, at the end of 1951, the country of Libya was organized from three provinces. Muhammad Idris al-Sanusi (1890–1983), a Libyan spiritual and political leader, was put into power as King Idris I.

Words to Know

Anarchists: people who believe that society should be organized around voluntary associations, rather than large government organizations.

Atheism: the belief that there is no God.

Democracy: a form of government in which the citizens vote for their representatives.

Fundamentalist: a person who believes in living by a set of strict moral principles.

Sharia: Islamic law.

Socialism: a system in which there is no private property, and business and industry are owned by the workers.

Radio Cairo

The sort of political conflict that took place in Libya was also occurring throughout the Arab world, where England and France had divided the former Ottoman Empire into separate countries after World War I (1914–18). In Egypt, President Gamal Abdel Nasser (1918–1970) had a vision of joining these states into a single country that could stand up to their former European masters. Nasser also put **socialism** (an economic system in which there is no private property; business and industry are owned by the workers) into practice in Egypt. The Egyptian president spread his views through radio broadcasts from Cairo that could easily be heard in nearby countries.

Qaddafi vs. Khadafy

English-language publishers translating the name of Libya's leader into English use several spellings. Among them are:

- Muammar Qaddafi

- Moammar Khadafy

- Moammar Gadhafi

The pronunciation in English is mow-AH-mahr gah-DAW-fee, although the "G" sound may also be pronounced as a "K."

As a high school student, Qaddafi spent hours listening to Nasser's speeches, even memorizing some of them. Qaddafi was so enthusiastic that he organized a group of classmates to put Nasser's ideas into practice in Libya. Qaddafi's closest friends in high school were the same men who became his top assistants after he took power. In addition to supporting Nasser's idea of a unified socialist Arab state, Qaddafi insisted this his friends observe strict Islamic moral codes, such as not drinking alcohol. Qaddafi was eventually thrown out of school for leading students in marches in support of Nasser and criticizing King Idris.

After he was expelled from high school, Qaddafi enrolled in a military college in the Libyan city of Benghazi. There he continued his political activities, organizing a group of friends into the Free Officers Movement. After graduating from military college in 1965, he went to England for further military training. At the time, Libya had close ties to Britain and the United States. But Qaddafi wanted to rid Libya of foreign influences, and for the next three years he worked inside the military to promote the idea of overthrowing King Idris.

Birth of a nation

Idris had allied with Britain during World War II, and after the war Britain helped arrange for him to become the head of Libya. Idris was friendly toward Britain and the United States. He allowed both countries to have military bases on Libyan territory and let them practice bombing runs in the Libyan desert. At the time, Libya was desperately poor, with few economic resources and fewer than two million people. The financial and military aid provided by the United States in exchange for the bases was a major source of income. This changed abruptly in 1959, when high-quality oil was discovered in the Libyan desert. Libya signed agreements with American oil firms to drill and sell the oil in exchange for half the

profits. Suddenly, Libya went from a poor desert nation to one that had a huge income from oil. Like Saudi Arabia, which had undergone a similar transformation twenty years earlier, Libya became a strong ally of the United States, a major oil customer.

But in 1967 another event shook Libya: the so-called Six Day War between Israel and its Arab neighbors, including Egypt. (The Jewish state of Israel was founded in 1948 on Palestinian Arab lands previously governed by the British.) Libya did not take part in the conflict—its army was small and would not have been much help—but the defeat of Egypt and the other Arab countries raised intense emotions in many people, including Qaddafi.

Coup d'etat

Two years later, on September 1, 1969, a group of about seventy army officers seized control of the Libyan government from the monarchy, whose support had been declining

Mu'ammar Qaddafi was the son of Bedouin tribesmen, who typically herd animals in the desert and live in tents. The simple lifestyle of the Bedouin and their democratic decision-making helped shape Qaddafi's political ideas as leader of Libya. *Photograph reproduced by permission of the Corbis Corporation.*

The Bedouin

The Bedouin (pronounced BED-oo-in) are nomadic (meaning they move from place to place) Arabs who live throughout the Middle East, mostly in desert areas. They are Muslims who usually earn a living by herding camels and goats. They are known for living a simple life and for observing a strict Islamic moral code. Families wander recognized areas with their livestock. Each tribe, consisting of member families, is a group of equals, headed by a sheikh (pronounced sheek).

rapidly. It was a peaceful coup d'etat (pronounced coo day-TAH, the takeover of a government) that lasted just two hours. No deaths or injuries were reported. The Free Officers Movement claimed credit for the coup and put twelve of its members in charge of the country, calling them the Revolutionary Command Council (RCC). Among those twelve was Qaddafi, then twenty-seven years old. A week after the coup, the RCC promoted Captain Qaddafi to the rank of colonel (the highest Libyan military rank), and appointed him commander in chief of the armed forces.

The RCC insisted that it was ruling Libya as a committee. But Qaddafi's promotion to head of the armed forces and his forceful personality soon created the impression that he was in charge. It was typical of Qaddafi's role in Libya that he was not named head of state or head of government. Nevertheless, he was widely recognized as the man in control of the country.

Qaddafi's vision: The Third Universal Theory

Qaddafi had long dreamed of uniting the Arab people into a single country, just as Nasser of Egypt had. After he seized power, Qaddafi took Nasser's ideas further. In addition to forming one big Arab state, he wanted it to be ruled by Islamic law and socialist economic principles and to have greater social equality. Instead of Western-style **democracy,** he supported what he called "Popular Congresses," meetings of all citizens who could vote directly on all issues instead of relying on representatives sent to a congress or parliament. He also positioned Libya as the champion of all countries occupied as colonies by European powers, and he approved of terrorism as a way for those countries to achieve independence. Qaddafi called his policies the "Third Universal Theory," which he described in detail in *The Green Book,* published in three parts starting in 1976.

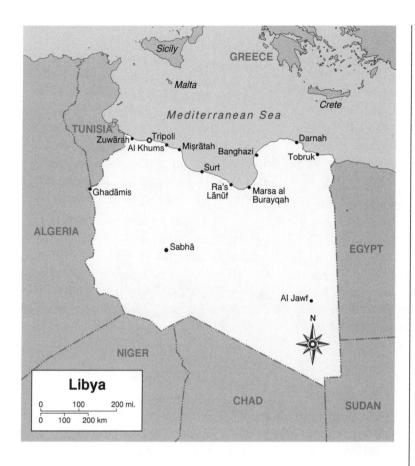

Libya's close proximity to Egypt allowed a young Mu'ammar Qaddafi to listen to radio broadcasts of Egyptian president Gamal Abdel Nasser, who greatly influenced Qaddafi.

At the time *The Green Book* was written, the world was largely divided into two camps: communist countries allied with the Soviet Union (today, Russia and its neighboring countries), and anticommunist countries allied with the United States. (Communism is an economic system that advocates the elimination of private property; under it, goods and the means to produce them are owned by the community as a whole and, in theory, are available through the government to all as needed. It is the opposite of capitalism, the economic system followed by the United States, in which individuals own property.) The conflict between the two sides, which lasted from 1945 to 1990, was known as the Cold War. Qaddafi's plan was to create a third system, a combination of Islamic law, socialism, and direct democracy. Qaddafi hoped his theories would help Arabs resist the influences of former

What Year Is It?

To promote Islam in Libya, Mu'ammar Qaddafi announced that the country would use the Islamic calendar. But which one?

At first Qaddafi switched from the standard Islamic calendar—which counts the years since the founder of Islam, Muhammad (c. 570–632), moved from Mecca to Medina (in present-day Saudi Arabia) and founded the religion—to a calendar that counts the years since Muhammad's birth. Then Qaddafi switched to a third calendar that counts the years since Muhammad's death. (In Islamic societies, it is customary to recite the phrase "peace be upon him" after the name of the prophet Muhammad. In writing, this is usually expressed by the initials "pbuh." This phrase is implied throughout this book.)

The changes were not observed by everyone in Libya. A Libyan newspaper printed in early 2001 (according to the Christian calendar) published a legal bulletin titled "No. 4 for 1431." The date on the newspaper was 1369. For most of the Muslim world, it was 1421.

colonial powers such as Britain and France, as well as the United States. The Third Universal Theory placed Libya in opposition to the Western countries, including the United States, but also kept it independent of Soviet influence during the Cold War.

Islamic cultural revolution

Qaddafi's ideas on how society should be organized were rooted in his Bedouin childhood. Bedouin tribal society, which is found throughout the Arab world, lives simply and strictly observes the rules of Islam. Tribes are headed by a sheikh (pronounced sheek), but male members discuss and vote on issues as a group of individuals.

Instead of setting up a standard democracy with an elected congress, as in the United States, Qaddafi insisted that Libyans should vote directly on laws and policies through Popular Congresses. At least twice a year, all Libyan adults were required to attend sessions of their local Popular Congress. On one hand, this guaranteed that people would have a voice in government. On the other hand, it meant that political parties had no role in government. This made it difficult to organize challenges to Qaddafi's policies.

In 1977 Qaddafi officially changed the name of his country to the Socialist People's Libyan Arab Jamahiriya. The Arabic word *jamahiriya* means "state of the masses." The new name implied that Libya was ruled directly by the people without need for a formal government. The idea reminded some people of ideas put forward by anarchists (people who believed that society should be organized around voluntary associations, rather than large government organizations) in the nineteenth century. To others, the new name seemed more symbolic than evidence of a real change.

As the leader of Libya, Qaddafi took steps to introduce Bedouin values and Islamic rules into everyday life. He issued decrees to make Islamic law (called **Sharia**) the basis for all laws and to practice a "pure" form of Islam. He banned alcohol, nightclubs, and immodest dress and behavior in public and began to use traditional Islamic punishments, such as cutting off the hand of a convicted thief or whipping people caught eating during the day in the month-long fasting period of Ramadan. Some of Qaddafi's decisions had confusing, even comical results, such as his order that Libya would observe the Islamic calendar (see box).

Qaddafi also set up religious schools to train Islamic teachers to spread his views of how Islam should govern into other countries, as well as to bring Islam into Africa to replace Christianity, which European missionaries had introduced in the nineteenth century. With Libya's oil money, he founded and paid for the Islamic Mission Society to build and repair mosques (Muslim houses of worship) and education centers around the world, from Vienna, Austria, to Bangkok, Thailand. These efforts were often unwelcome in other Muslim countries, which viewed them as attempts to take a hand in their internal affairs.

In the 1990s Qaddafi's views on Islam came into conflict with traditional Islamic religious figures, as well as with fundamentalist (extremely strict) Islamic organizations such as Egypt's Muslim Brotherhood. While the Muslim Brotherhood often used terrorist tactics to spread the influence of Islam, Qaddafi insisted that Islam should be promoted in the open.

By the 1990s radical (extremist) Islamists began to launch terrorist attacks against the Libyan government.

Islamic socialism

Although Qaddafi rejected communism because communists supported **atheism**, or a belief that there is no God, he believed in socialism, the economic system of which communism was an offshoot, just as Egypt's Nasser had. Starting in 1969, his new government took over many privately owned companies, including part of the oil industry, in which American oil companies had a major stake. This greatly increased Libya's income from oil. Qaddafi's takeover of American property upset the United States, which opposed socialism wherever it appeared. To make relations with the United States worse, Qaddafi insisted that American military forces leave all their bases in Libya, including the giant Wheelus Air Force Base.

Qaddafi put some of the state-owned oil income to use in improving the lives of his countrymen. He built roads and schools and provided a wide range of benefits for ordinary citizens. This made Qaddafi widely popular in the country. He was viewed as "the Leader" who took back from foreign powers what rightfully belonged to all Libyans and used it to improve their lives.

Creating a single Arab nation

In 1970 Qaddafi began talks with leaders of Egypt and the Sudan (and later Syria) to create a single Arab country. An agreement was announced in April 1971 for Libya, Egypt, and Syria to create the Federation of Arab Republics. Officially the federation came into existence on January 1, 1972, led by Egypt's President Anwar el-Sadat (1918–1981). But Sadat and Qaddafi soon disagreed on how quickly the countries should merge. In October 1973, Egypt and Syria launched a war against Israel (called the Yom Kippur War), but they left out Libya, to Qaddafi's intense irritation. Relations soured to the extent that Libya and Egypt fought a brief war along their border in 1977. The idea of the federation finally broke down completely in 1978, after Sadat negotiated a peace treaty with Israel.

Efforts by Qaddafi to unite with Tunisia, a neighboring Arab state, and with Syria without Egypt, also failed. In the 1980s Qaddafi unsuccessfully tried to form alliances with African states south of the Sahara desert.

Foreign relations and terrorism

Qaddafi had long opposed American and British influence in Libya. His insisting that the United States and its ally Great Britain abandon their bases in Libya combined with the seizure of property of American oil companies (along with most property owned by foreigners) soon made Qaddafi highly unpopular with the government of the United States.

In addition to spending on his countrymen, Qaddafi also used part of Libya's oil money to finance foreign groups fighting what he called "wars of national liberation" against the European powers. Qaddafi's contributions helped buy arms for use in terrorist attacks. Dozens of groups received Libyan aid, including the Irish Republican Army (IRA), which was fighting against British rule in Northern Ireland, and a variety of organizations fighting against Israel under the banner of the Palestine Liberation Organization (PLO). After disastrous wars between Arab nations and Israel in 1967 and 1973, terrorism became the principal tactic in the Palestinians' fight to destroy Israel and replace it with a Palestinian nation.

In the late 1970s and 1980s, a variety of Palestinian groups accounted for many terrorist actions in the Middle East and in Europe. Libya was closely associated with these groups through its financial support. Qaddafi also set up training camps for terrorists in the Libyan desert.

Aid to terrorist groups

Libya has been accused of supporting a wide range of terrorist organizations around the world, about fifty groups altogether. In the Middle East, these groups include the PLO, Hamas, and the Abu Nidal Organization. In Europe, the list includes the IRA and the Red Brigades in Italy. In Asia, it includes Islamic terrorist groups in the Philippines and radicals active in Japan.

In 1976 Libya and Algeria secretly agreed to provide guns and money to help groups in Europe that were seeking

A bomb planted on a Pan Am 747 exploded over the village of Lockerbie, Scotland, raining wreckage down on the town. The terrorist act killed 270 people, including 11 people on the ground. A Libyan agent was eventually convicted of destroying the plane. *Photograph reproduced by permission of AP/Wide World Photos.*

independence from Spain and France. These included the Basques in Spain and Bretons and Corsicans in France.

In the Western hemisphere, Libya has sent money to the Sandinistas in Nicaragua (a socialist party that the United States fought secretly in the 1980s) and to other left-wing groups in El Salvador. In 1983 a planeload of Libyan supplies meant for a Colombia guerrilla group called M19 landed in Brazil.

In September 1986 Qaddafi declared in a speech to the Organization of Non-Aligned States that he would "do everything in my power to divide the world into imperialists and freedom-fighters." (An imperialist nation is one that tries to extend its power by conquering or controlling other countries.) Groups that attacked the "imperialists" (first and foremost the United States, in his view) were entirely justified in their actions. "National liberation," he said, "can only be achieved through armed struggle."

Some analysts believe the wide range of groups supported by Qaddafi reveals his interest in attacking countries he sees as hostile to his government, rather than support for the terrorists he helps bankroll.

State terrorism

Qaddafi has also been accused of taking part directly in terrorist attacks. On April 5, 1986, a Libyan terrorist planted a 5-pound (2.3-kilogram) bomb in the Labelle Disco, a nightclub in West Berlin, Germany, that was popular with American soldiers. The explosion killed two American soldiers and a Turkish woman and injured more than two hundred others, including seventy-two Americans. The bombing was apparently revenge for an attack the month before, in which U.S. planes sank two Libyan patrol boats in the Gulf of Sirte in the Mediterranean. Libya had claimed control of the gulf in 1981, and the United States had been challenging this claim ever since. (Fifteen years later, the United States got proof that agents from Libya's embassy in East Germany were indeed responsible for the Berlin bombing. They were arrested, tried, convicted, and sentenced to twelve to fourteen years in prison.)

Ten days after the nightclub attack, U.S. Air Force jets bombed Tripoli, the Libyan capital, and the city of Benghazi. Their target apparently was Qaddafi himself. Although the Libyan leader escaped unharmed, the attack killed fifteen civilians, including Qaddafi's young adopted daughter.

On December 21, 1988, a bomb exploded on Pan American Flight 103 from London, England, to New York. The explosion killed 259 people on the plane and 11 on the ground in the village of Lockerbie, Scotland. After a long investigation, American and British investigators determined that Libyan agents were responsible and demanded that Qaddafi hand over two suspects. Qaddafi refused, and in 1992 the United States and Britain persuaded the United Nations (UN) to ban foreign trade with Libya until the suspects were handed over. This finally happened in April 1999. The two were tried in the Netherlands by Scottish judges; one was convicted and sentenced to life in prison.

The Pan Am attack was not the only such incident blamed on Libya. The following year, 1989, Libyan agents blew up a French airliner over the African country of Niger, killing 171 people, including 6 Americans. A decade later, France convicted six Libyans in absentia (in their absence) of the crime, including Qaddafi's brother-in-law. Shortly afterward the Libyan government effectively admitted its role by paying $31 million to the relatives of those killed.

The economic sanctions put into place by the United Nations proved costly to Qaddafi. The Pan Am bombing was widely criticized, and Libya became cut off from other countries. Qaddafi's long dream of uniting countries under his Third Universal Theory gained no ground, and Qaddafi lost his role as a leader of national liberation movements. In addition, international oil prices dropped and Libya's oil production fell, meaning much less money was available to finance Qaddafi's schemes at home and abroad. Many observers thought his decision to hand over the Pan Am bombing suspects in 1999 was evidence that he had changed his mind about supporting terrorism, and saw it as his bid to build more normal relations with other countries. But as the twenty-first century began, the UN sanctions against Libya continued.

For More Information

Books

Blundy, David, and Andrew Lycett. *Qaddafi and the Libyan Revolution.* New York: Little, Brown, 1987.

Cooley, John K. *Libyan Sandstorm.* New York: Hold, Rinehart, and Winston, 1982.

Tanter, Raymond. *Rogue Regimes: Terrorism and Proliferation.* New York: St. Martin's Press, 1998.

Periodicals

Borrel, John, and George Church. "Targeting Gaddafi: Reagan Readies Revenge on a 'Mad Dog.'" *Time,* April 21, 1986, p. 18.

Cooley, John K. "The Libyan Menace." *Foreign Policy,* Spring 1981, p. 74.

"Gaddafi of Libya: Prophet of Outrage," *Life,* February 1980, p. 102.

Grogan, David. "A Jackal at Bay." *People Weekly,* May 5, 1986, p. 42.

"Qaddafi, Muammar al." *Current Biography,* March 1992, p. 39.

"Survey of Arab Affairs." *Jerusalem Letters/Viewpoints,* June 1, 1992.

Takeyh, Ray. "The Rogue Who Came in from the Cold." *Foreign Affairs,* May-June, 2001, p. 62.

Tom Ridge

August 26, 1945
Pittsburgh, Pennsylvania

Director of the Office of Homeland Security

Tom Ridge and George W. Bush (1946–) shared several important experiences. Both attended Ivy League schools (Harvard for Ridge and Yale for Bush), and both had been governors of big states (Pennsylvania in Ridge's case, Texas in Bush's). So it was not surprising when Bush, who had become president eight months earlier, named his friend Ridge to be the Director of Homeland Security in September 2001, a job intended to organize the government response to the terrorist attacks of September 11, 2001.

The United States was still in a state of shock on September 21, just ten days after the attacks on the World Trade Center in New York City and on the U.S. military headquarters at the Pentagon near Washington, D.C., in which terrorists flew hijacked planes into the buildings, killing about three thousand people. President Bush appeared before a joint session of the Senate and House of Representatives to describe in a televised speech how he would respond to the attacks. Abroad, Bush said, he would focus on tracking down **Osama bin Laden** (c. 1957–; see entry), believed to be the ringleader of the attacks. At home, the highlight was appointing a single

"This historic proposal would be the most significant transformation of the U.S. government since 1947. The creation of this department would transform the current confusing patchwork of government activities related to homeland security into a single department whose primary mission is to protect our homeland."

person to organize antiterrorist efforts. At the time, few were thinking about the political consequences of the response; the main concern was national unity in the face of the attacks on the capital and the country's biggest city.

Modest origins

Although Bush and Ridge were born within a year of each other, their origins and childhoods were very different. Ridge's father was a veteran of World War II (1939–45), and after the war he and his family lived in government housing for veterans near Pittsburgh, Pennsylvania, a major steel manufacturing city. They later lived in Erie, another manufacturing town near Pittsburgh. The Ridges were politically active on different sides of the fence: Ridge's father was a Democrat, and his mother was a Republican.

Ridge was a good student in high school and won a scholarship to Harvard University, one of the highest-ranked colleges in the country, from which he graduated in 1967. From Harvard, Ridge went to the Dickinson School of Law, part of Pennsylvania State University. Ridge had graduated from Harvard at the height of the Vietnam War (1955–75), when many students were protesting U.S. involvement in the war, which many people saw as a civil war between communist and anticommunist forces in the Southeast Asian country. Ridge, however, accepted the call of his draft board (the draft was essentially a lottery that chose young men to fight in Vietnam) and became a member of the infantry, the famous "grunts" who battled the guerrilla fighters of the communist Vietcong. As a staff sergeant, Ridge was honored with a medal, the Bronze Star for Valor.

A law career, then politics

After his military service ended, Ridge returned to Pennsylvania to finish law school, after which he entered into private practice as a lawyer. Not long afterward, Ridge went into politics, beginning with a position as assistant district attorney in Erie.

In 1982 Ridge ran as a Republican candidate for the U.S. House of Representatives. He became the first enlisted (non-officer) veteran of Vietnam to be elected to the House. As a moderate (less extreme) Republican in a Democratic-leaning, working-class area, Ridge was reelected five times.

In 1994, after a dozen years in Congress, Ridge ran for the governorship of Pennsylvania and won. Four years later, Ridge was reelected, this time with 57 percent of the vote, an unusually high margin for a Republican running in a state in which registered Democrats outnumber Republicans by about half a million voters.

Ridge made cleaning up the environment a central goal of his term, attacking the air pollution from manufacturing plants around Pittsburgh and the urban pollution often associated with Philadelphia. He also demonstrated his conservative (more traditional) beliefs by reducing state taxes and signing more than two hundred death warrants for people convicted of capital crimes (crimes for which execution is a possible penalty).

As a Republican governor in a Democratic state, Ridge took a more moderate course than Bush did in Texas. In 2000, Ridge's name was mentioned as a possible running mate for Bush's presidential run. (Dick Cheney [1941–], a Texas oil executive and former U.S. representative from Wyoming, was eventually chosen instead.)

Ridge was about halfway through his second term as governor when President Bush asked him to become Homeland Security Director. He was sworn into his new job in early October 2001, just a month after the terrorist attacks on New York and Washington.

After a smooth start, a rocky path

In his speech on September 21, President Bush announced that he was creating the Office of Homeland Security, a cabinet-level office reporting directly to him. He said that Ridge "will lead, oversee and coordinate a comprehensive national strategy to safeguard our country against terrorism and respond to any attacks that may come. These measures are essential. The only way to defeat terrorism as a threat to our way of life is to stop it, eliminate it, and destroy it where it grows."

Ridge was sworn into his new job two weeks later, riding on a wave of national unity and determination to defeat the terrorists responsible for the September 11 attacks. In Congress, as in the country overall, politicians put party differences aside to concentrate on fighting Al Qaeda (pronounced al-KAY-duh), bin Laden's terrorist group blamed for plotting the attacks.

At the time of his appointment, no one paid much attention to the fact that Ridge was not technically becoming a member of the president's cabinet—although Bush had used the phrase "cabinet-level office"—which would have required him to be confirmed by the Senate. Instead, Ridge became part of the White House staff, instructed to help coordinate the domestic antiterrorist activities of such cabinet departments as Justice (in charge of the Federal Bureau of Investigation [FBI] and the Immigration and Naturalization Service), Transportation (in charge of the Federal Aviation Administration, which was responsible for the safety of civilian aircraft), the Central Intelligence Agency (charged with uncovering plots overseas), and Treasury (responsible for blocking the flow of money to terrorist groups).

Within six months, the difference between "cabinet officer" and "cabinet-level officer" became more obvious and more important.

The honeymoon ends

Less than a month passed before political strains began appearing in the nation's antiterrorism efforts. In November 2001, senators asked Ridge to appear as a witness before committees looking into the 9/11 attacks and the U.S. response. The White House refused. Normally, committees in the Senate or the House of Representatives can order cabinet members, who must be approved by the Senate before taking office, to testify. But the White House argued that Ridge was an adviser to the president, not a cabinet officer, and he could not be required to testify.

The president got his way, even when one congressional committee after another asked Ridge to testify and he refused, on orders from the White House. But the refusal had a political price. It annoyed and even insulted some senators, who traditionally feel it is their job to oversee the activities of the White House and to offer their advice on running the government.

Even as early as November 2001, the argument began to take on political overtones. Democrats in the Senate were sharply critical of the White House's refusal to let Ridge testify. Republican senators said they understood the position of the Republican-controlled White House.

In spring 2002 the political tensions increased after information came to light that the FBI had received some pieces of information that, if it had been handled differently, might have alerted the government to the plot against the World Trade Center and the Pentagon. But still the White House refused to allow Ridge to appear as a witness before congressional committees.

Now playing: *Divorce Court*

In March 2002 Ridge made his first major announcement: a plan to assign colors to days, based on how serious his office judged the threat of terrorist attacks to be. Based on an analysis of all available information from different government agencies, days were to be designated Green in case of a "low" risk of terrorist attack; Blue in the case of a "guarded" condition; Yellow in case of an "elevated" risk; Orange in case of "high" risk; and Red in case of "severe" risk. The color scheme reminded many people of a similar system for rating the chance of tornados.

At first conditions were judged to be Yellow. But as day after day passed in condition Yellow with no sign of terrorist activity, some writers in the news media began to question the seriousness and effectiveness of the Homeland Security program.

Then, in early May, two months after the color scheme was introduced, Ridge led reporters on a tour of his new command center, officially called an SCIF (Sensitive Compartmented Information Facility). Set up in an old U.S. Navy facility in Washington, D.C., it was located in an ordinary office building and guarded by private employees of Wackenhut, a civilian security company. During the tour, Ridge described the center as a place where a variety of government agencies could coordinate their actions in the case of a future terrorism emergency.

But reporters noticed that unlike emergency command centers set up by the White House or the Pentagon,

Homeland Security Director Tom Ridge addressing the Homeland Security and Defense Conference in Washington, D.C., November 27, 2001.
Photograph reproduced by permission of AP/Wide World Photos.

which are housed underground and designed to operate in the wake of a nuclear attack, Ridge's facility used normal commercial telephones (which failed widely during the 9/11 attacks) and 50-inch (127-centimeter) big-screen televisions available from discount electronics stores. On the day of the tour, one of the televisions intended to display video conferences by government officials during a national emergency was tuned into a daytime television program called *Divorce Court.* The Homeland Security program was accused of being a public relations show that lacked substance in fighting terrorism.

Shortly thereafter, the FBI director admitted that his agency had missed signals prior to September 11 that Al Qaeda was planning an attack. Some FBI agents complained that the national headquarters had refused to support their efforts to investigate one man who was later accused of being involved in planning the attack.

In the meantime, senators who were annoyed by the White House's refusal to let Ridge testify complained that other government agencies that he was supposed to coordinate rarely informed him in advance of taking their own antiterrorist actions or announcing their plans.

The role of politics in a national emergency

Shortly after 9/11, Bush declared war on terrorism, and public opinion polls showed that an overwhelming majority— more than 90 percent—of the American people supported the president. The crisis and the response seemed to put the fight against terrorism above politics.

It took less than six months for this feeling to give way to the more familiar give-and-take of politics, and Ridge became tangled in these quarrels even before he had time to take office supplies out of their packaging in his new crisis coordination center.

Elected senators strongly claimed they had a right to be consulted on how to run the nation's war on terrorism, while the president argued he should be left alone to direct the campaign as he and his advisers saw fit.

Ridge and his operations became a target of criticism, even ridicule, that was indirectly aimed at the president. Like the Harvard graduate who agreed to fight in the infantry in Vietnam, Ridge found himself taking political fire for his superiors in a fight where he was a foot soldier.

For More Information

Periodicals

Daalder, Ivo, and J.M. Destler. "Advisors, Czars, and Councils: Organizing for Homeland Security." *National Interest,* Summer 2000, p. 66.

Freedburg, Sydney, Jr. "Shoring Up America." *National Journal,* October 20, 2001, p. 3,238.

Kelly, Patrick. "Tom Ridge." *Current Biography.* February 2001, p. 47.

Maximilien Robespierre

May 6, 1758
Arras, France
July 28, 1794
Paris, France

Leader of the "Reign of Terror" during the French Revolution

> "Terror is the only justice that is prompt, severe, and inflexible."

In slightly more than one year, from mid-1793 until mid-1794, about seventeen thousand people died in France in the name of a political ideal. The victims ranged from the king and queen of France to **aristocrats** (the upper classes of society, which controlled the government) to ordinary people accused of minor crimes. Their trials were often brief and the outcome already decided. It was called the "Reign of Terror."

The Reign of Terror bore little resemblance to the "terrorism" of later centuries. The French Terror was carried out by a small group of men, members of the Committee of Public Safety, which led the government. They claimed they were trying to protect the French Revolution from enemies inside France and in other countries. Later, terrorism would become associated with people trying to gain power from the outside.

What the Reign of Terror did have in common with later terrorism was the use of violence to support deeply held political beliefs. The man most closely linked to this chapter in the French Revolution was Maximilien Robespierre, who headed the Committee of Public Safety and who eventually lost his own life to the same violence that he used against so many others.

Origins in Arras

Maximilien-François-Marie-Isidore de Robespierre was born on May 6, 1758, in the town of Arras, in northeastern France. His mother died in childbirth when Robespierre was nine years old. His father, a moderately successful lawyer, fell apart after his wife's death, and Robespierre was raised by his grandparents. Robespierre was educated at a college in Arras and then went to the respected College of Louis-le-Grand in Paris, where he studied law.

In 1781 Robespierre qualified as a lawyer and set up a legal practice in Arras. His practice was successful, and Robespierre was also active in the local cultural life. In particular, he embraced the ideas of Jean-Jacques Rousseau (1712–1778). Rousseau was a leading philosopher in the eighteenth century, a period when political philosophers in both France and England questioned the monarchy, or kings and queens. This was particularly the case in France, where, unlike in England, there was no parliament (governing body) to limit the power of the king. Rousseau's writings were not always consistent, but his influence was enormous. In particular, in his book *The Social Contract*, he wrote that society was responsible for creating good. (In an earlier work, he had written that man had been corrupted by society, and that man's natural state was that of a kind of "noble savage." The conflict between these two ideas cannot be resolved except by saying that Rousseau changed his mind.)

Rousseau argued that human beings join voluntarily with other humans in a "social contract" to improve the common condition. But Rousseau questioned whether the will of the majority always leads to the best outcome. He held that the goal of government should be to ensure freedom, equality, and justice for all, regardless of what the majority wants. If the government fails to act morally—to work for the common good, in Rousseau's view—it no longer has real authority over its citizens.

In Rousseau's opinion, French kings were not acting to secure the common good and had lost their moral right to rule.

Words to Know

Aristocrats: the upper classes of society, which controlled the government.

Guillotine: a machine that used a falling metal blade to cut off a person's head.

Jean-Jacques Rousseau was a Swiss-born philosopher who deeply affected Robespierre. Rousseau believed that government should be run to benefit all mankind. Robespierre was one of the leading advocates of creating Rousseau's ideal government from the French Revolution.
Photograph reproduced by permission of the Corbis Corporation.

In 1789, when the French king, Louis XVI (1754–1793), called together the Estates-General—a form of parliament that had not met since 1614—to raise money to pay for the government's wars, Robespierre was eager to become a delegate (representative of the people). Louis XVI had hoped for a tame session that would be limited to raising money. What he got was the French Revolution.

Storming the Bastille

Robespierre became a delegate to the Third Estate, which represented commoners, rather than aristocrats (the Second Estate) or the Catholic Church (the First Estate). The Estates-General met at the Palace of Versailles in early May 1789. After a month of arguing, in June the Third Estate decided to restructure the Estates-General and declared itself to be the National Assembly, which was to represent all people of France. The king had lost control of the process.

Robespierre, in the meantime, had joined a group called the Society of the Friends of the Constitution, which came to be called the Jacobin Club. The Jacobin Club wanted the Estates-General to start a democratic revolution that supported the "moral" authority of the people against the king and the aristocracy. The Jacobins became a kind of political faction, or party, in the new National Assembly in June.

Starting in July 1789, when a mob stormed a government fortress and prison called the Bastille (pronounced bass-TEEL), the king, the aristocrats, and the common people fought for power in France. The commoners far outnumbered the king and aristocracy, and once they had tasted power, there was no stopping them.

Robespierre was one of the commoners pressing for more power. After centuries of rule by the king and aristocracy, however, such a revolutionary idea gained ground only gradually.

While this struggle was going on, between 1789 and 1793, kings in other European countries became disturbed at what was happening in France. If the people of France could rise up and overthrow their king, who was to say the same thing couldn't happen in other countries? European kings began gathering their armies to invade France and restore Louis XVI to power.

By September 1792 foreign armies were advancing and supporters of the king in the French countryside were beginning to revolt against the central government in Paris. France was in crisis.

The storming of the Bastille on July 4, 1789, was the symbolic beginning of the French Revolution. It marked the start of nearly a decade of unrest and confusion as various factions of French society struggled for the upper hand in ruling France. *Photograph reproduced by permission of the Granger Collection, New York.*

The Committee of Public Safety

The unrest came to a head in September. The new National Convention (an organized parliament) assembled on September 20, 1792, and voted two days later to abolish (do away with) the monarchy. Louis XVI and his family tried to leave France secretly but were recognized and arrested. The National Convention accused Louis of treason (crimes against his country), convicted him, and sentenced him to death. He was executed by **guillotine** (a machine that used a falling metal blade to cut off a person's head) on January 21, 1793.

By spring, France faced a serious crisis. It was at war with most of the countries of Europe, and the war was not going well. At home, the French economy was in ruins, caused by the falling value of the currency and a naval blockade by Britain. Conservatives from the countryside disliked the rapid changes being made by the National Convention in Paris and began to challenge its authority. At the same time, the demands of the Paris Commune, representing the commoners of Paris, were growing. The Commune was calling for heavy taxes on the rich to support the poor.

In July the National Convention turned over effective control of the government to a dozen men who made up the Committee of Public Safety. Robespierre was elected to the Committee on July 28 and emerged as its leader (although officially all twelve members were equal).

The Terror

The situation continued to worsen throughout the summer. By September 1793, food shortages had grown serious, opponents in France were taking up arms against the government in Paris, and the military situation had become desperate, particularly with the loss of the Mediterranean port city of Toulon to the British navy.

To save the country from invasion, the Committee of Public Safety adopted a series of extreme measures that came to be known as the "Reign of Terror." In September, the Law of Suspects allowed revolutionary committees to arrest suspects for "treasonable activities." Maximum prices were set for many goods, especially food, with severe penalties for charging more. Louis XVI's queen, Marie Antoinette (1755–1793), was put on trial and executed by guillotine. And across France, people accused of opposing the revolution were charged with treason and executed.

In all, an estimated seventeen thousand people were executed during the Terror. Many thousands more fled the country. Throughout this period, three men were in charge of the Committee: Robespierre, Jacques-René Hébert (1757–1794) and Georges-Jacques Danton (1759–1794). However, much of the worst violence seemed to be the result of mob rule rather than part of an intentional plan.

In March 1794 Robespierre solidified his power on the Committee. He organized the arrest and execution of Hébert, and the next month of Danton. He reorganized the Committee of Public Safety and ruled France as a dictator.

In June 1794 the government changed the procedures for prosecuting people suspected of resisting the revolution. Suspects no longer had the right to a lawyer, and death was the only possible penalty for those found guilty. The excesses of the Reign of Terror had reached their height. In the six weeks between June 12 and July 28, 1794, nearly thirteen hundred people were sentenced to death, an average of twenty-eight a day.

The Terror ends

But just as Robespierre was taking the Terror to new heights, the original reason for his extreme measures—the looming invasion of the country—was coming to an end. Partly as a result of a universal draft, in which all men were required to serve in the military, and partly because more talented officers were being placed in charge, France began driving back the invading European armies. An important victory was achieved when France won the Battle of Fleurus (June 26, 1794) against the Austrians and Dutch.

At the same time, the increasing executions made many members of the Convention fearful of their own safety, including members of the Jacobin Club.

On July 27, Robespierre was accused of tyranny (using oppressive power) and barred from speaking to the National Convention. He and several key supporters were arrested. Soldiers loyal to the Paris Commune soon freed them, but the Convention promptly ordered them arrested again. During all this, Robespierre was shot in the jaw.

The next day, July 28, Robespierre and twenty-one of his associates were found guilty and put to death by guillotine. The following day, eighty more followers were executed. By November, the Jacobin Clubs had been closed. The Reign of Terror was over.

Robespierre and modern terrorism

The terrorism of Robespierre largely consisted of a revolutionary government killing people it saw as its enemies. In this respect, it is very different from the terrorism of the twenty-first century, which largely consists of private groups using violence against civilians or government targets to achieve political ends.

But there are similarities, starting with the use of violence to achieve political goals. Before the Reign of Terror, politics was largely played by aristocrats or rivals for the throne. The French Revolution introduced the idea that ordinary people had a right to participate in politics. The revolution also gave birth to the idea that the outcome of a political quarrel was of such importance that it could justify the deaths of hundreds or even thousands of people.

To a large degree, Robespierre and his fellow Jacobins were fighting not just to gain power for themselves but for the idea of democracy and popular rule. The fact that many ordinary French citizens died at the hands of the Committee of Public Safety seemed, to Robespierre, beside the point. It was an experience to be repeated during later revolutions, such as the Bolshevik Revolution in Russia in 1917, which put a communist government (one supposedly ruled by the people) in power but led to the deaths of millions of peasants.

For More Information

Books

Lefebvre, Georges. *The French Revolution from 1793 to 1799,* translated by John Hall Stewart and James Friguglietti. New York: Columbia University Press, 1964.

Rude, George F. E. *Robespierre: Portrait of a Revolutionary Democrat.* New York: Viking Press, 1976.

Schama, Simon. *Citizens: A Chronicle of the French Revolution.* New York: Vintage Books, 1990.

Scott, Otto J. *Robespierre: The Voice of Virtue.* New York: Mason and Lipscomb, 1974.

Periodicals

Hornblower, Margot. "Liberte, egalite, fraternite? 200 Years Later, the French Are Still Quarreling about the Revolution." *Time,* May 1, 1989, p. 48.

O'Brien, Conor Cruise. "Virtue and Terror." *New York Review of Books,* September 26, 1985, p. 28.

Robert M. "Bobby" Shelton

1929
Tuscaloosa, Alabama

Grand Wizard of the Ku Klux Klan

"We don't want violence but we ain't gonna let [them] spit in our face either."

Photograph reproduced by permission of the Corbis Corporation.

During the growing campaign by African Americans during the 1950s and 1960s to achieve equal rights with white Americans, another campaign began to deny equality to citizens with black skin. This campaign was led by the Ku Klux Klan (KKK), an organization that often used violence, or threats of violence, to stop black Americans from exercising their rights under law.

In the 1960s, Robert M. Shelton was the Grand Wizard (the leader) of the largest organization of several that called themselves the "Ku Klux Klan." He was the public head of a shadowy organization officially named the United Klans of America, Knights of the Ku Klux Klans, Inc. Its headquarters were in his hometown of Tuscaloosa, Alabama. But given the secret nature of the activities carried out by the Klan and by its imitators, it was often unclear who was behind the cross burnings, beatings, and **lynchings** that plagued much of the South during the 1960s.

Tuscaloosa, Alabama

Robert Marion Shelton was born in Tuscaloosa, Alabama, in 1929. His grandfather was a farmer and shopkeeper. His father was a "merchant," according to Shelton. Shelton himself grew up in Tuscaloosa, graduated from high school there, and took some college courses by mail. He also served in the U.S. Air Force for three years, during which he was stationed in Berlin, Germany. This was during the period in which President Harry S. Truman (1884–1972) gave the executive order that ended the **racial segregation** of the U.S. armed forces. (Racial segregation was a system in which black people and white people did not share public services such as schools or transportation.)

Shelton returned from the air force to Tuscaloosa. There he went to work in the B. F. Goodrich tire company and joined the United Rubber Workers union. Sometime in the early 1950s, he also became active in one of several splinter organizations of the KKK, an organization that dated its beginnings to the period immediately after the U.S. Civil War (1861–65; see box pp. 240–41).

The 1950s saw the first stirrings of change in Alabama society. While Shelton was growing up in the 1930s and 1940s, racial segregation was the norm in most southern states, especially Alabama and Mississippi. Blacks and whites in the South had lived separately ever since the original KKK in the late 1860s had discouraged black citizens from claiming their legal rights. Schools, public transportation, restaurants, and churches were strictly segregated.

But starting with the U.S. military just after World War II (1939–45), **civil rights** lawyers began attacking local laws that kept the two races apart. Slowly, federal courts began ruling in their favor.

Rocky start in the Klan

It was during this time that Shelton became active in the KKK in Alabama. In the early 1950s, he joined one version of the Klan under the legal name U.S. Klans. Always a soft-spoken man, and often described as humorless, Shelton had strong organizational skills that more than made up for his apparent lack of public speaking ability. In the spring of 1960, the Alabama Klan leader, Eldon Lee Edwards, dismissed Shelton on grounds of "incompetence, untruthfulness, and lack of cooperation." Shelton said it was a disagreement over finances.

Words to Know

Civil rights: the nonpolitical rights of citizens to equal opportunity under the law.

Communist: a person who believes in the economic theory in which the people—usually represented by the government—owns all goods and their means of production.

Integration: incorporation of individuals or groups as equals.

Lynching: the execution of someone by a mob.

Prejudices: irrational dislikes.

Racial segregation: a system in which black people and white people did not share public services such as schools or transportation.

Subversive: attempting to overthrow or destroy the political or social order.

White supremacists: people who believe that the white race is superior to the

By that time, however, Shelton had enough influence among Klan members in Alabama to form his own offshoot, which he called the Alabama Knights. Since KKK traditions, such as wearing white hooded robes and burning crosses on lawns to terrorize residents, could be used by any group, Shelton's Knights soon became one of the leading Klan organizations in the state.

The next year, Shelton attended a meeting in Indian Springs, Georgia, with the leader of another small Klan in Georgia. They planned to discuss joining forces. Shelton arrived with eight military-style guards dressed in white shirts, red ties, khaki paratrooper pants, black boots, and marine helmets. His show of force resulted in the merger of Shelton's Alabama Knights with the Georgia Klansmen. Shelton, at age thirty-one, was named Imperial Wizard of the new organization, which he called the United Klans of America. He moved its headquarters to Tuscaloosa.

Politics

As the federal courts struck down laws limiting civil rights on the basis of race, whites in many southern states resisted, and no states were more resistant than Alabama and neighboring Mississippi. Although the KKK was not at its heart a political group, in the late 1950s it began trying to get segregationists elected to public office.

In 1958 Shelton and his fellow Klansmen helped elect Governor John Patterson over a racially moderate candidate, George C. Wallace (1919–1998); afterward, Wallace declared that he would never be outdone in making racial appeals to voters. Soon after, Shelton was promoted to the job of salesman at B. F. Goodrich and was very successful in selling tires to the state government. (Shelton was eventually dismissed by the tire company for spending too much time on the Klan and later earned a living selling air conditioning before devoting himself full-time to the KKK.)

In 1962 Shelton's Klan members supported Wallace to succeed Patterson as governor of Alabama. Wallace was elected on promises to maintain racial discrimination in Alabama. It was a partnership that would last many years, sometimes secretly, as Wallace went from the Alabama state house to a run for president of the United States. Throughout his career, Wallace was hailed as the champion of the "little guy," the white worker who felt left behind as southern blacks made significant progress in being treated equally under the law.

White resistance

In the early 1960s the African American civil rights movement rapidly gained ground in the South. College students integrated public restaurants (or made them available to all races) by staging "sit-ins": they sat at the lunch counter and waited quietly, sometimes for hours, to be served, even if the restaurant owner was unwilling to do so. Throughout the South, public universities were integrated by federal court orders. Public schools were integrated, also by the order of federal courts acting under a 1954 U.S. Supreme Court ruling (*Brown v. the Board of Education*) that the concept of "separate but equal" public school systems was a violation of the Constitution.

The KKK was at the forefront of white resistance. In particular, the Klan tried to frighten black citizens to stop them from exercising their rights. In rural areas, whites dressed in the pointed white hoods of the KKK burned crosses outside the homes of black farmers or town officials to scare them. Black men (and sometimes women) were murdered, hanged from trees as a warning to other black citizens not to try to change things.

Shelton and the KKK played a kind of game with the news media throughout all this. Shelton was often quoted as stating that the Klan did not support violence, but that he could understand how some white people were upset at the change in social relations between whites and blacks. In 1961 Shelton was placed under a court order not to interfere with whites trying to integrate interstate bus transportation—who were known as Freedom Riders—when they entered Alabama.

Members of the Ku Klux Klan adopted white robes and the burning cross as symbols of their racial hatred. *Photograph reproduced by permission of the Corbis Corporation.*

(Despite the order, when the Freedom Riders got to Alabama their bus was attacked and they were badly beaten.) The Klan also paid for lawyers to defend Klan members arrested for attacking civil rights workers.

Spokesman for the resistance

Shelton emerged in the 1960s as the leading spokesman for whites who hated the new racial equality being forced on them by federal courts. Where other segregationists made fiery speeches, Shelton's mild manner spoke for thousands of lower- and lower-middle-class whites throughout the South. His

United Klans rapidly grew into tens of thousands of members—the actual numbers were never revealed—and was by far the largest of the organizations using the Ku Klux Klan name.

Shelton did not mind making statements that seemed ill-educated or unsophisticated, which may have appealed to the sort of people likely to join his organization. He told the *New York Times Magazine* in 1964 that "my research shows that the full moon brings out the animal instincts, increases their excitement, and they [black people] become violent, restless, inclined to get in trouble and brawls."

Shelton's **prejudices** (irrational dislikes) were not limited to African Americans. He also opposed labor unions that fought for workers' rights (despite having once joined a union himself) and products made overseas. He opposed the fluoridation of water (the addition of chemicals to drinking water to prevent cavities) as well as the National Mental Health Association, which he thought was a communist plot. He particularly disliked Jews.

New tactics

In mid-1963 several Klans announced a change in tactics: nonviolence. With little to show for their terrorist attacks on civil rights workers, some Klan leaders hoped they might be more successful with a more reasonable approach.

In his own appearances, Shelton began to stress the Klan's anticommunist positions over its antiblack and anti-Jewish positions. (Communism is an economic and political system in which citizens—represented by the government—own all property and businesses. In theory, the government is supposed to distribute all profit to all its citizens equally. Communism is at odds with the American economic system, capitalism, in which individuals own property in varying levels.) Shelton cooperated with white politicians, such as Governor Wallace, to accuse civil rights activists of being influenced or funded by communists. He also threw the Klan's support to Senator Barry Goldwater (1909–1998), the 1964 Republican presidential nominee running against President Lyndon Johnson (1908-1973). But it made little difference; Johnson won in a landslide.

Shelton's effort to turn away from traditional Klan behavior also did not succeed with potential recruits, for whom burning crosses and terrorizing African Americans was an essen-

What Is the Ku Klux Klan?

"Ku Klux Klan" is the name used by a series of **white supremacist** organizations in the United States, starting just after the Civil War. (White supremacists believe that the white race is superior to the other races, particularly blacks.) The Klans were known for their use of terror against African Americans and others, including Roman Catholics and Jews.

There have been at least three waves of organizations operating under the name Ku Klux Klan. The first started in 1866 as a social organization for Civil War veterans in Pulaski, Tennessee. Its founder was a former Confederate general, Nathan Bedford Forrest (1821–1877). It quickly turned into an organization that used violence against the social changes brought about by Reconstruction. (Reconstruction was the period following the Civil War in which Congress attempted to reunite the country.) Members of the original KKK attacked Reconstructionist politicians throughout the South and raided the homes and businesses of freed black slaves. The Klan used violence, including beating and lynching (the execution of someone by a mob), to restore white supremacy in the South. Forrest tried to dissolve the group in 1869 after the violence got out of hand, but it continued for another two years. By 1871, the possibility of equal rights for African Americans in the South had been defeated for the time being, and the Klan quietly faded from the scene.

In 1915 a new version of the KKK was organized near Atlanta, Georgia. It was also devoted to preserving white supremacy, but it had a longer list of targets: African Americans, certainly, but also recent immigrants to the United States from southern Europe who tended to be Roman Catholic, as well as Jews and

tial part of the Klan experience. Any effort to clean up the Klan's image was doomed in September 1963 when a powerful bomb exploded at the Sixteenth Street Baptist Church in Birmingham, Alabama. Four young black girls died. It took fourteen years to bring the main bomber, Klan member Robert Chambliss, to justice, but the public image of the Klan was set: it was an organization that bombed children in churches. (Three other men were also linked to the bombing; one died in 1994, one was convicted in 2001, and the third was convicted the following year.)

A year and a half later, in March 1965, another incident in Alabama tipped the balance against Shelton and the KKK. A white woman from Detroit, Michigan, Viola Liuzzo, was shot

people sympathetic to the Bolshevik revolution in Russia (1917). The second Klan drew its members from mostly white small towns in the South and Midwest. Membership in the second Klan peaked in the 1920s, but it had disappeared by the end of World War II.

In the 1950s several separate organizations, mostly in the South, continued to use the name Ku Klux Klan, but their membership was tiny and their leadership disorganized. But in the early 1960s, as the civil rights movement began making significant progress, membership in the KKK began growing rapidly. In particular, the Civil Rights Act of 1964, which outlawed discrimination based on race, boosted membership in the southern states. As with the earlier organizations, the Klan of the 1960s drew members from lower- or lower-middle-class whites living in small towns in the rural South. Also like the earlier Klans, the new Klan used nighttime raids with members wearing white robes and pointed hoods to conceal their identities. A burning cross became its symbol of warning to African Americans linked to the new civil rights movement.

In 1965 four Klansmen were arrested for the murder of Viola Liuzzo, a white civil rights worker from Detroit, Michigan, who was shot and killed after taking part in a famous civil rights march from Selma to Montgomery in Alabama. President Lyndon Johnson (1908–1973), in a national television speech, vowed to use federal authority to stamp out the Klan.

After the 1960s the Klan became a marginal organization, allying itself with U.S. Nazis and other right-wing extremists. Although its costumes and symbols continued to anger African Americans, its influence and membership were very small.

and killed while driving civil rights marchers from Montgomery to Selma, Alabama. She was the second white from the North killed that week. President Johnson declared that he had had enough and announced a major crackdown on the KKK. He ordered the Federal Bureau of Investigation (FBI) to arrest and charge suspects in the murder with a federal crime: conspiring against Liuzzo's civil rights. Governor Wallace also promised state cooperation in pursuing the crime. (In many earlier cases, state authorities had failed to prosecute murders carried out in the name of civil rights.) Two of the three men linked to the murder were tried in state court but were found not guilty. However, all three were found guilty in federal court and sentenced to ten years in prison.

A bomb planted in the Sixteenth Street Baptist Church, Birmingham, Alabama, killed four young African American girls in 1963. The bombers were suspected of membership in the Ku Klux Klan headed by Robert Shelton. *Photograph reproduced by permission of AP/Wide World Photos.*

No Limit on Hate: The Mentality of the KKK

The explosion in Birmingham's Sixteenth Street Baptist Church, which killed four young black girls, horrified many Americans—but not all. At a KKK rally held in St. Augustine, Florida, shortly after the bombing, a Klan speaker from Texas, the Reverend Charles Conley Lynch, addressed the rally:

"I tell you people here tonight, if they can find these fellows [responsible for the bombing], they ought to pin medals on them. Someone said, 'Ain't it a shame that them little children was killed?' In the first place, they ain't little. They're fourteen or fifteen years old—old enough to have venereal [sexually transmitted] diseases, and I'll be surprised if all of 'em

didn't have one or more. In the second place, they weren't children. Children are little people, little human beings, and that means white people. . . .

"And in the third place, it wasn't no shame they was killed. Why? Because when I go out to kill rattlesnakes, I don't make no difference between little rattlesnakes and big rattlesnakes, because I know it is the nature of all rattlesnakes to be my enemies and to poison me if they can. So I kill 'em all, and if there's four less [of them] tonight, then I say, 'Good for whoever planted the bomb!' We're all better off. . . . I believe in violence, all the violence it takes either to scare [them] out of the country or to have 'em all six feet under!"

In 1965, the clock seemed to run out on the Klan. An organization that had survived throughout years of harassing and killing blacks found itself on the defensive. Even former supporters like Wallace turned on the Klan.

Endgame

Although Shelton used the same arguments and the same robes as the KKK had a century earlier, he was operating in a different world. Where the original KKK defeated the post–Civil War effort to achieve racial equality, Shelton failed completely. A century of experience and a world war, in which the murder of six million Jews by Nazi Germany (and the impressive performance of African Americans fighting in the U.S. Army), simply overwhelmed the racial hatreds spread by the Klan.

In 1965 and 1966, the U.S. House of Representatives Committee on Un-American Activities launched an investigation of the KKK. Shelton, who had claimed for years that communists influenced the civil rights movement, was in the witness chair of the same committee that had gone after American communism in the 1950s. Shelton refused to answer the committee's questions and was held in contempt of Congress. He went to jail for a year.

When Shelton was released from prison, the South had turned unfriendly to his beliefs. Road signs outside small towns criticized the Klan and urged its members to go elsewhere.

Cointelpro

In the late 1960s, things went from bad to worse for Shelton and the Klan. In the middle of the decade, the FBI had launched a program called the Internal Security Counterintelligence Program, Cointelpro for short, designed to stamp out organizations it found to be **subversive** (those that attempted to overthrow the government or social order) through harassment and investigation for possible wrongdoing. The Klan was one of its main targets.

Shelton's star within the Klan was fading. A young man from Louisiana, David Duke, began to emerge as the leading spokesman for white supremacists in the United States.

For More Information

Books

Chalmers, David Mark. *Hooded Americanism: The History of the Ku Klux Klan.* Durham, NC: Duke University Press, 1987.

Katz, William Loren. *The Invisible Empire: The Ku Klux Klan's Impact on History.* Washington, DC: Open Hand Publications, 1986.

Wade, Wyn Craig. *The Fiery Cross: The Ku Klux Klan in America.* New York: Oxford University Press, 1998.

Periodicals

Chalmers, David. "The History of the Ku Klux Klan: Rule by Terror." *American History Illustrated,* January 1980, p. 8.

Chalmers, David. "The Hooded Knights Revive Rule by Terror in the 'Twenties." *American History Illustrated,* February, 1980, p. 28.

Long, Margaret. "The Imperial Wizard Explains the Klan." *New York Times Magazine,* July 5, 1964, p. 8ff.

Weisberger, Bernard. "When White Hoods Were in Flower." *American Heritage,* April 1992, p. 18.

Fusako Shigenobu

September 1945
Tokyo, Japan

Leader of the Japanese Red Army

In November 2000, citizens of Japan were startled to see a handcuffed middle-aged woman emerge from a train arriving in Tokyo. When she spotted the waiting cameras, she raised her hands and gave the thumbs-up sign, shouting at reporters: "I'll fight on!"

Her name was Fusako Shigenobu. For three decades the police had been looking for her as the leader of one of Japan's most mysterious terrorist organizations: the Japanese Red Army (JRA). Surprisingly, she had been captured in the small Japanese town of Takatsuki, near Osaka. For nearly thirty years, she had been based in Lebanon, where her group conducted terrorist raids as allies of Palestinians fighting against Israel.

According to police, Shigenobu was disguised as a man when she checked into a hotel in Takatsuki. Although age and her disguise might have hidden one of Japan's most wanted terrorists, her style of smoking cigarettes evidently gave her away: she puffed a cigarette as if it were a pipe and blew perfect smoke rings.

"The mission's purpose was to consolidate the international revolutionary alliance against the imperialists of the world."

Photograph reproduced by permission of the Corbis Corporation.

An adolescent in the 1960s

Shigenobu was born in Tokyo in 1945, a month after World War II ended with Japan's surrender to the United States. Her father had been a member of Japan's ultraconservative political faction that was blamed for starting World War II. But he was too minor to attract the Americans' attention, who put other members of the faction on trial after the war. Instead, he ran a small grocery store during Shigenobu's childhood. Her excellent academic performance during junior high school grew worse after she realized that her parents could not afford to send her to college.

After high school, Shigenobu took a job with Kikkoman, a company that made soy sauce. She used her earnings to pay for night classes at Meiji University in Tokyo in 1964.

It was then the era of the Vietnam War (1955–75), and Japanese students—like students worldwide—took part in antiwar, anti-American protests, including protests against the presence of American troops on the Japanese island of Okinawa. (The Vietnam war began when communist troops of North Vietnam invaded South Vietnam. [The country had been divided in 1954 after an international conference.] The United States, fearful of the spread of communism in Southeast Asia, aided and fought alongside the anticommunist South Vietnamese. The North eventually overran the South and reunited the country under a communist regime.) Some student protests were led by the Socialist Student League, one of whose leaders was a young man named Takamaro Tamiya. Shigenobu met Tamiya during a protest, and the two became romantically involved. Their relationship led Shigenobu deeper into the radical student movement.

The Red Army is founded

The protests had little effect in Japan, however, and sometimes the police shut them down. Some students decided they needed to take more drastic measures. The result was a group calling itself the *Sekigun,* or Red Army. The founders hoped it would become a full-fledged military organization, with arms, explosives, and battle helmets painted blood red. They wanted to set up offices in Mexico, Brazil, and San Francisco and coordinate a worldwide uprising and a revolution in Japan.

Members of the new Red Army were determined to get started right away, and in 1969 they attacked several Osaka police stations with Molotov cocktails. (A Molotov cocktail is a firebomb consisting of a bottle filled with gasoline, with a rag stuffed in the top to hold it in. The rag is set on fire and the bottle is thrown at its target.) Later, they attacked another police station in Tokyo. In November 1969 police arrested more than fifty Red Army members at a training camp near Mount Fuji, one of Japan's most famous landmarks. They were accused of planning to attack the police headquarters in Tokyo and the residence of Japan's prime minister.

In March 1970 the Red Army staged Japan's first hijacking. After a Japan Airlines Boeing 727 took off from Tokyo, nine neatly dressed hijackers took out daggers and swords from cardboard tubes and burst into the pilot's compartment, demanding that the plane head for Pyongyang in the secretive communist country of North Korea. At first the plane landed in Seoul, South Korea (which authorities tried to

The Japanese Red Army's (JRA) first terrorist attack was the hijacking of a Japan Airlines plane to North Korea in 1970. It was the first plane hijacking in Japan and marked the beginning of a long string of incidents staged over the next two decades by the JRA. *Photograph reproduced by permission of the Corbis Corporation.*

disguise as the North Korean capital's airport), but the hijackers were not fooled. Eventually the plane, carrying ninety-nine passengers and seven crew members as hostages, went to North Korea. The hijackers were allowed to stay after they released their hostages, who, with the hijacked plane, flew back to Japan a few days later.

In 1972 fourteen members of the JRA died after an internal disagreement ended with a shoot-out among its members. The violence, including a later shoot-out with police, basically ended the group's role in Japan. But by that time Shigenobu was long gone.

To the Middle East

In 1971 Shigenobu had married a fellow radical, Takeshi Okudaira, and moved with him to Beirut, Lebanon. At Palestinian guerrilla camps in Syria and Lebanon, both underwent "military training," which consisted of lessons in firing rifles and throwing hand grenades. Their presence in the Middle East was a result of making contact in North Korea with **George Habash** (1926–; see entry), leader of the Popular Front for the Liberation of Palestine (PFLP), one of the most violent Palestinian terrorist groups fighting to replace Israel with a Palestinian state. (The state of Israel was founded in 1948 on land that in biblical times was the Jewish homeland but in the mid-twentieth century was under British control. After the Holocaust, the period during World War II [1939–45] in which six million Jews were killed, the United Nations established the state—on territory that Palestinians hoped would be used to create a homeland for them. Since that time Israel and its Arab neighbors fought a series of wars over territory and the right of Israel to exist.)

To many people, the alliance between the JRA and the PFLP was hard to understand. Observers at the time believed the Japanese had become frustrated with their failure to start a revolution in Japan. In fact, Japanese police had effectively shut down the group in a series of raids. Their cause was hurt more by the discovery that some members had been tortured to death for having argued with the group's political positions.

Once in the Middle East, Shigenobu became a key leader of the JRA. Intelligence officials believe she headed the group's finances and the planning for its most daring raids from a headquarters in the Bekka Valley in Lebanon (an area largely controlled by Syria during the JRA's most active period).

The JRA soon began making terrorist attacks on behalf of the Palestinian cause. One of the first and most notorious of these raids was an attack on Lod Airport in Israel in May 1972. Terrorists from the JRA entered the passenger terminal of Tel Aviv's main airport and began throwing hand grenades and firing machine guns. The attack killed twenty-six people, including sixteen people from Puerto Rico who were on a religious pilgrimage to the Holy Land. About eighty others were injured. Among those killed in the attack was Okudaira, Shigenobu's husband.

A decade and a half of terror

Over the next fifteen years, the JRA was one of the most active terrorist groups in the world. It conducted a string of dramatic terrorist attacks that were often—but not always—on behalf of the Palestinian cause. Among the incidents blamed on the group:

Working with two other gunmen, Kozo Okamoto (center) killed 26 people at Israel's Lod Airport on behalf of the Popular Front for the Liberation of Palestine in 1972.
Photograph reproduced by permission of the Corbis Corporation.

- **July 1973:** The JRA, along with some Arabs, hijack a Japan Airlines plane to Libya. The passengers are eventually released and the plane is destroyed.

- **January–February 1974:** JRA terrorists attack a Shell Oil refinery in Singapore and hijack a ferryboat and its passengers. Eventually the hostages are released unharmed.

- **September 1974:** JRA seizes eleven hostages from the French embassy in the Hague, capital of the Netherlands. The attackers are given a plane to carry them to Syria.

- **August 1975:** Ten JRA attackers seize fifty-two hostages and the U.S. consulate in Kuala Lumpur, Malaysia, including the U.S. consul and a senior Swedish diplomat. They demand the release of seven prisoners held in Japanese prisons, including several JRA members. Five of the prisoners are released and allowed to fly to Tripoli, Libya. The hostages are then set free.

- **September–October 1977:** JRA hijackers seize a Japan Airlines plane in Bombay, India, and force it to fly to neighboring Bangladesh. The Japanese government agrees to exchange nine JRA prisoners and pay $6 million in ransom for the 159 hostages on the plane. The hijackers are flown to Algeria.

Following the Indian hijacking, the JRA stopped its attacks for nine years. In 1986, however, its terrorist activities began again, sometimes under the name Anti-Imperialist International Brigade. These attacks include:

- **May 1986:** In Jakarta, Indonesia, mortar shells are fired at the U.S. and Japanese embassies. Later, fingerprints of Tsutomu Shirosaki, a member of JRA, are found in the hotel room from which the mortar shells were fired. (A mortar is a military weapon with a short barrel and a wide mouth.)

- **May 1986:** A JRA member, Yu Kikumura, is arrested with a bomb in his baggage at Amsterdam's Schiphol Airport. He is sent to Japan but released on a legal technicality.

- **April 1987:** The U.S. embassy and United States Information Service offices in Madrid, Spain, are attacked with rockets on the first anniversary of an American bomb attack against Libya. The JRA claims responsibility.

- **June 1987:** The U.S. and British embassies in Rome, Italy, are attacked with rockets and car bombs on the same day. The JRA claims responsibility, and arrest warrants are issued for two JRA members based on photo identifications.

- **April 1988:** Kikumura (who was arrested at Schiphol Airport a year earlier) is arrested at a rest area on the New Jersey Turnpike carrying three antipersonnel bombs. He is convicted of possessing explosive devices and sentenced to thirty years in prison.

- **April 1988:** Two days after Kikumura's arrest, a United Service Organization nightclub popular with American troops in Naples, Italy, is bombed. Five people are killed, including one member of the U.S. Navy. Italian police identify the fingerprints of a JRA member.

- **July 1988:** Two unused, improvised mortars are found near the U.S. embassy in Madrid. The JRA claims responsibility for planning an attack timed for the Fourth of July, in revenge for an Iranian airliner being shot down by the U.S. Navy in the Persian Gulf.

Decline and fall of the JRA

The JRA's level of activity fell significantly during the 1990s. At the time the Palestinian terrorist groups it associated with were experiencing a decline in their influence as the Palestine Liberation Organization (PLO) began peace negotiations with Israel.

U.S. government antiterrorist experts, who believed the group had had between twenty and forty members, estimated that it had fallen to fewer than ten members by 2001. In October 2001 the U.S. State Department dropped the group from its list of terrorist organizations on the grounds that it had not been active since 1999. In May 2000 Japanese officials arrested four JRA members after they were driven out of Lebanon. And the Japanese never gave up hope of persuading the government of North Korea to return the JRA members involved in the original 1970 hijacking.

Shigenobu, who was still high on Japan's list of most wanted criminals, remained out of sight until 2001, when her unusual style of smoking cigarettes gave away her presence in Japan. Despite the continuing terrorist violence in the Middle East, the end of the Cold War (a conflict between the United States and the Soviet Union that lasted from 1945 until 1990) had made it harder for terrorists to find a sympathetic country in which to hide. A peace agreement between Israel and the PLO in 1993 further reduced the JRA's list of hiding places, not to mention employers looking to hire terrorists. And over the course of thirty years, the JRA had little to show for its long string of terrorist attacks.

As with another Japanese terrorist suspect—**Shoko Asahara** (1955– ; see entry), leader of the Aum Shinrikyo sect—she was expected to remain in prison for a long time as Japan's slow legal system ground on. (Asahara's trial had lasted for seven years and was still proceeding in 2002.)

For More Information

Books

Imamura, Anne E., editor. *Reimaging Japanese Women.* Berkeley, CA: University of California Press, 1996.

Periodicals

"Arrest of a Fugitive." *Maclean's,* November 20, 2000, p. 123.

Jachnowitz, George. "Why Terrorism?" *Midstream,* February-March 2002, p. 9.

"The Japanese Red Army." *Department of State Bulletin,* November 1989, p. 64.

Sterling, Claire. "Terrorism: Tracing the International Network." *New York Times Magazine,* March 1, 1981, p. 16.

Ahmed Yassin

c. 1936
Al Joura, Palestine Mandate

Religious leader of Hamas

One of the worst threats to Israel is a man who is paralyzed below the neck and confined to a wheelchair. Sheikh Ahmed Yassin is the religious leader of Hamas, the organization that has done as much as any other to change the Israeli-Palestinian conflict from a political struggle to a religious war.

Yassin has never been accused of murder or setting off a bomb himself. But his organization, Hamas, has been the main source of suicide bombers, a deadly and terrifying form of warfare against both military and civilian targets.

Childhood

Yassin was born in 1936 or 1938—accounts vary—in the small village of Al Joura, located in a region then called the Palestine Mandate. The land came under British rule after the defeat of the Ottoman Empire in World War I (1914–18), but some Jews wanted to found a Jewish homeland there, and some Arabs wanted to found an independent state of Palestine on the same land.

"There is a misconception in the world of the meaning of the word jihad; it comes from juhad and it means effort. . . . I can be a teacher and be practicing jihad, I can be a builder and be practicing jihad and I can be a fighter. . . . All people are part of the jihad whether they know it or not."

Photograph reproduced by permission of AP/Wide World Photos.

Words to Know

Figurehead: a symbolic leader who has no real power.

Fundamentalist: a person who believes in living by a strict set of moral principles.

Koran: Islam's holy book.

Mosques: religious meeting places in Islam, similar to churches.

Quadriplegic: a person who is unable to move his arms or legs.

Secular: nonreligious.

In 1948 the Jewish state of Israel declared its independence. Immediately the armies of surrounding Arab states attacked the new country. Thousands of Palestinian Arabs fled their homes, including Yassin's family, which moved to a refugee camp called Shati in the Gaza Strip (a piece of Egyptian territory on the Mediterranean coast just south of Israel). Some refugees and their children still lived in the camp as the twenty-first century began, as repeated efforts to defeat Israel and found an Arab Palestinian state failed. But for many Palestinians, the dream never ended.

In 1952, as a teenager, Yassin was playing at the beach, doing somersaults, when he fell on his head, breaking his neck. The accident left him a **quadriplegic** (unable to move his arms or legs), confined to a wheelchair for the rest of his life.

Despite his handicap, Yassin continued his studies and became a teacher. On the side, he gave private math lessons. One of his students was the son of the Egyptian governor of Gaza, who also suffered a physical handicap. The governor recommended Yassin as someone who would make an excellent teacher of Islamic studies. As a teacher and a preacher in **mosques** (religious meeting places in Islam, similar to churches), Yassin became involved with the Muslim Brotherhood, a radical Islamic **fundamentalist** group. (A fundamentalist is a person who believes in living by a strict set of moral principles.) The Muslim Brotherhood was known for being opposed to the government of Egypt. Yassin was arrested during a visit to Cairo on suspicion of links to the Brotherhood, but he was soon released. He returned to Gaza as a recruiter for the organization.

Entering the political scene

Yassin remained active in the Muslim Brotherhood while working as a religious teacher in Gaza. He founded the Islamic Center in Gaza, a cultural organization to help counter the influence of the **secular** (nonreligious) Palestine Liberation Organization (PLO). Yassin received support from Israel in setting up the Islamic Center, which developed into an important social and political organization, and soon become a deadly enemy of Israel.

After the Six Day War (June 1967) between Israel and neighboring Arab states, Yassin was active in the Palestinians' continuing resistance to Israeli occupation of Palestinian territory, including the Gaza Strip. He was arrested in 1978 by Israel and jailed for seven years on charges of smuggling weapons. He was released from jail in 1985 as part of a prisoner exchange between Israel and a terrorist organization called the Popular Front for the Liberation of Palestine-General Command.

The founding of Hamas

Two years later, in 1987, Palestinians launched a popular uprising against Israeli rule called the Intifada. The Intifada rocked both Israel and the PLO, which by then was negotiating a peace agreement with Israel. Yassin founded Hamas—the name means "zeal," or extreme enthusiasm, in Arabic—as a way to gain influence over the Intifada and challenge the role of the PLO as the main organization representing Palestinians.

Hamas was effectively a branch of the Muslim Brotherhood in Palestinian territory, and Yassin became its chief religious leader. Hamas soon settled into a double role. On the one hand, it organized and trained Palestinians to carry out terrorist attacks against Israel, especially suicide bombings. (In a suicide bombing, the bomber straps explosives to his or her body and sets them off in the middle of a crowd, killing himself as well as the people around him.) In this way, Hamas came to be seen as a leader of the Intifada, which had actually started as a mass revolt by Palestinians. Hamas received enormous political benefits from the uprising.

On the other hand, Hamas organized educational and welfare activities. These enabled the organization to raise substantial sums of money from sympathetic Arab states, such as oil-rich Saudi Arabia, and even from Arab communities in the United States.

The Muslim Brotherhood

The Muslim Brotherhood was the first Islamic fundamentalist organization in the modern era. It has been highly influential in the Arab world for more than seventy years. It was founded in 1928 by an Egyptian teacher, Hassan al-Banna, who supported a return to strict Islamic teachings in the Koran (Islam's holy book).

The Muslim Brotherhood was founded at a time when Egypt was emerging from centuries of rule by the Turkish Ottoman Empire, which had been defeated by Britain and France in World War I (1914–18). At the time Egypt, like other parts of the former empire, was controlled by Great Britain. Some Egyptians were eager to modernize Egyptian society, which largely meant adopting the culture and economic practices of Western Europe. The Muslim Brotherhood was a reaction against that modernization. The dream of the Brotherhood's founder was to use Islam as the basis for reorganizing Egyptian government and society. Within a decade of its founding, the movement had branches through North Africa and as far east as Palestine, Lebanon, and Syria.

In its first decade, from 1928 to 1939, the organization was mostly aimed at young Egyptians. It concentrated on moral and social reform and operated educational programs. In the next decade, between 1939 and 1948, the Brotherhood took on a more political role. This was a period when Egypt was struggling to free itself from British influence. Members of the Muslim Brotherhood occasionally used terrorist tactics, and many members joined the fight against Israel in 1948. In the

Leading from prison

In 1989 Yassin was convicted of taking part in a plot to kill Palestinians who had collaborated (cooperated) with the Israeli army. He was sentenced to life in prison. He remained in jail for eight years, steadily gaining fame as a symbol of Palestinian resistance. The fact that he was confined to a wheelchair, unable to move around without help, added to his fame.

In the meantime, the military branch of Hamas, known as the al-Kassam Brigades, became a leading practitioner of suicide bombing (which Hamas called "martyr operations"). At first all suicide bombers were men, but later some young women also joined their ranks. It proved to be almost impossible to pre-

same year, the Brotherhood was linked to the assassination of Egypt's prime minister, Mahmud Nuqrashi, and was temporarily banned in Egypt.

For a few years after the war against Israel, the Brotherhood worked with Egyptians resisting British rule, led by President Gamal Abdel Nasser (1918–1970). But in 1954 the Brotherhood was outlawed again after being linked to an assassination plot against Nasser. For the next thirty years, the Muslim Brotherhood operated as an underground organization in Egypt.

The Brotherhood spread far beyond Egypt and set up branches in the largest Arab countries, especially Syria, Lebanon, and the Sudan. In the period after World War II (1939–45), many Arab states were trying to modernize their economies and societies. This put them on a collision course with the Brotherhood, who wanted to return to the rules of Islam that had been written down thirteen hundred years earlier. In many countries, the Muslim Brotherhood was outlawed but continued to operate as a secretive, underground organization, preaching its message to young men.

In Syria after 1980 membership in the Muslim Brotherhood was punishable by death. Syrian troops were reported to have killed about ten thousand people in the process of crushing an uprising by the Brotherhood in 1982.

In 1984 the Egyptian government lifted its legal ban on the Brotherhood but kept a close eye on its activities.

vent suicide bombings, since there is no way to tell a suicide bomber from anyone else on the street, until the bomb goes off.

The bombers are convinced that their deaths will help the cause of Islam, and that they will be rewarded with eternal life in paradise, according to their understanding of the **Koran**, Islam's holy book. Often, their families also receive significant financial support.

Life after prison

In 1997 Israel was forced to release Yassin along with many other jailed Palestinian leaders. That year, two Israeli secret agents were arrested in Jordan in a failed attempt to assassinate another Hamas leader. The king of Jordan, who had

Masked Hamas activists tote imitation weapons and burn an Israeli flag during a 1997 demonstration celebrating Hamas leader Ahmed Yassin's release from an Israeli prison. About four thousand people watched as the activists marched around wearing white death shrouds with fake explosives strapped to their waists. *Photograph reproduced by permission of AP/Wide World Photos.*

established peaceful relations with Israel, was furious that Israel had sent assassins into his country. As his price for not ending the peace, Israel agreed to release a number of jailed Palestinian resistance leaders, including Yassin. The release was a huge political gain for Yassin as a leader and for Hamas as a symbol of Palestinian resistance.

Yassin emerged as an important public figure representing Hamas. In his wheelchair, Yassin clearly was not going to take up arms against Israel himself. Any direct attack by Israel against him would be seen as picking on a crippled, elderly religious figure, an unwise move in a world where television images can affect public opinion worldwide.

For his part, Yassin dropped his previous strong opposition to negotiating a peace agreement with Israel. The PLO, working with the Israeli government and the United States, had reduced the contributions to Hamas, and consequently shut down much of the organization's welfare activities. In turn, public support for Hamas fell sharply.

The possibility of peace

Going against the political and military wings of Hamas, Yassin expressed limited support for negotiating a peace agreement with Israel, but only if Israel would withdraw to the territory it had occupied before the 1967 war, the same position held by the PLO. Other Hamas leaders bitterly criticized this position and asked Yassin to resign.

In October 1997, Yassin said in a television interview with the Al-Jazeera news agency:

> We do not hate the Jews as Jews. We do not fight the Jews as Jews. We are fighting [people] who take our rights and our land, and our homes and our houses. . . . The Palestinian people want to return to their homes. For that reason, we are prepared to live with the Jews in the best possible circumstances, in brotherhood and a spirit of cooperation.

In September 2000, a second Palestinian Intifada began a new wave of violence in Israeli-occupied territory and in Israel itself. Hamas claimed responsibility for about half the suicide attacks launched against Israel in the first year of the uprising.

By 2001 Yassin had been largely reduced to a **figurehead,** a symbolic leader who has no real power. But his major contribution remained: the introduction of a strong religious element into what had been largely a political struggle between Palestinian leaders like **Yasir Arafat** (1929–; see entry) and the Israeli government. By introducing the power of religion, which plays a central role in the lives of many Muslims, Yassin immensely complicated the peace process in the region.

For More Information

Periodicals

Abu-Amr, Ziad. "Hamas: A Historical and Political Background." *Journal of Palestine Studies,* Summer 1993, p. 5.

Darwish, Adel. "Grasping the Nettle." *The Middle East,* November 1999, p. 16.

"Deceptive Frailty." *The Economist,* December 19, 1992, p. 40.

McGreary, Johanna. "Radicals on the Rise: The Militant Islamic Group Hamas Enjoys a Boost in Popularity as It Goes about Its Business of Slaughtering Israelis." *Time,* December 17, 2001, p. 50.

Shahin, Mariam. "Simple Facts and Contradictions." *The Middle East,* December 2001, p. 8.

"Yassin, Ahmed." *Current Biography,* July 1998, p. 51.

Ramzi Yousef

c. 1968
Unknown

Terrorist who bombed the World
Trade Center in 1993

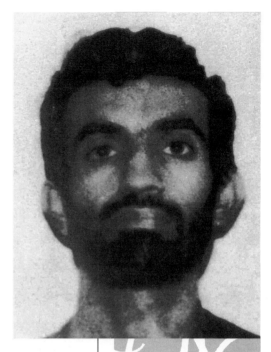

I f Ramzi Yousef had had his way, September 11 might never have happened. Almost a decade before the World Trade Center buildings in New York City were destroyed on September 11, 2001, Yousef had tried to destroy the twin towers by setting off a bomb in the underground parking garage of one building in hopes it would topple onto the other. His plot failed, but only because he could not afford a bigger, better bomb, he later said. It did succeed, however, in turning Ramzi Yousef into America's "most wanted" terrorist.

Ramzi Yousef is one of the most mysterious terrorists yet caught. Although he is serving a life sentence in federal prison, with no chance of freedom, authorities are not sure of his name, his age, or his birthplace. More interesting, they do not know who helped pay for at least two years of global terrorism that included the first bombing of the World Trade Center, a bomb placed on board a Philippines Airlines plane, and perhaps other plots including an attempted assassination (murder) of Pakistan's prime minister and of Pope John Paul II, during the Pope's visit to the Philippines in 1995.

"Yes, I am a terrorist and I am proud of it. And I support terrorism so long as it was against the United States Government and against Israel, because you are more than terrorists; you are the one who invented terrorism and using it every day. You are butchers, liars and hypocrites."

Photograph reproduced by permission of the Corbis Corporation

261

Officials have wondered whether Yousef might have been working for Iraq's dictator, **Saddam Hussein** (1937–), or perhaps for **Osama bin Laden** (c. 1957–; see entries), the Saudi Arabian who is blamed for sponsoring a second attack on the World Trade Center on September 11, 2001. For his part, the man known as Ramzi Yousef is not telling.

Unclear Beginnings

Despite a massive, worldwide manhunt for Yousef after the World Trade Center bombing in 1993, authorities have never been able to penetrate the veil of mystery surrounding his origins—or even his proper name.

In 1994, Yousef said in an interview with the Arabic-newspaper Al Hayat that his father was a Pakistani, his mother was a Palestinian, and that he had a grandmother who lived in Haifa, Israel. (Some language experts believe he speaks Arabic with a Palestinian accent, which would support his claim to a Palestinian mother.) He claimed that he grew up in a working-class suburb of Kuwait City called Fahaheel, crowded with Palestinian exiles. Palestinians living in Kuwait, a tiny, oil-rich country on the Persian Gulf, were poorly treated. It seems possible that Yousef was known as Abdul Basit Mahmud Abdul Karim (usually shortened to Abdul Basit). He learned to speak Arabic and Urdu (the main language spoken in Pakistan). He also learned to speak English.

Yousef (or Basit) apparently resented his treatment as a youth in Kuwait, and came to blame the United States for his own problems, since the United States was the strongest supporter of Israel, a country carved out of Palestine in 1948 to be a homeland for Jews, six million of whom were targeted and systematically murdered by the German military during World War II (1939–45). Most of the Palestinians living in Kuwait were refugees (or children of refugees) from the 1948 war in which neighboring Arab nations attacked a well-armed Israel and lost even more territory to the new nation. Many were bitter about the experience—including, it seems, Ramzi Yousef.

At age eighteen, Yousef apparently left Kuwait for England, where he enrolled in Swansea Institute in Wales to study electronic engineering. There are records of a student named Abdul Basit studying at the technical college in Swansea, Wales, from 1986 to 1989 and receiving a degree in computer-aided electronic engineering, just as there are records of someone named Abdul Basit living in Kuwait. There are records of Yousef leaving Kuwait in August 1990, three weeks after Iraq invaded the country to start the Persian Gulf War (1990–91). He was said to have used an Iraqi passport, and to have admitted having relatives living in Iraq, which gave rise to speculation that he might have been working for the Iraqi government as a spy. Other reports say that the real Abdul Basit was killed during Iraq's invasion of Kuwait, and that "Ramzi Yousef" stole the identity of a real person—maybe with the help of Iraqi authorities during their occupation of Kuwait in 1990—in order to hide his own.

Apparently returning to the Middle East in 1989, Yousef (or Basit) may have been attracted to the growing battle in Afghanistan, where Muslims (followers of Islam) were fighting to drive out the army of the Soviet Union (now called the Russian Federation). Russian troops had entered Afghanistan in 1979 in order to support a communist government. (Communism is an economic theory that does not include the concept of private property; the public, represented by the government, owns the goods and the means to produce them in common.) A decade later, thousands of Arabs and other Muslims had volunteered to fight in Afghanistan to drive the Russians out. Among those helping to organize and pay for these volunteer fighters was a Saudi Arabian millionaire named Osama bin Laden, who later was accused of coordinating terrorist attacks aimed at the United States.

Much later, a U.S. Secret Service agent testified in court that Yousef claimed he had been trained for six months at a camp inside Afghanistan in the art of making explosives, and that he had become an instructor at a different camp near the border between Afghanistan and Pakistan. None of Yousef's statements has been proved by other evidence.

Whether Ramzi Yousef became involved with Osama bin Laden in Afghanistan, where bin Laden sponsored camps for Arabs volunteering to fight against the Russian occupation, or whether he was employed by the intelligence (spy) agency of Saddam Hussein in Iraq, it seems clear that he became an expert in building bombs, especially the kind used by terrorists.

According to some published reports, in 1991 Yousef traveled to the Philippines and joined forces with Abu Sayyaf, a group of fundamentalist Muslims fighting to separate the

Who Is Sheikh Omar Abdel Rahman?

Sheikh Omar Abdel Rahman was a blind Islamic preacher from Egypt who had an intense hatred for the government of his native country. In the early 1990s, he was headquartered in the New York City area, where he often preached at small mosques, including one in Jersey City, New Jersey, just west of Manhattan.

Born in Egypt in 1938, Rahman was arrested in Egypt and charged with involvement in the assassination of Egypt's President Anwar el-Sadat (1918–1981). He was found not guilty, but the United States put him on a list of suspected terrorists who were supposed to be kept out of the country. But in 1990, as a result of an error, he was admitted to the United States and was given a "green card," a document that non-citizens need to work.

Rahman is blind as a result of diabetes that began when he was under a year old. In 1993, when Ramzi Yousef encountered him, Rahman was frail and could barely walk. But his weaknesses did not stop him from preaching hatred towards the United States, as well as towards the government of Egypt headed by President Hosni Mubarak (1928–). Rahman was a familiar figure among some Arab Muslims living in New York in the early 1990s.

Rahman was born in Gamaliya, Egypt, in the Nile delta. Despite his diabetes and resulting blindness, he is reputed to have learned the Koran (Islam's holy book) by age eleven, and graduated with a master's degree in theology from Cairo University. Later he earned a doctorate at al-Azhar University in Cairo. He was married at least twice, and had a total of ten children with his two wives.

In the late 1960s and 1970s, Rahman taught in southern Egypt. There, he harshly denounced the government of President Gamal Abdel Nasser (1918–1970), and later President Sadat, for

southern part of the Philippines, inhabited mainly by Muslims, from the mostly-Catholic northern part of the country. One former member of Abu Sayyaf was quoted in press reports as saying Yousef was bitterly anti-American, and wanted to wage a campaign of terrorism around the world.

Ramzi Yousef's Story Begins

The part of Yousef's story that is known for certain began on September 1, 1992, when he landed in New York City

failing to establish an Islamic state in Egypt, one governed by the strict rules of the Koran. He was accused of being the spiritual leader of al-Jihad, the organization of fundamentalist Muslims that assassinated Sadat in 1981. The government's case was not proved, and Rahman was released and eventually came to the United States.

Most of the men accused of plotting to bomb the World Trade Center in 1993 were followers of the Sheikh, although Rahman himself was never charged. Five months after that bombing, in June 1993, Rahman and ten of his followers were arrested in Queens, New York, and charged with plotting to blow up other New York landmarks, including the headquarters of the United Nations, the Federal Bureau of Investigation's building in Manhattan, and two tunnels beneath the Hudson River that connect Manhattan with New Jersey. Two years later, Rahman was found guilty of conspiracy to blow up the buildings and sentenced to life in prison.

In 1997, U.S. officials said they had found evidence that Ramzi Yousef, convicted of bombing the World Trade Center in February 1993, had connections with Sheikh Rahman.

After his conviction, Rahman said in an interview with *Time* magazine: "Self-defense is legal in all religions. This is called jihad in Islam. The West has misinterpreted this concept. People who are defending their lands are called terrorists. Of course, this inter-pretation is useful to the West. It legitimizes attacks against any country in the Third World [poor developing countries]. Americans call them terrorists, and they take it to the U.N. [the United Nations, an international peacekeeping organization] in order to take legal action. And the U.N. does whatever the U.S. tells it to do."

on a Pakistani airliner. He was dressed in "harem pants" and a "puffy-sleeved shirt," according to officials, looking as if he might have come from Afghanistan. He had no visa (a document that would allow him to enter the United States), and instead showed an identity card with the name Khurram Khan. When this was challenged by immigration officials, he offered an Iraqi passport bearing the name Ramzi Ahmed Yousef and asked for political asylum (when a nation grants an individual the right to stay in its country so that person will not be detained in another). He told American officials he belonged to a Kuwaiti guerrilla (secret military) group, and would be tortured if he went back to Iraq.

Immigration officials detained Yousef for entering the United States without a visa, but there was a problem: the small facility used to hold suspicious immigrants was already filled with other prisoners. So instead of holding Yousef, the officials granted him temporary political asylum until a hearing could be held and then they released him. Unknown to Immigration officials then, Yousef was not traveling alone. His companion on the trip was Ahmad Ajaj. He was detained for carrying a false Swedish passport and a set of books that described how to make bombs. Ajaj was detained and kept out of the United States.

Having passed Immigration, Ramzi Yousef went to Jersey City, New Jersey, a suburb of New York located almost directly west of the World Trade Center. The twin towers of New York's tallest buildings could easily be seen in the distance, symbols of America's economic power and domination. In New Jersey, Yousef joined a group of Arab immigrants who were followers of Sheikh Omar Abdel Rahman, a blind Egyptian who preached at the Al-Salam mosque located on the third floor of a building in Jersey City above a check-cashing-store and a Chinese restaurant.

Yousef was something of a mystery man to the Arabs he lived with in New Jersey. He had introduced himself as an Iraqi, but said little else. Some thought his accent was not right, and believed him to be a Pakistani. The more observant Muslims criticized him for not wearing a beard.

According to telephone records found later, in November 1992 Yousef began ordering supplies for making bombs. Later, the residue (traces) of chemicals were found in an apartment occupied by Yousef and another man, Mohammed A. Salameh. Yousef apparently changed identities several times in the short period he spent in the United States, and moved from place to place often, ending up in a building at 40 Pamrapo in Jersey City.

On November 30, Salameh rented a storage locker under the name Kamal Ibraham. Later, the Federal Bureau of Investigation (FBI) inspected the locker and found nitric acid, sodium azide, and sodium cyanide, as well as sulfuric acid and urea—chemicals used to make explosives.

On February 23, 1993, two men, one of whom was Salameh, turned up at a Ryder truck rental location and inspected available vehicles. They settled on a Ford Econoline van for $200 a week with 100 free miles. Since Salameh did not have a credit card, he put down a cash deposit of $400. The money would later prove his undoing.

The Attack and Escape

About four o'clock on the morning of February 26, 1993, a Friday, the van drove into an all-night service station, followed by a blue Honda. The van driver—later identified as Salameh by the station attendant—spent $18 to fill the gasoline tank completely, perhaps to add more fuel for the explosion that was to come. One man made a call from a pay telephone, and a few moments later, a red car joined the group. The three vehicles then set off for lower Manhattan.

The van was parked in the underground parking garage beneath the World Trade Center.

At 12:18 P.M., the van exploded with a tremendous force, sending flames shooting up one of the twin towers. Six people were killed and over one thousand were injured, many by flying debris. The explosion knocked out power to the building and sent thousands of workers scrambling down smoky, dark stairwells. Traffic and business in lower Manhattan was completely snarled. The cost of the damage was estimated at $500 million. It was, in 1993, the biggest terrorist attack yet launched in the United States. According to officials who later arrested him, Yousef claimed his aim was to topple the tower so that it would tip and crash into the other twin tower, bringing down both buildings. But, Yousef said, he did not have enough money to build a bomb sufficient to do the job.

Four days after the bomb exploded, a letter arrived at the *New York Times* claiming credit for the bombing and criticizing the United States policy of supporting Israel in the Middle East. It was signed Liberation Army Fifth Battalion.

In the meantime, New York City police started immediately looking for the people responsible for the explosion, and on Sunday, two days after the bomb ignited, they had a

New York City police and firefighters inspect the bomb crater inside the World Trade Center one day after the February 26, 1993, attack by Islamic terrorists. Six people were killed and more than one thousand injured. *Photograph reproduced by permission of the Corbis Corporation*

major breakthrough. Police found a twisted piece of the Ryder truck that contained the vehicle identification number, a unique number that goes with every car and truck manufactured. It did not take long to trace the vehicle to the Ryder truck rental agency in New Jersey.

On Friday, just a few hours later, Salameh had returned to the rental agency asking for his deposit and claiming that the truck had been stolen the previous night. The rental agent refused to refund the money, and demanded that Salameh file a police report. Two days later, on Monday, Salameh returned and again demanded his deposit back. Later, there was speculation that he needed the money to buy a ticket out of the country. Again, he was turned down. Finally, on Thursday, he returned to the rental agency yet again. This time, FBI agents were waiting to arrest him.

In the meantime, his partner, Ramzi Yousef, had already fled, flying first class to Pakistan.

Disappeared. . . . and a new plot

For almost three years, Ramzi Yousef seemed to disappear. Authorities thought he might be in Afghanistan or western Pakistan. In March 1993, a bomb destroyed the home of Benazir Bhutto, prime minister of Pakistan, and Ramzi Yousef was blamed, but no definitive proof was found of his involvement. In March 1994, police in Bangkok, Thailand, foiled a plan to bomb the Israeli embassy there; again, Yousef was named as a suspect but never caught and definitive proof was not found.

In another event that was later linked to Yousef, a bomb exploded on a Philippine Airlines plane on December 11, 1994. The plane was on a flight from Manila to Tokyo, with a stopover in the city of Cebu, the Philippines. Investigators later developed evidence that Yousef, using the name Armaldo Forlani, had flown on the first leg of the flight and hidden a bomb under seat 26K on the Boeing 747 jumbo jet, then got off the plane at Cebu. A Japanese businessman flying in that seat was killed when the bomb exploded during the second leg of the flight. The plane, although crippled, was able to land safely. Philippine authorities were terrified that the bomb could signal a planned attack on Pope John Paul II, who was scheduled to visit the Philippines the next month (January 1995).

Yousef's plans were cut short by a fire in his apartment on January 6. Neighbors noticed smoke pouring from an apartment and called the fire department. Inside, firemen found what amounted to a bomb factory—and a laptop computer left behind by Ramzi Yousef.

The computer proved to be a goldmine of information. On it investigators found a plan to murder the Pope during his visit to the Philippines, as well as detailed plans to explode bombs on about a dozen commercial airliners flying across the Pacific to the United States, presumably using the same sort of bomb that had been planted on the Philippines Airline plane a month earlier. Authorities said the computer contained departure times for commercial airliners, and times for the bombs to explode.

But Ramzi Yousef was nowhere to be found. After fleeing the apartment building, he had disappeared.

Reward

It had been almost three years since the World Trade Center bombing, and U.S. officials were determined to find Ramzi Yousef. The U.S. Government offered a $2 million reward for his capture, and publicized it by means of matchbook covers distributed widely in Pakistan.

In Islamabad, Pakistan, a Muslim born in South Africa walked into the U.S. embassy and told them he knew where Ramzi Yousef could be found. But, he warned, Yousef was on the verge of leaving in just a few hours.

Quickly, agents of the U.S. Drug Enforcement Agency and the U.S. State Department joined with Pakistani police. They surrounded an inexpensive guest house called Su Casa and went to room 16 on the upper floor. Pakistani police burst into the room—and found Ramzi Yousef lying on a bed. Beside him, in a suitcase, were two remote-control toy cars, filled with explosives.

Within a few hours, Pakistani officials completed paperwork required to send Yousef back to the United States. On the twenty-two-hour flight, according to the U.S. agents who accompanied him, Yousef admitted his role in the World Trade Center bombing, as well as boasting about his plans to blow up as many as a dozen airplanes flying across the Pacific Ocean. U.S. Secret Service Special Agent Brian Parr testified against Yousef at his trial, at which Yousef was charged with both the World Trade Center explosion and the Manila airliner plot. Agent Parr also said Yousef said his true name was Abdul Basit Mahmoud Abdul Karim.

In November 1996, a man tried under the name Ramzi Yousef was found guilty of trying to blow up the World Trade Center and sentenced to life in prison. Before sentencing, he told the judge in the courtroom:

> You keep talking also about collective punishment and killing innocent people to force governments to change their policies; you call this terrorism when someone would kill innocent people or civilians in order to force the government to change its policies. Well, when you were the first one who invented this terrorism.
>
> You were the first one who killed innocent people, and you are the first one who introduced this type of terrorism to the history of mankind when you dropped an atomic bomb which killed tens of thousands of women and children in Japan and

when you killed over a hundred thousand people, most of them civilians, in Tokyo with fire bombings. You killed them by burning them to death. And you killed civilians in Vietnam with chemicals as with the so-called Orange agent. You killed civilians and innocent people, not soldiers, innocent people every single war you went. You went to wars more than any other country in this century, and then you have the nerve to talk about killing innocent people. . . .

The government in its summations and opening said that I was a terrorist. Yes, I am a terrorist and I am proud of it. And I support terrorism so long as it was against the United States Government and against Israel, because you are more than terrorists; you are the one who invented terrorism and using it every day. You are butchers, liars and hypocrites.

Who was Yousef Ramzi?

"Yousef Ramzi" was sentenced to spend the rest of his life in prison. But the details of his life remain unknown. Was he an agent of the Iraqi government? Officials in Kuwait claimed that he had collaborated with Iraqi soldiers when they occupied Kuwait in 1990, and the fact that he entered the United States in 1992 with an Iraqi passport persuaded some investigators to think so.

Was he part of Osama bin Laden's global network of terrorists? In 2002, U.S. officials said that a key figure in bin Laden's plan to bomb the World Trade Center on September 11, 2001, Khalid Shaikh Mohammad, was also linked to Yousef. According to officials, Khalid Shaikh Mohammed helped Yousef coordinate, and pay for, his plan in Manila to blow up airliners crossing the Pacific.

It seems possible that the truth about Ramzi Yousef will never be known. Even if he were to decide to tell all, would investigators believe him? Or would they conclude that he was telling a new set of lies, perhaps to lure them off the scent of the truth?

Sitting in the Federal maximum-security prison in Florence, Colorado, Ramzi Yousef isn't talking.

For More Information

Books

Mylroie, Laurie. *Study of Revenge: Saddam Hussein's Unfinished War Against America*. Washington, DC: AEI Press, 2000.

Reeve, Simon. *The New Jackals: Ramzi Yousef, Osama bin Laden and the Future of Terrorism.* Boston: Northeastern University Press, 1999.

Periodicals

"An Enigmatic Personality Whose Mission Was to Punish America." *New York Times,* September 6, 1996, p. A14.

"Broad Terror Campaign is Foiled by Fire in Kitchen, Officials Say." *New York Times,* February 12, 1995, page 1.

"Charged as Terror Master, Surrounded by Mysteries, Many Origins and Aliases for Bomb Suspect." *New York Times,* May 29, 1996, p. B1.

Duffy, Brian. "The Long Arm of the Law: How Federal Agents Nabbed the 'Evil Genius' Accused of Blowing up the World Trade Center." *U.S. News & World Report,* February 20, 1995, p. 50.

Farley, John. "The Man Who Wasn't There." *Time,* February 20, 1995, p. 24.

"Funds for Terrorists Traced to Persian Gulf Businessmen." *New York Times,* May 26, 1993, p. A12.

"Pieces of Terrorism: Accounts Trace the Trade Center Explosion." *New York Times,* May 26, 1993, p. A12.

Weaver, Mary Ann. "Children of the Jihad." *New Yorker,* June 12, 1995, p. 40.

Index

References to photos are
marked by (ill.); **boldface**
indicates main entries and
their page numbers.

Japanese Red Army 248
major acts of terrorism 23,
28, 69
Palestine Liberation
Organization (PLO) 21–23
See also Hamas, Palestine
Liberation Organization
(PLO), Popular Front for the
Liberation of Palestine (PFLP)
Palestine Liberation Organization
(PLO) 152
Abu Nidal Organization 201
Arafat, Yasir 23
Fatah 23
Intifada 157
Palestine Mandate 67, 117
Palestinian Authority 26
Palestinian Secret
Organization 199
PanAm flight 103 bombing 217,
216 (ill.)
Paranoid schizophrenia 166
Patterson, John 236
Pentagon attack 91
Peres, Shimon 26, 27 (ill.)
Persian Gulf War 81–82
Personality disorders 167
Peru
Red Banner 146
Shining Path 146, 147–148
PLO. *See* Palestine Liberation
Organization (PLO)
Plunkett, Joseph Mary 131
A Poisonous Cocktail? 36
Popular Front for the
Liberation of Palestine
(PFLP) 152, 154
Baader-Meinhof Gang 45
Carlos the Jackal 116
Japanese Red Army 248
major acts of terrorism 154
Prairie Fire 101
Presidential Medal of
Freedom 195
Proll, Thorward 44
Proudhon, Pierre Joseph 56

Q

Qaddafi, Mu'ammar 206–218,
206 (ill.)

R

Rabin, Yitzak 26, 27 (ill.), 157
Radical Abolitionists 108
Radio Cairo 207
Rahman, Sheikh Omar Abdel
264–265
Raspe, Jan-Carl 49
Red Army Faction. *See* Baader-
Meinhof Gang
Red Army. *See* Japanese Red Army
Red Banner 146
Reign of Terror
Terror 230
Republic of Ireland. *See* Ireland
Ressam, Ahmed 88
Revolutionary Catechism 59
Revolutions of 1848 56
Reynolds, Albert 17
Ridge, Tom 219–225, 219 (ill.),
224 (ill.)
**Robespierre, Maximilien
226–233,** 226 (ill.)
Rousseau, Jean-Jacques 227,
228 (ill.)

S

Sabri Al Banna 197–205,
197 (ill.)
Sadat, Anwar el- 25, 71, 73, 156
assassination of 265
Salameh, Mohammed A. 266
Sanchez, Ilich. *See* Carlos the
Jackal
Sarin gas. *See* Tokyo subway sarin
gas attack
Sayyaf, Abu 264
Schleyer, Hanns-Martin 49
Scrutton, Hugh 164, 165,
165 (ill.)
*Secrets of Developing Your
Supernatural Powers* 32
Sekigun. *See* Japanese Red Army
September 11, 2001 attacks 91
Sharon, Ariel 29
**Shelton, Robert M. "Bobby"
234–244,** 234 (ill.)
Shigenobu, Fusako 245–252,
245 (ill.)
Shining Path 142, 146, 147–149,
147 (ill.)